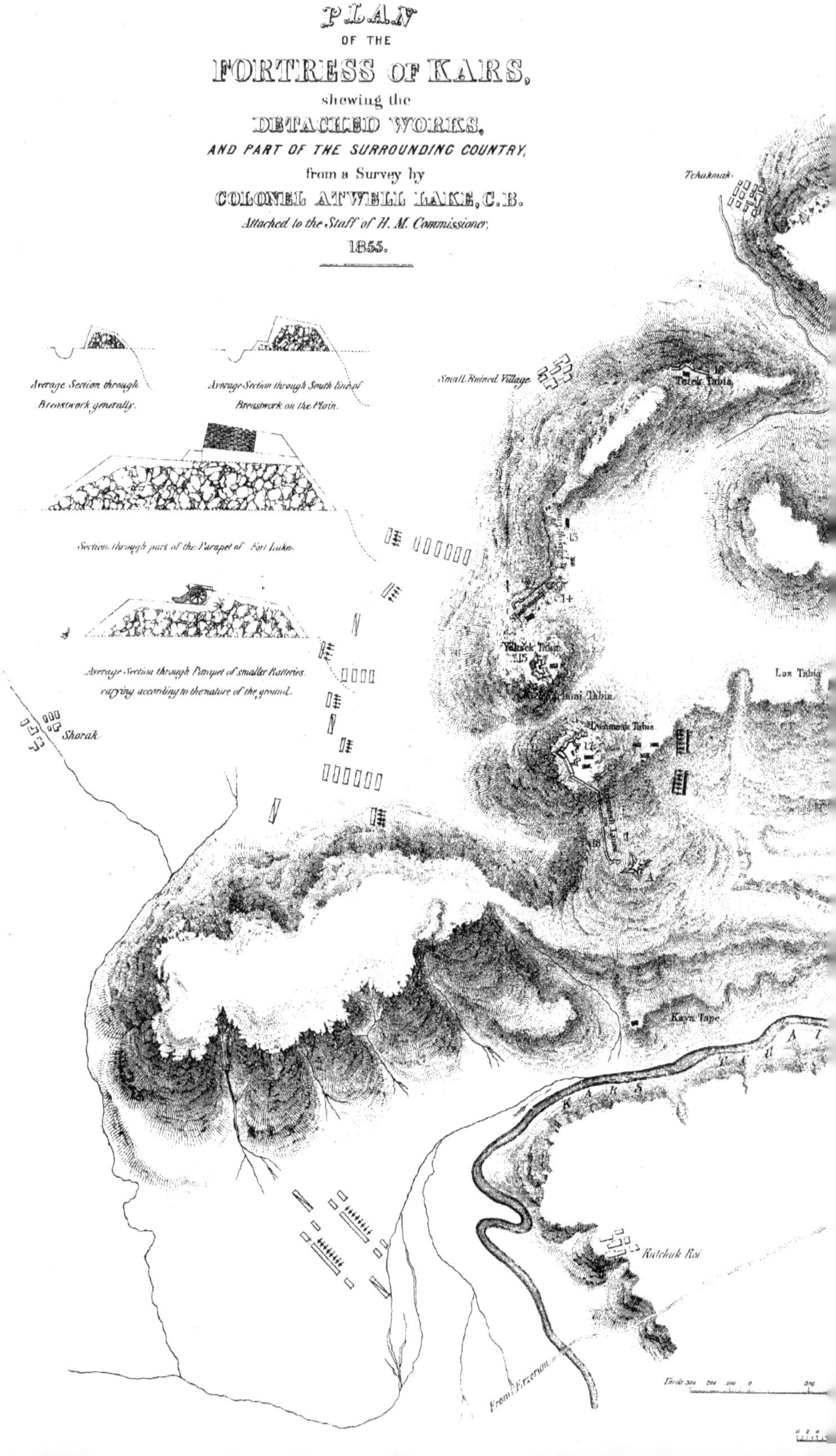

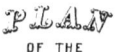

PLAN
OF THE
FORTRESS OF KARS,
shewing the
DETACHED WORKS,
AND PART OF THE SURROUNDING COUNTRY,
from a Survey by
COLONEL ATWELL LAKE, C.B.
Attached to the Staff of H. M. Commissioner,
1855.
Average Section through Breastwork generally.
Average Section through South line of Breastwork on the Plain.
Section through part of the Parapet of Fort Lake.
Average Section through Parapet of smaller Batteries, varying according to the nature of the ground.
Tchakmak
Small Ruined Village
Tetek Tabia
15
14
Laz Tabia
Tohmash Tabia
Shorak
Kaya Tape
KARS
Kutchuk Koi
From Erzerum
Yards

THE DEFENCE OF KARS.

"Distinet hostem
Agger murorum."—*Æneidos* Lib. xi. line 381

"Hambre y frio, entregan al hombre á su enemigo."—*Spanish Proverb.*
"Hunger and cold deliver a man up to his enemy."

TURKISH INFANTRY SOLDIERS.

NARRATIVE

OF THE

DEFENCE OF KARS,

Historical and Military.

BY

COLONEL ATWELL LAKE, C.B.,
(UNATTACHED);
ONE OF HER MAJESTY'S AIDES-DE-CAMP, AND LATE OF THE MADRAS ENGINEERS;

FROM AUTHENTIC DOCUMENTS,

AND FROM NOTES TAKEN BY THE SEVERAL OFFICERS SERVING ON THE
STAFF OF HER MAJESTY'S COMMISSIONER WITH THE
OTTOMAN ARMY IN ASIA MINOR.

ILLUSTRATED BY LIEUT.-COLONEL C. TEESDALE, C.B.,
AND WILLIAM SIMPSON, ESQ.

LONDON:
RICHARD BENTLEY, NEW BURLINGTON STREET,
Publisher in Ordinary to Her Majesty.
1857.

TO

MAJOR-GENERAL

SIR W. FENWICK WILLIAMS, BART., OF KARS, K.C.B.
&c. &c. &c.

𝔚𝔥𝔬𝔰𝔢 𝔇𝔢𝔢𝔡𝔰,

APPRECIATED BY HIS QUEEN AND COUNTRY,

AND WRITTEN IN THE HEARTS OF THE SOLDIERS WHOM HE LED,

REQUIRE NO EULOGY BEYOND THEIR SIMPLE RECORD,

THIS BOOK

IS DEDICATED

BY HIS ATTACHED COMPANION IN ARMS,

ATWELL LAKE.

LONDON,
April, 1857.

PREFACE.

On taking up a volume purporting to be a "Narrative of the Blockade of Kars," the general reader may very possibly ask the question, "What can "we now be told on this subject with which we "have not already been made acquainted?"

It is very true that several works have lately been published, giving an account of much that took place during the blockade; but, as yet, no connected history of all that occurred in Asia Minor, having reference more particularly to the defence and ultimate surrender of Kars, has been offered to the public.

I wish most sincerely that the task which I have undertaken had fallen into abler hands, in order that more justice might have been done to a subject which has occupied the attention and elicited the approbation of the people of England.

A perusal of the following pages will show the reader that there has been no attempt at any flowery or overstrained description. My desire has been to state facts simply as they occurred, to bestow praise where it has appeared to be deserved, and to abstain (as far as is consistent with that truthfulness which is expected from every annalist) from throwing blame on those who may have reasons, unknown to me, for their actions.

I consider it the duty of every Engineer Officer, as far as it lies in his power, to contribute, whenever an opportunity may occur, to the cause of science in fortification; and there are few officers to be found who are unwilling to gain information, however trifling, from the experience of others.

As regards the Defences of Kars, there may, perhaps, be no great novelty in their construction, but they, at least, contain a lesson upon the value of field-works, thrown up in great haste, and under difficulties of no ordinary nature.

PREFACE. ix

My original intention was to write a purely professional work, trusting that it might be read with attention by members of the Corps of Engineers, both in the Royal and Indian Armies, as well as by other military officers, to whom, generally, the art of fortification has, of late years, become an interesting study; but I was induced, at the solicitation of many whose opinions I value, to make the volume more comprehensive, by giving an account, in detail, of all that occurred in Asia Minor in connection with the operations at Kars.

To enable me to carry out this project with greater accuracy, I was under the necessity of seeking for information from those officers who were employed at a distance from the more immediate scene of action.

It has been mentioned, in my former work on Kars, that when General Mouravieff was informed that I had destroyed a plan of the fortifications, which I had made at intervals, prior to and during the continuance of the blockade, he most kindly offered to give me a copy of one which he had ordered his own Engineer Officers to prepare. This generous intention, however, the Russian Commander was unable to fulfil, owing to my departure from Tiflis before the plan was completed. He nevertheless so far redeemed his promise as to give me a plan of Kars, as it stood before the field-works were added to the existing fortifications.

Soon after my arrival at Penza—the town wherein I was destined to pass the period of my captivity—I accidentally found some papers, the existence of which I was, up to that moment, perfectly ignorant of, containing the angles and other notes I had taken whilst making the survey; so that I was enabled to pass my leisure hours in making a new plan, similar, in every respect, to the one I had destroyed.

I must here offer my best thanks to Mr. H. A. Churchill, Private Secretary to Sir Fenwick Williams, who afforded me his valuable assistance, whenever his other duties permitted him, in sketching the surrounding country, and thus enabling me to render the survey more complete than I could otherwise have made it, owing to the numerous calls on my own time.

To the Right Honourable Lord Panmure, Her Majesty's Secretary of State for War, my warmest acknowledgments are due, for having obligingly offered me the use of the establishment belonging to the Topographical and Statistical Depôt; and to Lieutenant-Colonel Jervis, the Director of that Institution, for the satisfactory manner in which he has lithographed the several plans and drawings which illustrate my book.

To Major-General Sir Fenwick Williams, who has kindly permitted me to have access to many official documents in his possession, and to Lieut.-Colonel C. C. Teesdale, whose aid has been invaluable in enabling me to supply from his journal many facts and dates which the loss of my own deprived me of the means of referring to, I beg to offer my sincere thanks.

I beg also gratefully to acknowledge the aid I have received from Majors Stuart and Cathcart, and from Captain Cameron, in furnishing me with many interesting details connected with the proceedings which took place at Erzeroom and at other places in the neighbourhood during the time that Kars was closely blockaded; and I offer my best thanks to Mr. W. Simpson, the talented Crimean artist, for the spirited sketches which he was good enough to draw expressly for my work.

I have only to solicit the kind indulgence of the Public for all errors and defects which will doubtless be discovered in this volume. I ask them to look upon it as the production of one whose sole object has been to give to the world a true and unvarnished record of events, on the result of which the safety of Asia Minor depended.

While many an able writer has been found to chronicle the gigantic and glorious operations that took place in the Crimea, no one has hitherto come forward to give a detailed and authentic account of the proceedings which occurred, on a much smaller scale, in Kars and its vicinity.

I therefore took up my pen to supply the omission; and, in so doing, my object has been to fulfil a duty which I owe to those brave officers and soldiers in the Turkish service who gallantly stood by my countrymen and myself in the hour of danger; and who, under great hardships and privations, evinced an endurance which has justly gained for them the admiration of all Europe.

To the critics and reviewers who may deign to notice my book I will only say, that if they treat me with as much leniency as they were pleased to extend towards me when, on a former occasion, I appeared before the public in the character of an author, I shall be more than satisfied.

ATWELL LAKE.

London, March 1857.

CONTENTS.

CHAPTER I.

PAGE

Appointment of General Williams as British Commissioner in Asia Minor—Officers of his Staff—Defeat of the Turks at Kuruk-Déré—State of the Ottoman Army at Kars—Corruption of the Pashas—Ismail Pasha—General Guyon—Muster of Turkish Troops—Condition of the Officers and Men—Major Teesdale—Kerim Pasha—State of the Garrison at Kars - - - - - - - - 1

CHAPTER II.

Health of the Soldiers—Worthlessness of Shukri Pasha, Commandant—Merit of Kerim Pasha, second in command—Appointment of more British Officers—Colonel Lake arrives at Kars—Exertions of General Williams—Insurrection in Koordistan, suppressed by General Williams on his own responsibility—Surrender of Izzideen shere Bey - - 29

CHAPTER III.

Description of the Fortress of Kars in 1855—New Works planned and executed by Colonel Lake - - - 42

CHAPTER IV.

Fortifications completed to a certain extent—Pontoon Bridges thrown across the river—Duty of English Officers—Strength of the Garrison—Description of the manner in which promotion takes place in the Turkish Army—General Williams and his Aide-de-camp employed at Erzeroom—Routes by which Erzeroom is approachable from Kars—Fortifications at former place—Provisions sent to Kars—Reports of Russian advance—Arrival of Vassif Pasha—His character—Camp pitched at Kars - - - 58

CHAPTER V.

Increase of Kars Garrison—Sickness very trifling—State of Hospital—Enrolment of Bashi-Bozouks—Lāz Riflemen collected—Their character—Ramazān—Mushir's unwillingness to issue orders on the subject—He is at length persuaded to do so—Arrival of General Williams at Kars, June 7th—Intentions of Enemy no longer doubtful—His Movements—Turkish Outposts attacked—Advance of Russians against the Lower Works, June 16th—Enemy repulsed and forced to retire — Account of Stores and Magazines — Grain at Kupri-keui taken by the Russians - - - - 72

CHAPTER VI.

Russian Army advances—Halts at Magharadjik—Appearance of the Force—Army of the Caucasus described—Enemy sends to Chiplakli and destroys Grain—Post taken—Private Letters sent into Garrison—Works extended and described—Staff of Kars Army—Feyzi Pasha—Commissariat—Peculation discovered—Townspeople are armed—Reconnaissance by the Enemy, 26th of June—Again on the 13th of July—General Mouravieff on the 1st of August proceeds towards the Soghanli-Dāgh—His return to Kars - - - 99

CONTENTS. xvii

CHAPTER VII.
PAGE

Skirmishes take place daily—An Ambuscade is planned, and fails—Reasons given for passive resistance—Enemy attacks Kanli Tabia, August 7th, and is repulsed—Tachmasb Heights fortified still further — Other Works constructed — Stone Bridge thrown over Kars-Tchai—General Kméty—Hussein Pasha—Inner Line of Defence on the Plain—Construction of Fortifications necessarily rude   -   -   -   -   116

CHAPTER VIII.

Enemy pitches Camps at Boskali, Chalgour, and Ainalli—Desertion commences to take place—Punishment awarded—Deserter taken and Shot—Lāz Riflemen become mutinous—Their punishment—Horses sent away for want of food—Vēli Pasha's Force—Correspondence between General Williams and Colonel Lake—Instructions given to Vēli Pasha—Erivan Force advanced, and Vēli Pasha retired—A Turkish Spy found and executed—Batoom Army—Heavy siege-guns arrive from Gumri—Kanli Tabia strengthened—Correspondence about Transport—Seven hundred Horses killed   -   129

CHAPTER IX.

Garrison attacked by Cholera—Turkish medical subordinates not well educated—Post arrives September 23rd—News from the Crimea, and from Omer Pasha—His Advice to the Garrison—General Williams writes to Sheikh Shamyl, and receives an answer—Three British Officers arrive at Erzeroom—They attempt in vain to get to Kars—Their subsequent Movements   -   -   -   -   -   -   156

CHAPTER X.

The Enemy attacks Pennek—The Turks take to an ignominious flight—Captain Cameron's description of it—Disappearance of Ali Pasha—Reasons for the Attack—Supposed connivance on the part of the Turks—Major Stuart and Captain Cameron remain at Erzeroom—Major Peel arrives September 21st—News of the fall of part of Sebastopol arrives at Erzeroom—Proceedings at Kars—The Blockade continues—The Cherkess and Assatin described—Cruelty to a child—Steps taken for protecting foraging parties   -   178

CHAPTER XI.

The Enemy advances, September 29th—Preparations to resist the Attack—Action commences—Yārim-Ai Tabia taken—Yuksek Tabia in danger—General Kméty—General Kavalieffsy killed—Vassif Pasha and Těk Tabias open fire—Fight at Tachmasb—Chasseurs—Attack on English Batteries—They are taken by the Enemy—Fire opened from Fort Lake and Kāradāgh—Reinforcements sent to former Battery—Enemy is driven out of English Batteries—Russians retreat   195

CHAPTER XII.

Not a shot fired from the Citadel—Action continues at Tachmasb—Daring act of a Russian Battalion—Order given to the Enemy to retire—Retreat is commenced—Impossibility of pursuit—Gallant conduct of Officers—Messrs. Zohrab and Rennison—Names of Officers who distinguished themselves—Conduct of Turkish Troops—Gallantry of the Enemy—Burial of the slain—General Williams notices conduct of his Staff—Probable loss on the side of the Enemy—Hospital arrangements—General Williams' official Despatch regarding the Battle -   -   -   -   -   -   -   -   211

CHAPTER XIII.

Cholera again breaks out—Gloom spread over the Garrison—Omer Pasha's silence—Officers receive the Medjidiyé—Turkish rank conferred on British Officers—Provisions begin to run short—Difficulty of sending out a Post—Evil resulting from neglect of orders—People caught in their attempt to escape from Kars—Turks found lying dead on the road—Increasing sickness of Troops—Addition to the Works   -   234

CHAPTER XIV.

Parapets raised in places—Sentries withdrawn from the front—Reported advance of Selim and Omer Pashas—Effects of starvation—Cold becomes intense—Difficulty of carrying fuel to the Heights—Conduct of Feyzi Pasha—Enemy begins to hut himself—Attempts made to keep up the strength of the Troops—Annoyance from the Enemy at night—Garrison kept on the alert—Barrack constructed   -   -   -   248

CONTENTS. xix

CHAPTER XV.

PAGE

Orders sent to Erzeroom by General Williams—Interview between Major Stuart and Vēli Pasha—The latter declines advancing without orders—He refuses to state the number of his Troops—The Condition of his Army—The State of Selim Pasha's Force—Vēli Pasha at length advances—Major Stuart visits Selim Pasha—Reputed character of the latter —Excuses made by him for his delay—General Williams writes to him, and offers him some advice—He is urged in vain to advance—Impossibility of collecting Bashi-Bozouks   260

CHAPTER XVI.

English Officers continue to visit Selim Pasha daily—False account of expected reinforcement—Major Stuart writes to Selim Pasha—His reply, and statement of his Force—The Pasha's arguments not well founded—General Williams writes to Major Stuart—Mr. Consul Brant's opinion of Selim Pasha—He urges the expediency of sending up another General—Some account of Omer Pasha's movements—The feasibility of a retreat from Kars is discussed—It is at first decided upon—All hope of succour is at an end, and a retreat is at length found to be impossible—The vigilance of the Enemy is increased   -   -   -   -   -   -   274

CHAPTER XVII.

An Aide-de-camp is despatched with a flag of truce to the Russian Camp—General Williams visits General Mouravieff —He announces the surrender of Kars to Lord Clarendon— Terms of the capitulation — Approval of Her Majesty's Government — General Mouravieff appreciates a brave defence—Terms are approved of by the Mushir, but objected to at first by the Turkish Officers—All is at length arranged satisfactorily—Generals Kméty and Kollmann escape— Reception of the Turks by their Enemy—Destination of British Officers—Peace is concluded   -   -   -   -   293

CHAPTER XIX.

The means which were undertaken for succouring Kars— Nothing required but food and ammunition to enable the Turks to hold Kars — Omer Pasha's first arrival on the coast—His movements—The rainy season puts a stop to his campaign—General Mouravieff continues to blockade Kars—The two courses which were open to Omer Pasha—Objections of the Consuls to the proposed plan—General Mouravieff's ideas on the subject—The opinion of Her Majesty's Government conveyed in Lord Clarendon's letter   323

CHAPTER XX.

The practicability of the route between Trebizonde and Erzeroom—Particulars of the route—Letter on the subject from Mr. Consul Stevens — No necessity for heavy guns—An advance by way of Batoom considered—Objections to such a proceeding—General Mouravieff's ignorance of the amount of ammunition—Concluding remarks   -   -   -   -   336

ILLUSTRATIONS.

Turkish Infantry Soldiers	*To face title.*
Turkish Cavalry Soldiers	„ page 60
Russian Bashi-Bozouks	„ „ 91
Russian Infantry Soldiers	„ „ 100
View of the Russian Camp at Chiftli-Kaya	„ „ 294
Plan of the Fortress of Kars	
View of the Town and Fortress of Kars	

NARRATIVE

OF THE

DEFENCE OF KARS.

CHAPTER I.

Appointment of General Williams as British Commissioner in Asia Minor—Officers of his Staff—Defeat of the Turks at Kuruk-Déré—State of the Ottoman Army at Kars—Corruption of the Pashas—Ismail Pasha—General Guyon—Muster of Turkish Troops—Condition of the Officers and Men—Major Teesdale—Kerim Pasha—State of the Garrison at Kars.

WHEN the late war with Russia, which commenced in the year 1854, exceeded the limits to which it was at first earnestly hoped it might be confined, Her Majesty's Government naturally turned its thoughts to the state of affairs in Asia Minor, particularly as related to its defences, so vital in importance to the security of the British possessions in the East, and therefore determined to send out a Commissioner to serve with, and report upon the proceedings of the Turkish armies in that country.

Colonel Williams, C.B., of the Royal Artillery (now Major-General Sir Fenwick Williams, Bart., of Kars, K.C.B.), was nominated for this important situation. A better selection could not possibly have been made. This officer had served for many years on the Turco-Persian frontier, and his intimate knowledge of the character of the Turks, combined with no ordinary talent for diplomacy, rendered him in every respect a most competent person to undertake the duty.

The following extract of a letter from the Earl of Clarendon contains his nomination and instructions:—

"*The Earl of Clarendon to Lieutenant-Colonel Williams.*

(Extract.) "Foreign Office, August 2, 1854.

"I have to acquaint you that you have been selected as the officer to attend, as Her Majesty's Commissioner, the Head-Quarters of the Turkish army in Asia, and to act in that capacity in communication with, and under the orders of Lord Raglan; and to perform whatever services, in connection with that army, his Lordship may see occasion to prescribe to you.

"You will accordingly proceed with as little delay as possible to Lord Raglan's Head-Quarters, communicating on your passage by Constantinople with Her Majesty's Ambassador, who will be instructed to obtain from the Turkish Government all possible facilities for your performance of the duties intrusted to you.

EARL OF CLARENDON'S LETTER.

"You will receive from Lord Raglan detailed instructions for your guidance, and it is therefore only necessary for me to enjoin you to endeavour to maintain the most friendly relations with the officers of the Turkish army with whom you may come in contact, as also with any French officers who may be appointed to accompany that army in a similar capacity to that in which you are employed.

"You will communicate to me, for the information of Her Majesty's Government, all matters of political interest which may come under your observation, and you will keep me fully informed of the operations in which the Turkish army is engaged. You will also be at liberty to correspond with Her Majesty's Mission at the Court of Persia, when it may appear to you that the interests of the service on which you are engaged may be promoted by your doing so.

"You will furnish Lord Raglan with copies of all Despatches which you may have occasion to write to this office, or to any of Her Majesty's diplomatic or consular agents: and you will send your despatches for this office under flying seal to Her Majesty's Ambassador at Constantinople.

"You will furnish Her Majesty's Ambassador with any information which his Excellency may specifically require of you; but with regard to any representations which you may think it expedient should be made to the Porte, you will, unless otherwise instructed by Lord Raglan, apply to his Lordship on the subject, in order that, if he should concur in your opinion, he may himself request Her Majesty's Ambassador to bring the matter before the Porte."

Soon after the receipt of this letter Colonel Williams, who, in the February following, received the local rank of Brigadier-General, proceeded to Erzeroom to take up his appointment, accompanied by Lieutenant C. C. Teesdale, of the Royal Artillery (on whom the local rank of captain was subsequently conferred), as his Aide-de-camp. The Brigadier-General was afterwards joined by Dr. Sandwith, who, in addition to his duties as medical attendant on the officers attached to the Commission, was also appointed Inspector-General of Hospitals in Asia Minor. Some few months after this, Mr. H. A. Churchill, at that time attached to the Persian embassy at Teheran, joined the Commission as Secretary to General Williams, a post for which his perfect knowledge of several Eastern languages specially qualified him. He had previously served under Her Majesty's Commissioner, who, owing to the intelligence he then displayed, again applied for his services.

General Williams proceeded, in the first instance, to Constantinople, where, prior to setting out for the purpose of taking up his appointment, he received very minute instructions from Lord Raglan, the

Commander-in-chief of the British army, who was at that time in Varna.

Lord Raglan well knew the difficulties which Her Majesty's Commissioner would have to encounter in carrying on the duties connected with his new situation, owing to the jealousy and intrigues of the Turkish authorities with whom he would be necessarily associated; and his Lordship therefore felt it incumbent upon him to point out in detail the several subjects requiring General Williams' particular attention.

His orders were contained in the following clear and concise letter:—

"*General Lord Raglan to Colonel Williams.*

"Sir,   "Varna, August 20, 1854.

"Her Majesty's Government having been pleased to nominate you Commissioner at the head-quarters of the Turkish army in Asia, and to act in that capacity in communication with me and under my orders, I have the honour to request that, in obedience to their commands, you will lose no time in proceeding to Kars, and assuming the duties confided to your charge.

"You will, however, in the first instance, take advantage of your being at Constantinople, for the purpose of obtaining the necessary equipment, to solicit Her Majesty's Ambassador to get from the Turkish Government introductions to the authorities with whom you will have to communicate in the accomplishment of the objects of your Mission.

"You will also seek to obtain from his Excellency the advice which his great local experience, his knowledge of public men in this country, and his unrivalled power of discrimination, enable him to give better than any other man.

"The instructions of the Secretary of State are ample, and would render unnecessary that I should add anything thereto, were it not that the variety of accounts that have been given of the Mushir's army obliges me to impress upon you the expediency of trusting to no reports you may receive, but of endeavouring to ascertain, by close personal observation, its actual composition, the numbers each arm can bring into the field, distinguishing the Regulars from the Irregulars, the state of the arms in possession of the troops, whether Cavalry or Infantry, the quantity of musket ammunition (rounds per man) in the hands of the men and in reserve, the number of pieces of artillery and their calibre, how horsed, and with what number of rounds per gun, and how carried: whether the Infantry and Cavalry are formed into brigades and divisions, and under general officers, or whether there is no formation beyond that of a regiment or battalion; whether the troops are regularly supplied with provisions, and the horses with forage;

and, lastly, whether the army is paid, and to what period.

"You will also make it your business to discover whether the officers exercising commands of importance are efficient, and whether they support each other, or are occupied in intriguing to supplant those with whom they are associated.

"You will make all these inquiries free from any spirit of party or bias in favour of or prejudice against any individual, and you will attend especially to the judicious injunction of the Earl of Clarendon to establish and maintain the most friendly relations with the French officer whom I have reason to hope Marshal St. Arnaud will attach to that army for the exercise of the same functions as those intrusted to you.

"You will correspond with me by every opportunity, and you will take care to send your despatches to the Secretary of State under flying seal to Viscount Stratford, and to keep his Excellency informed upon all military as well as political matters.

"I have, &c.,

"(Signed)   RAGLAN."

Prior to General Williams' departure from Constantinople he heard of the defeat of the Turks by the Russians at Kuruk Déré, between which place and Hadji Véli Keui a very sanguinary engagement had taken place.

It appeared that, on the 29th of July, 1854, the Russians attacked the Turkish Division at Byazid, and that the latter had retreated without showing much resistance. Considerable stores of grain, biscuit, and ammunition had been laid up at that place by the Turks, which, of course, fell into the hands of the enemy; and, on the news of the disaster being received by the authorities at Kars, it was determined, at a Council of War, to retrieve the disgrace which had fallen on the Turkish arms, by attacking the Russians in the position they then held near their own frontier, before the force, which had been detached to Byazid, could return to join the main army.

In accordance with this determination, during the night of the 4th of August, all the necessary preparations were made for carrying their purpose into effect. After a somewhat stormy debate, owing to the difference of opinion among the several Commanders who were assembled at the Council, the plan of attack was at length finally decided upon, and, had it been carried out to the letter, there seems but little doubt that the result of the affair would have been very different to that which followed.

It was intended that the attacking forces should arrive in front of the enemy at day-dawn, but the right wing, consisting of about ten thousand regular infantry, under the command of Kerim Pasha, whose personal courage far exceeded his skill as a General in the field, did not succeed in taking up its position until six A.M.

The left wing, numbering about twelve thousand infantry, was commanded by Vēli Pasha, and did not reach its ground until two hours later. The advanced guard was under General Kméty (Ismail Pasha), General Guyon acting as chief of the staff.

In addition to the force above enumerated, there were about five thousand Bashi-Bozouks and militia, and between seven and eight thousand irregular troops, of which four thousand five hundred were horsemen of a most inferior description, and almost useless. The same observation may be applied to the regular Turkish cavalry, of whom there were about four thousand present, and who, from the want of proper training, the unfitness of their arms and accoutrements, and the bad condition of their horses, were of little or no use. The field-train consisted of fifty-two guns and a thousand artillerymen, who, as usual, fought bravely, and did their duty in a most satisfactory manner.

The Russian army was under the chief command of General Prince Bebutoff, an officer who had seen much arduous service, and who had the reputation of possessing much talent and energy. It consisted of the following troops :—

25 battalions of infantry.
2 regiments of Don Cossack cavalry.
2 regiments of Circassian Cossack cavalry.
2 regiments of dragoons.
6 regiments of irregulars.
60 field-pieces.

Contrary to expectation, the Russian division, which had gained the victory at Byazid, rejoined the main army prior to the advance of the Turkish force, so that the enemy was considerably stronger than was anticipated.

The whole Russian army attacked the right wing of the Turks, which was broken before the left wing and centre could get into position, owing to some misunderstanding on the part of the officers in command of the two latter columns, and to which may, in a great measure, be attributed the disasters which followed. After five hours' fighting, the Turks, finding that any further resistance would be in vain, retreated to Kars, leaving General Kméty, with a small force of cavalry and a few guns, to watch Hadji Vēli Keui.

During the action ten Turkish and six Russian guns were dismounted, which, owing to the superiority of the Russian over the Turkish cavalry, were all taken off by the former. The loss on either side it was difficult to estimate, but there is no doubt that the beaten army suffered very severely. Mr. Consul Brant puts the probable number of Turks at two thousand killed and wounded, and an equal number taken prisoners, while Her Majesty's Ambassador at Constantinople, in writing on the subject, states that "the " reduction of their efficient numbers may be safely " stated at ten thousand." This amount, however, may be supposed to include the soldiers who, disheartened by defeat, deserted by hundreds, if not by thousands.

The loss the Russians experienced must necessarily have been very considerable, owing to the long continuance of the action and to the steady fire of the artillery, which is described as having been most effective; but it is impossible to give even an approximating number.

The result of this disastrous affair soon became apparent in the total disorganization of the Kars army, and the consequent desertions which took place almost every day.

At the conclusion of the engagement the enemy retired to his former camp, both sides having been permitted, by mutual consent, to bury their dead the following day. It is difficult to imagine why Prince Bebutoff did not follow up the advantage he had gained by his victory. The chances are that, if he had pursued the retreating army, he would have found them so dispirited by defeat that he would not have met with much opposition, and he might possibly have possessed himself, with but trifling loss, of the fortified position of Kars, which was at that time by no means in a defensible state. It is needless now to descant on the difference which such a step would have created in the campaign of the following year, when the Russians suffered so severely in their determination to take the place, which would, in all probability, have cost them, comparatively speaking, but few lives.

It would be equally difficult to conjecture what the intention of the Turks was in making the attack, for even had they been victorious, they could not have expected to gain much by the step. General Williams, in a letter to Lord Clarendon, dated August 27, 1854, when alluding to the Kars army and its defeat, wrote thus :—

" The bad management of that army throughout
" the summer has been unhappily crowned by the
" disasters of a night march of a half-disciplined
" force to attack at day-dawn one perfectly handled
" and well organized : the onset, if even conducted
" with prudence and crowned with success, could
" not have led to any important results, particularly
" at this advanced season of the year ; for I feel
" assured that, by inquiries on the spot, I shall find
" that the Turkish army did not possess either
" provision, materials, or carriage adequate to an
" advance into the interior of Georgia in face of an

" intelligent enemy having the entire resources of
" that country at its command: this injudicious
" movement (by whomsoever advised) has only pro-
" duced a further distrust of the Turkish soldier,
" not only with respect to their officers, but also as
" regards their own prowess."

In contemplating the results of this battle, and beholding the utter destruction of the bands of discipline in the Turkish host, some idea may be formed of the task in store for any one subsequently intrusted with its reorganization, and charged with the guidance of its future movements and destiny.

The Turkish officers were the first to set the example of cowardice: the soldiers exhibited the sad spectacle of an aggregate of brave men scattered to the winds without a chief to direct them. The brave Generals Kméty and Guyon did all that might have been expected from such able and gallant officers; but they were foreigners, and a discomfited Mussulman army would be slow to listen to Christian leaders when their own chiefs abandoned it.

The heights of Kars proved at last the beacon which attracted and guided the shattered forces towards a haven of rest: those heights which afterwards were so industriously fortified by their hands, and so gloriously defended by their stout hearts and unbending valour, presenting to the world a specimen of Mussulman courage and constancy, as well as confidence in a Christian Commander, which will for ever shed a glorious ray around the Ottoman arms.

On the 15th of September General Williams arrived at Erzeroom. His first care was to inspect all the caravanserais where the troops, coming from Kars, were to take up their winter quarters. He also visited the hospitals where the wounded were located, for the purpose of seeing that they were carefully attended to.

Soon after leaving Trebizonde, he had a foretaste of the way in which business was carried on with regard to the unfortunate army of Kars. In the middle of the road he found a beautiful brass gun, lying, with its small stores and all its equipments complete, without a man near it; and from the state of the sponge, it was very evident that it had remained for days, if not for weeks, unmoved and uncared for. Several more guns were seen in the same state before the end of the day's march, and this formed the ground of the first remonstrance addressed by Her Majesty's Commissioner to the Turkish authorities.

It is no doubt a difficult thing to move heavy guns along such roads, but it was quite feasible to do so in the present instance, as was afterwards fully shewn. The Turk, however, having once been brought to a standstill, lights his pipe and says that "God is great," but he never overcomes his own *vis inertiæ* sufficiently to go to work again.

It was very evident that the reoccupation by the Turks of the frontier station, which they had lost possession of prior to the battle of Kuruk Déré, was of the utmost moment. Persia was at that time a neutral power, but was imagined to be better disposed towards England than towards Russia. It was, therefore, of the greatest consequence that the communication which had been cut off by the capture of Byazid by the Russians should be reopened.

Under these circumstances General Williams lost no time, after his arrival at Erzeroom, in laying the facts of the case before the Governor-General. The result of his interview with Ismail Pasha is given in the following extract of a letter addressed by Her Majesty's Commissioner to Lord Clarendon :—

"*Colonel Williams to the Earl of Clarendon.*

(Extract.) " Erzeroom, September 17, 1854.

" Having in view the reoccupation of Byazid, and the consequent resumption of commercial intercourse with Persia, I waited on his Excellency Ismail Pasha, the Governor-General; and having placed in the proper light the disgrace which the Sultan's arms had suffered by the cowardice of Selim Pasha in abandoning that frontier station,

I told his Excellency that I would use my utmost endeavours with the Mushir of the Kars army to detach a force sufficient to vindicate the insults which a band of Cossacks and a few regulars of the enemy were daily offering them in that vicinity; but I added that his Excellency's assistance was absolutely necessary to the success of my plans.

"Ismail Pasha replied that nothing annoyed him so much as the conduct of Selim Pasha; he added, 'I have more than once asked the Mushir to open this road, and I will second you to the utmost, if he sends me word to that effect, after you have seen him at Kars.'

"Ismail Pasha, at my request, promised to have supplies of biscuits, flour, and rice, ready to be forwarded to the station where the road branches toward Byazid, the moment he heard from me, inclosing the Mushir's orders to that effect: he further assured me that he would collect as many entrenching tools as possible and despatch them with the above enumerated supplies.

"It will now depend on the Mushir either to mar or to further this operation, and I shall use every effort to induce him to do his duty."

The Ottoman Army, to which General Williams was accredited, was at this time in a most disorganized state, having been, by gross mismanagement on the part of its Commanders, signally defeated by the Russians, the previous year, in the battle before alluded to. Desertions from the ranks had taken place to an enormous extent, and the remaining troops, dispirited, for a time, by their late disasters, totally demoralized in every way, and under the guidance and tuition of officers, themselves wholly ignorant of their duty, were in a very unfit state again to encounter the enemy in the field; though, as it was afterwards proved, the latent sparks of their natural courage were only smouldering in their bosoms, and had not, even under overwhelming misfortunes, been wholly extinguished.

The Turkish Pashas and superior officers, at all times most corrupt, had robbed the unhappy soldiers of their just dues to enrich themselves; and the ragged state of their clothes, and the non-receipt of a single piastre of pay for several months, were quite enough to lead them to imagine that they were completely neglected by their Government.

In this wretched state did General Williams find the Ottoman army on his arrival in Asia Minor. He lost no time in bringing it to the notice of the proper authorities at Constantinople, stating, at the same time, all that was required for the equipment of the troops in clothing, arms, and ammunition. How far these requisitions were attended to need not here be shown, the subject having been discussed in higher quarters by those who have the best right to pass comments on the conduct of functionaries holding important situations.

The Vali of Erzeroom, Ismail Pasha, was an Arnaout, and a very old man: he evidently meant well, but his age was unfortunately too great to fit him for much exertion, either mental or bodily. Her Majesty's Commissioner, having made such arrangements as he considered necessary, proceeded, with his Aide-de-camp and the Inspector-General of Hospitals, to Kars, where he arrived on the 22nd of September, 1854.

On his approach he was met by General Guyon, at that time holding a commission in the Turkish army. He was by birth an Irishman, and was one of the most distinguished officers in the wars of Hungary against Austria. He had tried hard to improve the Kars army, but he found it a very difficult task, and he seemed to be almost disheartened. He soon after left the place, and was not again employed. He was a thoroughly brave and chivalrous man, but fell a victim to the intrigues of jealous cowards.

The troops were encamped on the lowest part of a considerable plain just at the foot of the town of Kars: it could scarcely be called a fortified camp, though there were a few ditches running round it which bore the name of entrenchments, but which would have been of no use whatever in case of an attack.

MUSTER OF TURKISH TROOPS AT KARS.

General Williams occupied himself, as at Erzeroom, in visiting the hospitals, which, owing to his expected arrival, had been put into a tolerably decent state. As an instance of the manner in which the duties of the medical department had been carried on, prior to the superintendence of Dr. Sandwith, the following anecdote is given. A wretched man had a cataplasm prescribed for him: for a wonder, it was made; but instead of being applied in the usual way, he was forced to *eat* it!

The General next inspected the infantry: he was told that upwards of twenty-two thousand men were present. Doubting Turkish veracity, he counted them, and found that they numbered considerably under fifteen thousand.

The following memorandum, which was forwarded to Her Majesty's Ambassador at Constantinople, shows the actual numbers:—

"*Memorandum respecting the State of the Turkish Army at Kars.*

"September and October, 1854.

"INFANTRY.

" In the muster-roll, as given by the generals of division, the numbers fictitiously put down are—

1st division	9,662	men and officers.
2nd division	8,243	,,
Reserve	4,669	,,
Total	22,574	,,

Men.—Disposable number in camp :—

Regulars	7,200
Rediff	3,400
	10,600
Add men off duty, sick	2,000
Encamped about an hour from Kars.	2,000
Total	14,600

They were fine-looking fellows, but miserably clothed; their faces well bronzed, and their bright eyes showing how much was in them, if only properly treated. In order to make as great a display as possible, every available officer and man was paraded; and, on riding past one of the columns, General Williams remarked a number of officers standing together without any men. The Mushir (marshal) turned round, and asked who they were; whereupon the colonel of a rediff (militia) regiment, named Déli Zechariah Bey, who had the reputation of being half mad, dashed through the whole staff, and said aloud, "Effendim, they are men " who have let their soldiers go on a visit to " Georgia." They were, in fact, the officers of a regiment that had been destroyed or taken prisoners at Kuruk Déré, the previous year. It by no means follows that Turkish officers share the fate of their men.

False muster-rolls were kept for a double purpose. First, because the pay and rations of those soldiers who did not exist went to the Pashas; and, secondly, it was done to conceal from the Sultan and his Government the real losses consequent on the rout at Kuruk Déré.

The Turkish authorities were, no doubt, both surprised and annoyed to find any one taking the trouble to institute such minute and searching inquiries into affairs which had, up to that period, been left entirely under their own control. Her Majesty's Commissioner, however, was not to be imposed upon by plausible stories; he had lived too long among the Turks to be easily deceived by any specious reports which they might think fit to lay before him, and at once resolved to satisfy himself, by a personal inspection, of the truth of the several statements with which those in command endeavoured to mislead him.

Having detected roguery and peculation to a very great extent, General Williams felt it his duty to bring the circumstance to the notice of Her Majesty's Government; and in a despatch which he forwarded from Kars to the Earl of Clarendon, dated 25th of October, 1854, after alluding to the steps he had taken for the formation of magazines to contain such articles of consumption as would be required for the daily use of the garrison during the winter months, he adds—

"I also ascertained from the Vakeel of the Defterdar, who is in charge of these establishments, that rations for thirty-three thousand men are issued daily from them! Your Lordship can therefore estimate the difficulties we shall encounter during the winter if this enormous fraud is continued. The real effective being fourteen thousand men, such a course will diminish the number of days' rations to one-half, and soon bring famine into Kars.

"On the day following the inspection of these magazines, I was invited by the Mushir to see the second battalion of the Rediff of the Guard march to Olti; two hundred and fifty men were counted by three persons present, yet the Colonel, Edhem Bey, approached the Mushir and reported four hundred under arms! I avoided a public scandal by exposing the man before his regiment, but on my return to camp I waited on Zarif Mustafa Pasha, and having first laid before him the daily plunder of our magazines by the false muster-rolls of the Colonels, and brought to his notice the impudent attempt of Edhem Bey to deceive him and myself as to the effective of the battalion above alluded to, I begged him not to suppose that I assented to such an assertion, and intimated to him that I should inform my Government of these facts.

"His Excellency seemed much disconcerted, and

" said, 'the army did not draw too many
" ' rations.'

" He has just informed me that he quits the
" army to-day for Erzeroom. I have already in-
" formed your Lordship of the sentiments I gave
" him on that point. I believe all the gold and
" silver ever sent to this army to be in his coffers,
" but, as soon as he quits the camp, I shall wait
" on Kerim Pasha, the Kaimakam, and request
" him to assemble his Colonels; I shall then ex-
" pose the whole robbery, and thus, I hope, save
" the garrison from starvation during the long
" winter which awaits them.

" When the winter subsistence of this garrison
" and that of Erzeroom are taken into considera-
" tion, together with the vast supplies which the
" operations of the ensuing year will involve, it
" must be admitted that the districts of the pro-
" vince of Erzeroom cannot meet such demands,
" and I therefore trust that the central government
" will order supplies from every part of Asia Minor,
" Bagdad and Moossul included, to be sent towards
" Erzeroom without delay."

General Williams was not contented with merely reporting to his own Government the result of the inquiries he found it necessary to make, but he adopted more active and immediate measures for the purpose of remedying, as much as possible, the evils which existed. Proper accommodation for the men was one of the subjects which engaged his attention at this time, for he had ascertained that many of the Pashas were occupying houses which would have conveniently held two hundred and fifty men, while the soldiers were stowed away like so many herrings in a barrel. This alone would account for the terrible mortality of the preceding year; for the very fact of hundreds of human creatures being literally packed into a small space not calculated to hold a tenth part of the number, was sufficient to produce all manner of sickness among the troops, in many cases terminating in death.

It was not peculation alone that Her Majesty's Commissioner had to complain of among the superior officers, though that was carried on to an extent almost incredible; it was brought to his notice that intoxication and debauchery were practised openly by those whose duty it was to set a good example to their men. The consequences arising from this baneful habit were but too apparent in the want of proper subordination; and General Williams assembled some of the superior officers in order that he might point out to them the impropriety and the danger of the course they were pursuing. Prior to leaving Kars he addressed the following letter on the subject to Her Majesty's Government:—

"*Colonel Williams to the Earl of Clarendon.*"

"My Lord,   "Camp near Kars, October 28, 1854.

"Agreeably to the determination expressed in my despatch of the 26th, I induced Kerim Pasha, the Kaimakam, to assemble the Colonels of this army, and I at once proceeded to state to his Excellency and those chiefs of regiments my astonishment and regret at the gross peculation carried on daily at the magazines, by means of their false muster-rolls; I told them plainly that I had represented everything to Her Majesty's Ambassador at the Porte, to your Lordship, and to Lord Raglan; I warned them that I should not cease my endeavours to collect sufficient food for this garrison, and begged them to recollect the dreadful mortality of last year, which I principally attributed to these wholesale peculations.

"I further told them that I was acquainted with the nocturnal intemperance reigning in the camp, and pointed out the consequence of such a state of things, should the enemy be induced to attack it at night. Kerim Pasha (who, I must say, has implicitly followed my advice since the departure of the Mushir) assured me before the assembled colonels that he would put a stop both to pillage and intoxication. I hope I shall be able to inform your Lordship that he has carried his promise into execution.

"I have, &c.,

"(Signed)   W. F. Williams."

On the 11th of November, 1854, General Williams quitted Kars, and returned to Erzeroom, leaving, as his representative, Captain Teesdale, his Aide-de-camp, on whom the rank of Major in the Turkish Army was conferred by the Sultan.

This promotion was communicated to the English Government by General Williams in the following terms :—

"*Brigadier-General Williams to the Earl of Clarendon.*

" MY LORD, "Erzeroom, February 3, 1855.

" In forwarding the enclosed copies of Lieutenant Teesdale's further reports, I have to inform your Lordship that Kerim Pasha received by the post before the last a firman from His Majesty the Sultan, according the rank of Major in his armies to that officer. It is, I am bound to say, a just tribute to his merit, for he has deservedly won the goodwill and respect of the troops composing the garrison of Kars.

" I have, &c.,
" (Signed) W. F. WILLIAMS."

His instructions were to look after the feeding of the troops, and to superintend their drill as far as the weather would allow, endeavouring, at the same time, as much as possible, to establish something like discipline among them.

KERIM PASHA.—STATE OF THE GARRISON. 27

The Mushir having by this time left Kars, the command of the army devolved on Lieutenant-General Kerim Pasha, a very fine old soldier, who afterwards greatly distinguished himself. Major Teesdale carried on his arduous duties with the greatest tact and energy, having ingratiated himself so well with the Turkish authorities, that any suggestion he made was immediately attended to. The season was too far advanced to do much more to the fortifications than to construct a small open battery on the hills, which will be referred to hereafter, and to connect two others on the plain below by means of a breastwork, the snow which falls at Kars being too heavy to allow of any work being carried on during the winter months. His time, therefore, was entirely taken up in trying to get adequate and proper supplies of provisions into Kars, and in devising the best means for procuring transport to effect this desirable object.

Despite all the efforts that were made, it was only possible to keep the men alive from day to day: their food was even then most indifferent; and the barley, which was intended for the horses, had to be used in making soup for the men. An extract from a letter addressed by Major Teesdale, at Kars, to General Williams, at Erzeroom, and dated 28th January, 1855, will explain, better than any other description, the state of the garrison at that period—" With Kerim Pasha I have been

"holding some sanitary conversations. I have
"visited the bakeries, and done what I could to
"make an improvement in the bread. The poor
"fellows are much in want of a few vegetables, if
"you could get any for them. The great want and
"universal cry is, of course, *money*. We could get
"on well enough with that, and, although it may
"be a bold thing to say, I think we have got them
"tight enough by the head to make them account
"for the greater part of the supplies. The Ara-
"bistan artillery will, in my opinion, be unfit to
"take the field in the spring, unless funds be pro-
"vided for repairing the harness, or, at least, to
"furnish the materials for doing so."

CHAPTER II.

Health of the Soldiers—Worthlessness of Shukri Pasha, Commandant—Merit of Kerim Pasha, second in command—Appointment of more British Officers—Colonel Lake arrives at Kars—Exertions of General Williams—Insurrection in Koordistan, suppressed by General Williams on his own responsibility—Surrender of Izzideen shere Bey.

THE great enemy which the garrison had to contend against about this period was the scurvy, which may be accounted for by the too simple nature of the diet, composed wholly of bread and meat. Vegetables of any sort were scarcely ever to be procured, and the want of regular exercise also tended greatly to increase this terrible sickness: in other respects, the health of the men was astonishingly good. Of twelve thousand men, scarcely two hundred were ever in hospital at one time; and the only way to account for this is by the fact of the garrison being composed of old hardy soldiers, the thrice-sifted remnant of what was once the army of Anatolia, sixty thousand strong.

Shukri Pasha, who had been sent from Constantinople as Provisional Commandant, seemed to have arrived at Kars with the fixed determination to render himself as obnoxious as possible to General Williams. In character he was a worthless profligate, possessed of no education, and without the smallest zeal for the real good of the army. This latter is sufficiently proved by his conduct, and the short duration of his stay at Kars, which did not exceed forty-eight hours. During this time he distributed one month's pay to the officers and soldiers, who were all from eighteen to twenty-four months in arrears, gave a drinking party, at which he did nothing but cry down Her Majesty's Commissioner and his proceedings, and finally left without having made an inspection of the troops, or taken a single step to make himself acquainted with the real state of the garrison.

He did not, however, meet with that prompt punishment which might have been insisted upon by the proper authorities at Constantinople, after the repeated representations made of his conduct by General Williams, but was allowed to remain in office to neutralize, by his apathy and neglect, all the efforts which were being made.

With the aid of an energetic man such supplies could have been thrown into Kars as would have enabled the garrison to hold out for a year, but Shukri Pasha thwarted and bearded the Commissioner in every possible way.

This man's character is well described in the

following extract from a letter addressed by Mr. Consul Brant to the Earl of Clarendon:—

"*Consul Brant to the Earl of Clarendon.*

(Extract.) "Erzeroom, December 7, 1854.

"You will have perceived that Shukri Pasha, the *locum tenens* of the new Mushir, Ismail Pasha, was prepared to thwart Colonel Williams in his energetic exertions to save the remnant of the Kars army from annihilation by sickness and famine, and to put it into a state of efficiency.

"I have since been informed, from a source that I may depend on, that a plot has been got up among the superior officers of the army, to persuade his Excellency Ismail Pasha, on his arrival, that Colonel Williams' interference is unauthorised and most prejudicial; and to induce his Excellency to invite the Colonel to an interview, in which he will be requested to produce his credentials from the Seraskier, and in case such are not shown, he will be told that any further interference in the affairs of the army will not be tolerated. I have warned the Colonel of this plot."

Kerim Pasha, the Rēis or second in command, appeared, on the contrary, anxious to do his utmost to meet the views of General Williams' representative, and, unlike ordinary Turks, he took the trouble of going, step by step, through every case which was brought before him, and, among others, that of

Achmet Pasha, a general officer, who was accused, among many other crimes, of having wantonly cut down his own men, and of having murdered a wounded soldier two hours after a battle was over. He was found guilty, and sent the following day to Erzeroom, where he was kept for a long while in arrest; but it was never known whether he was ultimately punished or not according to his deserts.

It may not, perhaps, be out of place to mention here a circumstance which showed pretty plainly that, however willing the commanding officer appeared to be to work with Her Majesty's Commissioner, other officers of high rank showed some slight symptoms of disaffection. Major Teesdale, in writing to General Williams on this subject, says: " Ayoupp Bey, the Colonel from Kaghisman, was re-" primanded in the Medjlis by Kerim Pasha. There " is an affair connected with this, which, slight as it " may appear, will do mischief if not crushed in the " bud. It appears that, when Kerim Pasha had " spoken his mind plainly to Ayoupp Bey, and dis-" missed the members of the Medjlis, some of the " Colonels got together, and expressed great dissatis-" faction at what had been said. Nearly the same " thing occurred among the Livas, when Achmet " Pasha was convicted, but they were quieter " then."

It will be admitted that the duty which Major

Teesdale had to perform was by no means a sinecure. The manner in which he conducted it called forth the warm approval of General Williams; and on his quitting Kars he carried with him the esteem and regard of all those in authority with whom he had been associated. His letters to Her Majesty's Commissioner during this period, written in a most clear and concise style, stated, from time to time, all that was required for the comfort and efficiency of the men, and brought to his notice such of the officers as he considered worthy of promotion or deserving of punishment.

Kerim Pasha well deserved the character given of him in the following extract from a letter addressed by Her Majesty's Commissioner to the Earl of Clarendon.

"*Colonel Williams to the Earl of Clarendon.*

(Extract.) "Erzeroom, December 21, 1854.

"The continued and marked consideration shown by Kerim Pasha, not only towards me, but also with regard to the British officer left in the entrenched position of Kars, demands my warmest thanks; and I doubt not that his Excellency will receive from Her Majesty's Government an expression of its acknowledgments and approbation for a line of conduct so diametrically opposite to that of Shukri Pasha. The moment he was emancipated from the withering influence of the late Mushir, Zarif Mustafa

Pasha, Kerim Pasha showed himself in his real character. He is a friend of justice: he is grateful for the efforts making by England for the defence of his country; and I trust that he will be allowed to command, next spring, a division of those soldiers whom he is now holding in hand with such praiseworthy zeal."

General Williams, in his despatches to the Home Government, had represented, in the following terms, the necessity for assistance being granted to him in the arduous task he had undertaken, by having placed at his disposal the services of as many officers of the different branches as could be spared:—

" I conceive that ten thousand men will be the
" extent of the force which Kars can accommodate
" within its walls, during the approaching winter,
" without engendering disease which would cost us
" more than a battle; but as the enemy might
" possibly make demonstrations against it in early
" spring, ere the bulk of the enemy could rendez-
" vous under its walls, I have requested the Mushir
" to prepare a house for two or three European
" officers, who might, during my absence with the
" Head-Quarters at Erzeroom, supervise the drills
" and sanitary arrangements of this garrison during
" the winter, and be ready, in case of need, to show

" it how to perform its duty in giving any enemy
" a warm reception.

" In accordance with these views, I beg to pro-
" pose that an officer of our artillery and engineers
" should be placed at my disposal for these pur-
" poses; and I will take care that they are com-
" fortably lodged during the long winter about to
" set in. If a rifle officer be added to the party, it
" would enable the men to be exercised and in-
" structed in ball-firing, when the weather per-
" mitted, a vital point, to which the officers of this
" army do not pay the least attention."

This requisition was at once attended to by the appointment of Captain William Olpherts of the Bengal Artillery, and Lieutenant Henry Langhorne Thompson of the 68th regiment of Bengal Native Infantry. These officers proceeded, with the local rank of Major and Captain respectively, to join Her Majesty's Commissioner without delay. They were followed, not long afterwards, by Brevet-Major Atwell Lake of the Madras Engineers, on whom the local rank of Lieutenant-Colonel had been conferred by Her Majesty's Government.

Towards the end of the month of March, 1855, the two former of these officers arrived at Kars, when Major Teesdale proceeded to Erzeroom for the purpose of rejoining General Williams. On the 31st of the same month Lieutenant-Colonel Lake, who had remained one day with Her Majesty's Commissioner *en route,* in order to receive his instructions, assumed charge of the post just vacated at Kars by Major Teesdale.

It is now necessary to turn once more to Erzeroom, and to show what had been going on in that city since General Williams' return in November, 1854. On his first arrival at that place he lost no time in making incessant exertions to put the army in an efficient state, and to obtain all the supplies necessary for that purpose; but he had not only to contend against the proverbial idleness, incorrigible debauchery, and prejudices of the Turkish authorities with whom he had to deal, but he experienced the pain and mortification of finding that no attention was paid to his requisitions, and no notice taken of his numerous despatches.

Nothing daunted, however, by all the obstacles thrown in his way—more than enough to cool the ardour of any one of a less sanguine temperament—General Williams redoubled his exertions, leaving no stone unturned to enable him to effect his object.

It will readily be allowed that his duties were of a most arduous nature. His task might, indeed, have been an easier, as well as a pleasanter one, if he had only met with that amount of cooperation on the part of the Turkish authorities, which, as Her Majesty's Commissioner, sent out to the Ottoman army for a special purpose, he had every right to expect. He felt, however, that, in the position which he had the honour of holding, the interests of the Government to which he was accredited should be his first and principal care; and that not only the organization of the army, with all the details connected therewith, but the interior economy of the local Government, which apparently stood so much in need of reform, should occupy his immediate attention. He allowed no private pique or personal feelings to influence his conduct, but proceeded steadily in his endeavours to master all the difficulties and impediments which were thrown in his way by the Turks.

During the period that Her Majesty's Commissioner was busily employed in laying out and superintending the fortifications at Erzeroom, he received direct intimation of an insurrection having broken out in Khoordistan, headed by a great and influential chieftain, named Izzideen shere Bey.

It may be observed, that the province of Khoordistan, a large and fertile tract of country situated in Turkey in Asia, is famed for the robust and hardy nature of its inhabitants, who are of most unsettled habits, and who acknowledge neither the Turkish nor Persian sway. They are divided into several tribes, each tribe being commanded by its own chief, who is himself wholly independent of any government. They neither speak the same language nor dress in the same costume as the Turks or Persians. The Christian villagers subject to their rule were formerly treated with great injustice and tyranny, but through the representations of European consuls, and by the interposition of the ministers at Constantinople, a very great amelioration had been effected with regard to these oppressed Armenian Christians.

The insurrection now alluded to commenced at Jezira-ben-Omer, and was known to be rapidly extending in the direction of Bitliz, Moosh, and Van. General Williams, from his long residence in that part of the country, and his intimate knowledge of the character of its inhabitants, perceived at once what the effects of this movement would be if it were not immediately checked. He knew that, if it once gained head, it would be necessary to detach the troops which were stationed between Erzeroom and Byazid, for the purpose of suppressing the insurrection, and this could not be done without leaving the line of communication between the Russian frontier and the capital of Asia Minor open to the enemy.

Under these urgent circumstances, General Williams determined, without waiting for instructions from Constantinople, to take upon himself the responsibility of communicating direct with the rebellious chieftain; and accordingly he at once despatched to the scene of action Major Mahmoud Effendi, a Polish officer, lately returned from the Danube, where he had acquired that rank, as well as a character for zeal and intelligence, which induced the General to select him for this important duty, with full powers and instructions as to the course he was to pursue.

The envoy, thus invested with the necessary authority, lost no time in opening a communication with the Khoordish chieftain, Izzideen shere Bey. It was not, however, from him alone that danger was to be apprehended, but from numerous other petty chiefs who were prepared to join him, so that the revolt would soon have become general; but, on the preliminaries having been arranged, Izzideen shere Bey was induced to surrender, trusting to the good faith of Her Majesty's Representative for the due fulfilment of the treaty; and at the same time the petty chiefs, finding that they would no longer be supported, returned to their allegiance.

Izzideen shere Bey, without hesitation, gave himself up to the British Vice-consul at Mussol, whither he proceeded, in company with Major Mahmoud Effendi, who, after delivering over his charge, returned without delay to Erzeroom, where he received the cordial thanks of General Williams, with an expression of his high approbation of the tact and ability he had displayed in carrying out a measure of so much importance. This young officer, it may be observed, was soon afterwards sent to Kars, and attached to the Chief of the staff, under whom he served with great credit until the surrender of the fortress.

Thus was suppressed, fortunately without bloodshed, this dangerous insurrection, which at one time looked so threatening, and which, had it been permitted to continue, would have very materially compromised the safety of the Anatolian army, by opening to the Russian detachment at Erivan a direct passage to the very heart of Khoordistan and Armenia, by which the enemy, being enabled to intrigue with the chieftains of North Khoordistan, might have received a vast accession of irregular cavalry, at all times ready to enlist under the banner of those who possess the means and inclination to pay them.

There can be no doubt that General Williams, in acting as he had thus done, incurred a responsibility of a very grave nature; so grave, indeed, that very few officers similarly situated, and not vested with full powers, would have dared to run the risk of failure. The result, however, fully demonstrated the expediency of this measure; and to the promptness and energy with which it was commenced and carried through, may be mainly attributed its complete success.

Izzideen shere Bey, it must be remembered, was a nephew of the celebrated Bēdir Khan Bey, the murderer of the Nestorian Christians, and possessed a name so powerful in Khoordistan, that, had he remained at large, he would have kept the whole country in a blaze. It was therefore of the most vital importance that the sparks of an insurrection, likely to be fraught with such incalculable danger, should be extinguished before it became too late. The terms * made with this political culprit were shortly afterwards confirmed by the Turkish Government, and he was sent to Constantinople, where, it is to be hoped, that, contrary to the custom which has prevailed in similar cases, he may be long retained; for the injudicious pardon and enlargement of chieftains, taken in actual revolt, have invariably led to a renewal of the same outrages, by encouraging them again to set all laws at defiance, the consequences of which may easily be imagined.

It cannot be denied that these insurrections are but too often engendered by the want of that faith on the part of the Imperial Government which ought always to characterize its dealings with a population naturally warlike and irascible; and it must be a subject of pride and congratulation to the people of England when they reflect upon the testimony which, in the case of Izzideen shere Bey, is borne by a semi-barbarous and almost wholly uneducated race to British honour and integrity, in the person of Her Majesty's Commissioner.

* The treaty guaranteed to Izzideen shere Bey the preservation of his life and property.

CHAPTER III.

Description of the Fortress of Kars in 1855—New Works planned and executed by Colonel Lake.

It may be as well, perhaps, before proceeding further, to give a short description of the fortress of Kars, and of the state the fortifications were in at the commencement of the year 1855.

Kars may truly be said to be the key to Asia Minor, and, as such, a place of great importance. It fell into the hands of the Russians in 1828, when besieged by a force under the command of the late General Prince Paskiewitch. It was at that time so very imperfectly fortified, that, though the Turks evinced a certain degree of courage, it surrendered after three days.

The town of Kars is situated in Armenia, 43° 16' east longitude, and 40° 15' north latitude, nearly seven thousand feet above the level of the sea. With a vast plain in front, and high mountains in rear, it is built in a kind of semicircle formed by the Kars-Tchai at the place where the river enters the narrow gorge of the mountains. The chief habitations are within the walls of the fortress, but there are also suburbs outside, the principal one of which is partly surrounded by a wall of defence, with two small bastions at the east and west angles.

The fortress itself is said, by local tradition, to have been constructed between the years 1578 and 1589, during the war with the Persians. It is in the form of an irregular polygon (the northern face resting on the steep rocks which form the right bank of the river), and is built of blocks of stone in cement, with a double " *enceinte* " of walls, and four towers or bastions. At the north-west angle is situated the citadel (considerably raised above the plane of the fortress), which is in itself a very strong place, and would be difficult to take were it not commanded by the mountains in rear.

There was—and indeed there still exists, though in a dilapidated state—a covered passage in masonry leading from the citadel to the river, built, doubtless, with a view to enabling the garrison to hold the citadel in the event of being driven to the last extremity; but so long as the position on the mountains in rear, forming the opposite bank of the river, remained imperfectly fortified, the citadel might be considered as nearly useless; for when once the enemy succeeded in establishing himself on the hills, it would become untenable. The inner wall of the fortress is flanked by numerous small round and square towers, placed at irregular intervals, and the outer wall forms altogether a circuit of 2600 yards.

The mountain of Kāradāgh, situated to the east of, and commanding the fortress, was, in 1828, fortified by a battery of earthwork and well furnished with cannon. There was also a tower, now in ruins, called the Castle of Temir Pasha, situated on the opposite bank of the river, to the west of the fortress, serving as a defence for part of the town.

This imperfect sketch will, perhaps, suffice to show the nature of the permanent works as they stood in the year above mentioned, when the place was attacked and taken by Prince Paskiewitch.

In a very interesting work, recently published by Lieutenant-General Monteith, entitled "Kars and Erzeroom," will be found a brief account of the capture of the fortress by the Russians in 1828. This officer was himself present at the affair, having joined Prince Paskiewitch shortly after the commencement of the Turkish war, and having accompanied him during a considerable portion of the campaign.

Having described the siege operations, which did not extend over many days, General Monteith proceeds to recount the surrender in the following

words :—" The Turks made a greater resistance on
" the western side, but with little success; for the
" whole of the lower fortress was soon occupied, and
" the Pasha gave up all hopes of a longer resistance.
" A white flag was now hoisted; Prince Paskie-
" witch demanded the surrender of the Pasha and
" of the Turkish garrison as prisoners of war, and
" the disarming of the militia and local troops, who
" were to be permitted to return to their homes.
" So great was the panic, that 1,000 Delhis, sta-
" tioned in the heart of the town, passed before the
" Russian troops without venturing to commit any
" act of hostility.

Emaum Pasha hesitated to accept these terms,
trusting to be relieved, and demanded two days
" to consider, declaring his determination to bury
" himself under the ruins of the part of the citadel
" he still occupied. The principal Mollahs brought
" this answer to the General, who replied, 'I will
" 'give you two hours to make up your minds.
" 'Mercy if you surrender, death if you resist!' As
" this threat was supported by forty pieces of artil-
" lery, ready to open on the confined space of the
" upper citadel, the garrison began to show signs of
" insubordination; and Emaum Pasha, fearing an
" insurrection, in despair brought the keys of the
" place, and gave himself up a prisoner. The gar-
" rison surrendered at ten A.M., and the Russian
" flag was hoisted on the ramparts.

" The fortress of Kars enjoyed at that time a
" character for strength which was very unmerited :
" the walls, though high, were weak, and yielded
" after a few shots had been fired against them.
" It is also so entirely surrounded by hills, that the
" garrison are exposed to a direct fire on every side,
" rendering it doubtful whether anything can be
" done to strengthen it without a number of
" detached works. Twenty-two mortars, and one
" hundred and twenty-nine cannon, with a con-
" siderable quantity of gunpowder and other am-
" munition, were found in the place, besides six
" thousand sacks of grain in the magazine. The
" loss of the Russians amounted to thirteen officers,
" and four hundred men killed and wounded; that
" of the Turks to two thousand killed and wounded,
" besides one thousand three hundred and sixty-
" one prisoners. The whole garrison, including the
" militia, had originally amounted to eleven thou-
" sand men; but eight thousand had either retired,
" or had been disarmed before the surrender of the
" fortress. Although there had been no capitula-
" tion, there was but very little plundering, and
" that little was immediately put a stop to, and a
" proclamation issued, promising protection to all
" who thought proper to remain. Order was per-
" fectly restored by the evening; and on the fol-
" lowing day the shops were opened, and the
" artisans continued their usual occupations. A

"council was then established, consisting of Prince
" Beckowitz, a Circassian Chief in the service of
" Russia, the Mufti, the Cadi, and some of the prin-
" cipal inhabitants, both Armenian and Mahomedan,
" only two being Russian employés. Even the
" police was continued as before; and during the
" two years that the place was occupied by the
" Russians, not a single complaint was made against
" the Russian authorities. The laws remained un-
" altered, the Cadi performed his usual duties, sub-
" ject to the inspection of an honest and upright
" man, and the Christians offered no complaints
" against the administrations."

It will now be necessary to describe the state of the place as it was found in 1855. It was not until about the middle of the month of April that the snow had sufficiently disappeared to enable the Engineer Officer, who had been intrusted with the duty of remodelling the works, to make a proper inspection of the existing fortifications. The fortress itself had remained much in the same state as it was in 1828. Time had not done much harm to the solid masonry of which the walls were composed; and about as little good had Turkish skill effected in the attempt to strengthen the position by throwing up outworks. Not one single redoubt (properly so called) had been constructed, nor had sufficient precaution been taken for the defence of the hills, by far the most important of all the points requiring attention. It is somewhat difficult to describe the exact nature of the works which had been raised, without showing a plan of them as they existed; but a brief sketch may perhaps be sufficient to convey some idea of them.

The total want of anything like an organized engineer corps in the Turkish army must surprise every one, while, at the same time, it will account for the wonderful notions the Turks have of fortification. The non-existence of such a corps is the more astonishing when it is considered that the Turkish soldiers, though so frequently beaten in the open field, have never failed to show extraordinary courage behind entrenchments, thereby evincing the necessity which exists for giving them some knowledge of the art, useful at all times and under all circumstances, of throwing up field-works. But this is a digression, intended only to bring forward some excuse for the unprofessional manner in which they had attempted to fortify this important place.

It had been deemed necessary, in order to prevent an enemy from coming too near the fortress, which in itself presented no great obstacles if regularly besieged, to surround the place with an entrenched line or breastwork; that is to say, commencing at some distance from the foot of the Kāradāgh mountain on the east side, and carrying it towards the river bank on the west. But from the nature of the ground, which rises considerably from the town to the plain in front for some distance, and then immediately falls, it was found absolutely necessary to carry the line a long way off, which made it so extensive as to become very inconvenient, when, as afterwards proved to be the case, the position had to be held by a limited garrison.

This breastwork, from being damaged by remaining under snow all the winter, and from having been, for the most part, constructed on principles altogether erroneous, presented a very ridiculous appearance when the snow melted. In several places there was a great hiatus, many hundred feet in length, and in no place was the line sufficiently high to prevent an ordinary pony from leaping over it. It afforded no cover whatever for the men; it had no banquette or trench in rear; little or no ditch in front; was raised on no particular profile, and was, in short, almost worse than useless. It had been discontinued many hundred yards from the river on one side, and nearly the same distance from the foot of the mountains on the other. The openings or passages through it, of which there were an unnecessary number, were wholly unprotected, and flanking fire seemed to be a thing utterly unknown.

At the eastern extremity of the south line of breastwork, three sides of a large rectangular redoubt, called Hāfiz Pasha Tabia (the word Tabia signifying a battery), had been constructed, but it was left entirely open and unprotected at the gorge: it had very insufficient parapets, and was unprovided with a magazine.

At the other extremity of this line a small irregular battery had been raised, called Kanli Tabia, open also at the gorge, with low parapets, without any magazine, and being altogether a most useless work as it then stood. Between these two batteries, and on the same line of breastwork, two small lunettes of better construction had been thrown up, called Yēni and Feyzi Bey Tabias, but neither of them was closed at the gorge, nor were they provided with magazines.

On the west line, facing the Erzeroom road, part of the breastwork had been raised and strengthened, and salients thrown out so as to form an open battery for guns "*en barbette.*" Nearly at the foot of the Kāradāgh Mountain, and on a badly-chosen site, a small battery called Koltuk Tabia, had been erected, intended to command the Gumri road, and to sweep the east line of breastwork. These works now described, together with the dilapidated remains of the wall which originally enclosed the principal suburb, and the two round batteries at the angles, called Chicheck and Yussuf Pasha Tabias, constituted the whole of the lower defences.

The Kāradāgh Mountain was fortified by long

straggling open works, difficult to describe, and with one small redoubt on the highest point, the whole being very much out of repair. To the northward of this position, on an eminence a very little lower than the Kāradāgh, and close upon the right bank of the river, a very large, and by no means badly-planned redoubt, called Arab Tabia, had been constructed, but, like the rest of the works, it had been left incomplete, with low weak parapets, no magazine, and unprotected at the gorge.

The fortifications on the opposite or northern side of the river, where the hills entirely command the town and fortress, consisted of but few works, badly planned, and totally unfit for the purpose of defence, with the exception of one small lunette, on the very edge of the precipice overhanging the river, which had been planned and constructed by Major Teesdale the previous year.

The most commanding spot of all, and indeed the key to the whole position, was to the north-west of the fortress, and on it had been constructed an unmeaning work, called Vēli Pasha Tabia, consisting of an irregular line of parapet, perfectly open in rear, pierced with embrasures built in stone and cement, while the remainder of the work was of earth. The site had no doubt been well chosen; but it was almost impossible to make a mistake in it, as the necessity for a work on this particular spot was too palpable to be overlooked.

To the right of this battery, and along a ridge running nearly parallel to the river, three small detached works had been constructed—one, the furthest off, and exactly opposite to, and commanded by, Arab Tabia has been before alluded to as having been planned by Major Teesdale; the other two were in the form of lunettes, open at the gorge and most injudiciously placed, as an enemy could, from the nature of the ground, approach almost close to them without being perceived. There was one other work, called Tchim Tabia, favourably placed on rising ground, commanding the river to the west of the town. This battery was small, and in the form of a double redan or *tête à queue d'hyronde*, capable of holding two guns " *en barbette.*"

These were all the works which formed the defences of Kars in April, 1855; and not only were they imperfect in form, and totally inadequate to the purpose they were intended for, but they were all more or less in a dilapidated state, completely unprotected in rear and without magazines.

The Officer of Engineers had proceeded to Kars with full powers from General Williams, and the Mushir commanding the army, to remodel the existing fortifications, and to construct such new works as he might consider necessary for the safety of the place. Instructions were also sent to Kerim Pasha, the Commandant at Kars, to attend to any requisitions Lieutenant-Colonel Lake might make for working parties or any other assistance. Accordingly eighty men were, as a preliminary step, told off under the most intelligent officer that could be found, Captain Hadji Agha, to form a band of sappers; and they were at once taught the art of making gabions and fascines, as well as profiles for the several works about to be constructed, in all of which they became in a short time very expert.

About the second week in April five hundred soldiers were set to work on the entrenched line, under the immediate superintendence of Major-General Hāfiz Pasha, an officer who possessed some knowledge of engineering, and who, during the whole of the blockade, was ever ready to afford most efficient aid in this department.

From the men never having worked before with European entrenching tools, and those in store being of inferior quality, it seemed at first almost hopeless to employ them to advantage; but being full of zeal, they soon became accustomed to them, and not only laboured cheerfully but performed their several tasks in as satisfactory a manner as could have been expected from an European working party.

The following list of engineer stores at Kars will prove how very inadequate the supply was:—

116 picks.	4 hatches.
135 shovels, iron.	6 adzes.
132 picks, made at Erzeroom.	5 axes.
	5 gimlets, large.
32 crowbars, iron.	13 ditto, small.
39 hammers, stone-breaking.	6 pincers.
	16 trowels.
472 turf-cutters.	33 tracing-lines.
20 trimmers.	28 sacks, horse-hair.
4 shovels, turf.	6 wedges, iron.
23 knives, grass.	3 saws, double-handed.
6 crowbars, blasting.	
4 fascine-chokers.	1 hammer, small, stone-breaking.
6 gabion gauges.	
12 sap-hooks.	400 pick-handles.
6 pickets.	200 platform planks.
4 ropes.	200 common ditto.
14 planes.	200 profile boards.
9 saws.	4 pairs of compasses.

Out of repair—

400 shovels.	50 picks.

In some places an entirely new line of breastwork was marked out, and the whole was put into a thorough state of repair, affording good and sufficient cover for the men. The necessary precautions were taken for protecting the openings, for the ingress and egress of troops, and, in order to command more effectually the several roads passing through the line, the batteries bearing upon them were strengthened, added to, and altered where necessary.

They were all closed at the gorges, and provided with proper magazines. "*Chevaux de frise*" were made, and put up in each battery and at every opening in the breastwork. Many small works, as seen in the plan, were constructed for the purpose of giving the requisite flanking fire, so that, after a short time, the lower works assumed a tolerably defensible appearance. A small three-gun battery was also erected on a commanding position, in the bend of the river, not far from the town, affording a very considerable range for the guns.

Koltuk Tabia was entirely demolished, and a new one, on a larger scale and totally different plan, was constructed, higher up the slope of the Kāradāgh Mountain, on a much more commanding site. While these works were being carried on below, nearly the whole garrison having, by this time, learnt how to handle the spade and pickaxe, the defences on the heights were not neglected.

On the spot where Tchim Tabia stood, a large enclosed redoubt, which afterwards bore the name of the Mushir, Vassif Pasha, was constructed, having a command, not only of the river, but of a great part of the town, and the permanent stone bridges. Two large magazines were made under the traverses, and the whole work was rendered as complete as possible. In this battery, as well as in most of the others, the body of the parapet was composed of loose stone built up with great neatness and dexterity, thickly covered with earth well beaten down, and the whole outer surface turfed over, so that the strength of the work was enormous.

The immense quantity of loose stone lying about in every direction, and much of it in large blocks, afforded very great facility for this description of work, and the Turks had a peculiar knack of building it up.

On the site of Vēli Pasha Tabia, taking in the greater part of the existing work to form part of the new one, a large and very formidable redoubt was now built, capable of containing a garrison of between two and three thousand men. Magazines were made, and a very large, strong, wooden blockhouse, loopholed all round, revetted thickly with earth and turfed over, so as to render it completely shot-proof, was constructed at the gorge. It was big enough to hold three hundred men, and was fitted up with sleeping places. This redoubt received from the Turks the name of Fort Lake.

The two lunettes on the heights before alluded

to were raised, strengthened, and closed at the gorges, and the same precautions were taken with the small work on the edge of the river bank. They were named respectively Zohrab, Thompson, and Teesdale Tabias; and the whole formed what was called the line of Ingliz, or English, batteries. The fortifications on the Kāradāgh were very considerably added to and strengthened. Arab Tabia was also put in a state of repair, and, being too large for any garrison likely to be spared for its defence, it was considered advisable, rather than incur the trouble of reducing its dimensions, to construct a reduite in the centre commanding the whole of the original work.

The bulk of the ammunition had hitherto been kept in the citadel in a most insecure place, and no precautions whatever had been taken to prevent accidents: it therefore became necessary to devise means for remedying this defect, which was accordingly done by altering one of the already existing buildings, and converting it into a magazine.

CHAPTER IV.

Fortifications completed to a certain extent—Pontoon Bridges thrown across the river—Duty of English Officers—Strength of the Garrison—Description of the manner in which promotion takes place in the Turkish Army—General Williams and his Aide-de-camp employed at Erzeroom—Routes by which Erzeroom is approachable from Kars—Fortifications at former place—Provisions sent to Kars—Reports of Russian advance—Arrival of Vassif Pasha—His Character—Camp pitched at Kars.

ABOUT seven weeks were spent in completing the fortifications and other works thus detailed, and nothing could possibly exceed the willing, cheerful, and able manner in which the Turkish soldiers laboured, wholly unaccustomed as they had before been to any work of the kind. It would have been most desirable (and had time permitted it was fully the intention of the Engineer Officer to have done so) to alter the position of the two lunettes composing part of the line of English batteries, for the defect in the site of these works, as before described, was very great. Still there were so many more important things to be attended to, that it was not deemed advisable to do more than to strengthen the parapets and close the gorges.

Two temporary bridges were thrown across the river in order to facilitate the communication between the lower works and those on the heights, and thereby to avoid the necessity of making a *détour* by the stone bridges situated further down. They were constructed of wooden pontoons which had been used for the same purpose the preceding year, of a very clumsy description, not even well adapted for such stationary work, still less for service in the event of the army having to take the field.

During all this time various duties devolved on the officers attached to the Commission, such as procuring information regarding the plans and movements of the enemy, examining the deserters who from time to time came in, and supervising the drill of the garrison, the infantry branch of which was under the guidance of Captain Thompson, and the artillery, for a short time, under that of Major Olpherts, who was afterwards sent, by order of General Williams, to join Vēli Pasha's army near Erzeroom, and did not again do duty at Kars.

The garrison, at this period, consisted of about thirteen thousand men, of whom ten thousand were infantry, fifteen hundred artillery, and fifteen hundred cavalry. The latter were very badly equipped; their swords were so short that they appeared almost ridiculous; the lances with which some of the regiments were armed were heavy and clumsy;

their clothes nearly threadbare; their horse appointments quite worn out, and the horses themselves much in the same state, scarcely one of them being less than eighteen years old. The drill of the cavalry had been shamefully neglected, and the men could neither ride nor manœuvre; the consequence was, they were dispirited, and this arm was nearly useless, except for outpost duty.

Some squadrons, relieved periodically, were stationed at villages close to the Russian frontier, but not much reliance could be placed on them. The artillery was altogether in a different state. The commanding officer, Colonel Ibrahim Bey, not only knew his own duty, but took care that his men should know theirs and perform it. Their clothes, like those of the other branches of the army, were somewhat shabby, but their appointments were decidedly better. The infantry differed a good deal. The first regiment of Arabistan, and the second regiment of Anatolia (the former commanded by Colonel Hussein Bey, and the latter by Colonel Cadri Bey, both of whom were afterwards promoted to the rank of Major-general), were at this time not only tolerably dressed and well armed, chiefly with percussion muskets, but they were very fairly drilled, and their commanding officers really seemed to take an interest in them.

Other regiments, again, particularly the Rediff, or militia, knew positively nothing whatever of their

TURKISH CAVALRY SOLDIERS.

drill, nor was it likely they should do so when many of their Colonels did not know the most simple evolutions, and some of them not even the ordinary words of command. This must ever be the case in an army where promotion to the rank of officer, and subsequently to the higher grades, depends solely and entirely on interest of the very worst description, and is never granted on account of merit. A man is one day a chibook-jee, or pipe-bearer to a pasha, and the next day he is perhaps a captain: the consequence of which is, that there can be no inducement for an officer of an independent spirit to study his profession, or to take any pleasure in his duties; for he well knows that, without interest of that kind which an honest and conscientious man would scorn to possess, or money wherewith to bribe the authorities, all hopes of promotion would be vain, and he must live and die a subaltern, insulted by the superior officers, and not respected by the privates.

The following extract from a letter of General Williams to Lord Clarendon places this subject in a strong but very just light:—

"*Colonel Williams to the Earl of Clarendon.*

(Extract.) "Camp near Kars, October 23, 1854.

"One of the greatest obstacles to be removed ere the Turkish army can be reorganized, is that presented by the determination of the officers who have risen from the ranks, to resist the introduction of young men brought up in the Sultan's military schools.

"Several months ago fourteen of these young men, after completing their studies at the Galata Serai, were sent to this army; they found themselves exposed to every description of insult and degradation; not one of them received a paid appointment in the état-major, and several have, in consequence, disappeared altogether from this army; I believe only four remain, and those subsist on the bounty of such superior officers as may find it to their own interest to employ them: in short, the officers at present in command, as well as those in subordinate posts, will always endeavour to keep the young cadets out of employ in order that their own promotion may secure for them those illicit sources of peculation on which they at present fatten, at the expense of the unfed and badly-clothed soldier.

"It is indeed lamentable to think how useless those expensive military establishments at Pera are rendered, by the conduct of the clerks and pipe-bearers who now occupy every post of command and responsibility in the Turkish army."

The Turkish soldier, if properly officered, might be made equal to any in the world. Though of indolent habits, he is by nature brave and hardy, capable of undergoing great privation and fatigue without complaining, and warmly attached to his sovereign. But more than this is necessary; and their gallant and almost unprecedented defence of the fortifications on the 29th of September must prove to all military men that confidence in their commanders is or was alone necessary to make them even more than a match for the famed army of the Caucasus.

During the period alluded to, General Williams and his Aide-de-camp had been incessantly employed with the fortifications round Erzeroom, as the snow had by this time cleared away. From early dawn until sunset, in all weathers, they were on the hills planning and superintending the works. The peasants used to get very tired of their labour, and were perpetually asking for rest, but they were kept at their duty by all kinds of devices. Sometimes the enlivening strains of music would cheer them; now and then a pasha would appear; and once or twice the Armenian bishop would come up to encourage his flock.

The pertinacity of Her Majesty's Commissioner in being always present seemed to astonish the authorities beyond measure, and the poor people were lost in wonder that a real pasha could give himself such trouble. The English officers were most ably assisted, while employed on the defences of Erzeroom, by Colonel Calandrelli, an Italian officer of artillery, who had made engineering his study, and who had assisted in holding Rome against the

French in 1848. He was a most energetic and talented man, and the news of his death from cholera, very soon afterwards, was received by all with feelings of deep sorrow and regret.

It was impossible for General Williams to leave Erzeroom at this time, though the news from Kars became daily more alarming, and the intentions of the Russians seemed to be no longer doubtful; for he well knew that the very moment his back was turned, the fortifications would cease to be made, and that no more provisions would be sent on. He felt sure that the old blight of apathy and indifference would again fall over the town; and such, indeed, turned out to be the case, when at length the General found it absolutely necessary to leave.

Erzeroom is approachable from Kars in two directions. The straight route is over the Dévé-Boynou Pass; the other, by the Childir road, enters the plain on the opposite side of the river; but to go by this latter route would necessitate an immense *détour*, and force an enemy to *déboucher* upon the plain under very disadvantageous circumstances; so that the direct road was the first to be attended to. Though it was a complicated piece of ground, it was finally made tenable against almost any odds: the Russians, at all events, never attempted it, though they were at one time within sight of the works.

General Williams, on the 21st of May, despatched

his Aide-de-camp to the hills which separate the plains of Erzeroom and Hassan Kaleh, to fortify a strong position which commanded the only approaches to Erzeroom on that side; but, on account of its being the season of the Ramazān, when the Turks neither eat, drink, nor smoke from sunrise to sunset, he experienced great difficulty in finding men; and the consequence was, the work was very considerably delayed.

The villagers and townspeople were employed on the fortifications, and were, of course, wholly ignorant of their duty. They were also unpaid, and but little zeal could therefore be expected. The levy was made at so many per village, and there were consequently a great number of grey-bearded old men and young children, who were but of little use. The latter used to do their best, and work merrily enough; but the old Babas would sit on a pile of their comrades' cloaks all day, and relate occasionally what the Russians did in 1828, when they were last there; and would wind up their story by exclaiming devoutly, " Inshallah! they won't come " any more!" with which exclamation another pipe was lighted, and no more work was done.

The first battery to be constructed had almost to be cut out of the solid rock, and it was consequently most tedious and difficult of execution. Very early in June, however, the work was accomplished, and Major Teesdale, leaving a large number of the in-

F

habitants to continue the remaining fortifications, rejoined General Williams, who was then starting for Kars, at which place the troops had, during this time, continued actively employed in the fortifications. All the wants of the army were, from time to time, brought by Lieut.-Colonel Lake, the senior officer attached to the Commission at Kars, to the notice of Her Majesty's Commissioner, and by him to that of the authorities at Constantinople.

Captain Thompson, who occasionally visited the outstations of Olti, Bardoss, &c., for the purpose of inspecting the troops who were located there, was directed to make inquiries at the several places he went to, as to what quantity of grain, if any, could be procured; urging upon the authorities the necessity for using their utmost endeavours to send into Kars, with all expedition, as large supplies as it was possible to collect. A hope was entertained that the appearance of an English officer in the districts might have a beneficial effect in arousing the energies of the authorities; but, as the result fully proved, their indolence, apathy, and intrigue were not to be conquered.

The ammunition, particularly for guns, was reported to be very deficient in quantity: the supply of food and stores of all kinds, especially forage for horses, was alarmingly low; and nothing but the untiring zeal and exertions of Her Majesty's Commissioner, who at last most fortunately took upon himself to purchase and send off, in considerable numbers, horse-loads of grain from Erzeroom to Kars, could have in any way replenished the nearly exhausted granaries.

At this time carriage was very difficult to procure at Erzeroom, but most fortunately General Williams heard of a caravan, taking merchandize into Persia, passing through the town at that moment; and after much trouble he succeeded in persuading the owners to leave their loads, and for a certain sum to convey stores to Kars. It will scarcely be believed, but yet such is the case, that the Medjlis, or council, at Erzeroom, objected to the arrangement on the plea of the cost! thus weighing the expenditure of, after all, a paltry sum of money, against the safety, not only of Kars and its garrison, but of probably the whole of Asia Minor.

It was from no hope of sparing their Government, that the authorities acted thus, or some excuse might be found for them by attributing their conduct to their ignorance, but it proceeded solely from intrigue, and from a dislike to spend money which they would, no doubt, have appropriated to themselves.

An extract from one of General Williams' letters to Lord Clarendon, dated from Erzeroom, shows very plainly the intrigues which were carried on by the pashas. He says:—

" There is evidently an active dispute between

"those in command in Kars and the authorities
"here; not a healthy rivalry of patriotism for the
"welfare of the soldier, but the abject one of
"getting these contracts and supplies in their own
"respective hands. I persevere, however, without
"any feeling of despair, notwithstanding the adverse
"circumstances under which I execute the duties of
"my office; for I cannot see how affairs can grow
"worse, and at that point one is justified in hoping
"for a better state of things."

Reports were now constantly flying about, that the enemy was making preparations for a movement towards Kars, but no authentic intelligence could be obtained until towards the latter end of May, when little doubt remained as to his intentions. Accounts had been brought in, from time to time, by people employed expressly for the purpose of procuring information, that large supplies of grain and provisions of different kinds were being collected at several places in the neighbourhood of Alexandropol, which tended to confirm the report that the army of the Caucasus was about to take the field.

It was at length ascertained that a large force had crossed the Arpa-Tchai, a river which separates the Russian from the Turkish territory. It was impossible to trust even those specially employed to bring intelligence regarding the enemy's movements, for they were all, more or less, corrupt, and, as it was afterwards proved beyond doubt, they sold their information to both armies.

Vassif Pasha, the new Mushir, who had been sent up from Constantinople for the purpose of commanding the army in Asia Minor, had arrived at Kars in the month of April, having remained some time at Erzeroom to consult with Her Majesty's Commissioner as to the several arrangements necessary to be made.

The selection of this officer for the important post conferred upon him turned out to be most judicious. He was a thoroughly upright, well-meaning man, with one sole object in view, namely, the good of the cause. He was ever ready to listen to the suggestions of General Williams, and invariably looked to him for advice.

Her Majesty's Ambassador at Constantinople, in a letter addressed to Lord Clarendon, gives the following just character of the new Commander-in-chief:—

"With respect to the qualifications of Vassif
" Pasha, the result of my inquiries, antecedent to
" the receipt of any instructions, was, that he is a
" man of military education, that he was engaged
" in active service against the Russians in 1829,
" that he possesses an independent fortune, and
" that no one suspects him of corruption. His
" language to me was that of an honest and con-

"scientious public servant. On the other hand he
"is no longer young, and his appearance denotes
"but little energy of mind or body.

"Your Lordship can hardly mean to hold me
"responsible for his success in command. The
"object of change in office or command throughout
"Turkey, when taken at the best, is not the pro-
"motion of known desert, but the removal of tried
"demerit. On such occasions the chances are
"quite as much in favour of change for the worse
"as of change for the better.

"As to the command of an army, I know but
"one man in the Sultan's service who enjoys the
"reputation of decided fitness for it, and that is
"Omer Pasha. In the present instance there is
"much to presume in favour of the new Com-
"mander. He shows public spirit in undertaking
"an irksome task and a difficult journey in the
"dead of winter. Besides, he is not the Com-
"mander-in-chief destined for operations in the
"field, but an acting Commander appointed to keep
"the army together, and, if possible, to improve it
"during the season of retreat.

"I hope he will act cordially in concert with
"General Williams. No efforts have been wanting
"on my part to make him do so."

Early in May, a camp was pitched at Kars within the entrenchments, and the whole garrison was paraded in review order before the Mushir. A general order was read to the troops, exhorting them to prove their devotion to the service of their Sultan, in the event of their being called upon to meet the enemy. Two guns were fired from every battery, and, with their bands playing and colours flying, they were at once marched off to their posts.

CHAPTER V.

Increase of Kars Garrison—Sickness very trifling—State of Hospital—Enrolment of Bashi-Bozouks—Lāz Riflemen collected—Their Character—Ramazān—Mushir's unwillingness to issue orders on the subject—He is at length persuaded to do so—Arrival of General Williams at Kars, June 7th—Intentions of Enemy no longer doubtful—His Movements—Turkish Outposts attacked—Advance of Russians against the Lower Works, June 16th—Enemy repulsed and forced to retire- Account of Stores and Magazines—Grain at Kuprikeni taken by the Russians.

By this time the garrison had been considerably increased : it had been deemed advisable to call in the troops stationed at Kaghisman and Ardahan, as well as the regiments and detachments at the several other out-stations. A battalion of chasseurs, and subsequently some guns and artillerymen, had also arrived at Kars from Erzeroom.

The amount of sickness among the troops at this period was unusually small : the few in hospital were men whose constitutions had been previously weakened by various causes, and the garrison was completely free from any epidemic. There were, indeed, a few cases of scurvy, but it did not seem inclined to spread. The hospital accommodation was of a most inferior description ; the wards badly ventilated, paper being, in most of the windows, substituted for glass, of which material there was a great scarcity; floors laid in mud, so that it was next to an impossibility to keep them clean. But as soon as the troops moved into camp, many of the houses, which had been occupied as barracks, were vacated, and became available for hospitals, as sickness increased.

Her Majesty's Commissioner had, on his arrival at Kars in the September of the previous year, made it one of his first duties to inspect the military hospitals, of which he had heard such indifferent accounts. He was anxious to satisfy himself as to the truth of these statements, before suggesting the alterations and improvements which might afterwards be found necessary.

The inspection which General Williams made was not altogether so unsatisfactory as might have been expected. He found, indeed, much to complain of; but, on the whole, a great improvement had taken place since the previous winter, when, to use his own words, " Nearly twelve thousand of the " miserable inmates perished in the hospitals, owing " to the want of medicines, bedding, food, fuel, and " light; their bodies, even before death released " them from their agonies, presenting spectacles too " loathsome to describe."

General Williams, in reporting the result of his visit to Her Majesty's Government, stated, that so utterly inadequate did he consider the buildings, as they then stood, to the accommodation of the sick which would, in all probability, crowd into them during the following winter, he had not failed to impress upon the mind of the Mushir the absolute necessity of providing more room, as well as of forming a magazine of fuel and food for the use of the hospitals.

That these instructions were wholly unattended to cannot be a matter of astonishment to those who know Turkish indolence and procrastination. The very admirable report drawn up by Dr. Sandwith, the Inspector-General of Hospitals, so clearly describes the state of the buildings, as they stood in September, 1854, as well as the nature of the Medical Staff of the Turkish army, that it is inserted at full length.

"*Report on the Medical Department of the Army at Kars.*

"Kars, September 24, 1854.

" The number of sick at present in the army at Kars amounts to between five hundred and six hundred, which, in an army of twenty-eight thousand suffering from the effects of recent engagements and defeats, is not extraordinary. To these, however, must be added about two thousand of the worst cases sent to the central hospitals of Erzeroom, a large per-centage of which died on the road.

" The hospitals which I visited with Colonel

Williams on the morning of the 23rd instant are large buildings, such as khans, mosques, &c., fitted up and furnished for the reception of the sick. These places are, on the whole, and considering the resources of the country, not ill adapted for their present service; their greatest fault being a want of ventilation, as the windows, having no glass, are covered up with paper. It was suggested to have fire-places and chimneys made, and fires kept constantly burning, which would establish a most wholesome ventilation. The floors, made of hard mud, were covered along the sides of the building with boards, raised three inches from the ground, and on these are placed the beds of the patients, consisting of a good straw mattress and a quilt stuffed with cotton, this quilt being enveloped in a covering of calico, which could be taken off and washed when necessary. The patients are supplied with clean shirts, calico drawers, night-caps, and bed-gowns; in short, the bedding and body linen of the patients, as far as I observed, and considering the circumstances, are unexceptionable.

"I observed no paper of prescriptions hanging over the bed of the patients, as is usual in hospitals, and seeing no bottles, I asked where the medicines were. I found that a great proportion of the patients were without remedies, others had tin bottles by their bedsides containing their potions. The apothecary who accompanied me was unable to say what these metallic bottles contained; but on tasting the fluid therein it was invariably found to be some infusion or decoction of harmless and useless herbs, such as marsh-mallow, bittersweet, and the like. All the severe surgical cases had been removed, others were already convalescent or dead, so that I was unable to ascertain by personal inspection the kind of dressings used. Many of the patients I saw were in various stages of typhus, dysentery, pneumonia, &c., and certainly required more energetic treatment than appeared to be in vogue. I was unable to obtain a sight of any statistical account of the diseases under treatment, but the above mentioned appeared to me to be the most frequent.

"Separating myself from Colonel Williams and his party, who were inspecting what was directed to be shown, I prevailed on one of the medical men to conduct me to the Pharmacy. We dived into a dark filthy passage, ascended a ladder, and came into three small mud rooms, which were shown to me as the Central Pharmacy. A short inspection of this at once explained to me the want of medicines in the hospital. A few large bottles and vases were labelled with about twenty specimens of drugs, but those labelled for medicines of any value I found empty: the others contained preparations, such as aqua styptica and tinctures, the use of which has long been discarded by modern medicine. There were also infusions of marshmallow, extracts of bitter-sweet, and sundry equally inefficacious drugs. The whole place was filthy and disorderly, and seemed more like the wreck of a plundered pharmacy than the depôt from which the sick of an army is supplied.

"The medical staff of the Turkish army is divided into physicians (hekim), surgeons (jerah), and apothecaries (ezaji). The former must be provided with a medical diploma before entering the Turkish service; or failing that, to produce certificates of a medical and surgical education, and be examined by the Professors of the Medical University of Constantinople. Besides the foreigners who arrive as candidates for employment in the army, the above-named University furnishes yearly a number of medical men, to whom are given the best places in the army. These are, of course, Turkish subjects, Mussulmans, Armenians, Greeks, and Jews. The Mussulmans are the most highly favoured with regard to place, but all are to my certain knowledge very incompetent, and all plunder the Government when afforded an opportunity.

"The cause of their incompetency is to be found at the fountain-head of the system: many of the Professors of the University are appointed by favouritism, and the school is consequently conducted in a slovenly manner, many places being made sinecures of.

"When a foreigner presents himself as a candidate for medical service, he finds no difficulty, generally speaking, in gaining admission into the army. If his previous education has been defective, he can, by a present to one of the chief apothecaries, or some equally influential person, make objections vanish, as in the case of a recent candidate for an apothecary's appointment, who had a list of the examination questions given him the day before he presented himself for examination.

"All the important operations in surgery are performed by the first class, or 'hekims.' In the army at Kars at this moment, as far as I can discover, there are but two or three of this class who have any claim whatever to be considered competent men, and these, I hear, are about to leave; others there are of this class who have been promoted through favouritism, but who are utterly ignorant of their profession. The Turkish surgery is in a deplorable condition, and nearly all those who are seriously wounded die. In the first place, five or six men capable of performing capital operations form a very insufficient allowance to an army in a campaign, but when these are let and hindered in every way, it may be said that the army is with-

INCOMPETENCY OF APOTHECARIES.

out a medical staff. The barber-surgeons, or 'jerahs,' are constantly on the watch for any unsuccessful case occurring from an operation performed by a 'hekim,' or first-class doctor, and a 'masbata,' or complaint of inefficiency, is addressed to the authorities by a number of them, who thus contrive to have him dismissed. The consequence is, that capital operations are seldom performed, and the sufferers from compound gun-shot fractures are left to die of gangrene, and limbs from which balls might be extracted are wrapped up and rot in poultices.

"None but the barber-surgeons attend the army during an engagement, and these men, having no anatomical or surgical knowledge whatever, are unable to apply a tourniquet or put a fractured limb in position. The apothecaries are intrusted with the task of compounding and dispensing the medicines according to the prescriptions of the physicians. They (the apothecaries) are supposed to have passed an examination at Constantinople, or elsewhere; but this branch of the department is the most corrupt of any, and I am told that a moderate present to the chief at Constantinople will pass any one as an apothecary. A physician attached to this army told me that having prescribed carbonate of iron, he was told by the apothecary that there was none left, but there was plenty of carbonate of ammonia: and, what is worse, I learned that any carbonate or sulphate was substituted for any other, either to save trouble or because none of the medicine ordered was to be found.

"I am told that ample sums are provided at Constantinople for the Drug Department, but the supplies on their way gradually diminish, until little is left at Kars to be turned into money by the Turkish employés. The depôts at Erzeroom are filled with large quantities of dried herbs, such as rose-leaves, poppy-heads, &c., the valuable medicines having disappeared: boxes also of old-fashioned specula vaginæ, obstetric instruments out of date, and other drugs on the market, are sent to the camp at Kars.

"After the late defeat of this army, a rich harvest was made by the apothecaries and doctors, who turned into money their medicines and instruments, and reported them as having been captured by the Russians.

"A regular system of embezzlement is pursued, from the highest to the lowest; and as charges could be brought and proved by any man against his superior, anything like discipline or subordination in this department is out of the question, and the efficiency of the Turkish soldier suffers in consequence.

"The only redeeming point in all this is, the material comfort of the soldier in the hospital. His bed is clean and comfortable, his attendants full of care for him, and his diet as good as circumstances will allow. All this is admirable in the hospitals at Constantinople which I have inspected; and though much inferior to what is found in the capital, the arrangements for the comfort of the soldiers in the hospital at Kars are very fair, and the absence of medicines is scarcely to be regretted, considering the ignorance of the medical officers, in whose hands active remedies, like edge tools, might do mischief.

" The absence of efficient surgical aid is far worse, since valuable lives and limbs are sacrificed either by utter abandonment or by mischievous dressings with stimulating salves and powders.

" I may, in conclusion, add, that many more details are to be learned by further inspection of the army, and much improvement may doubtless be effected in the hygienic condition of the Turkish soldier; the above report being but the result of a few hours' stay at Kars, added to what I have learned and observed during a residence of five years in Turkey.

"(Signed)   H. SANDWITH, M.D.
" *Staff Surgeon, Second Class.*"

Thus almost the only gratifying feature seemed to be, from the foregoing account, that the inmates of the hospital were treated with kindness and attention, and their persons were kept clean. This latter is one of the particular attributes of a Turk, and tends very considerably to preserve him in health.

It is doubtless the first duty, as well as the most ardent wish, of every Commander to see that his soldiers are properly cared for in sickness, and made as comfortable as possible; but in countries where civilization has not arrived at any great height, it is almost impossible to conceive the difficulties and obstacles which have to be surmounted.

About this time large bodies of Bashi-Bozouks came in offering their services. They were inspected by the Commander-in-chief, and such of them as were badly mounted, or were, from age or other causes, deemed unfit for duty, were rejected. Numbers, however, crept in, who only proved a useless burthen on the limited resources of this badly-provisioned army.

Emissaries were sent to collect and bring in as many irregular riflemen, inhabitants of the mountains of Lazistān, as could be found willing to serve. These wild mountaineers are a hardy and brave race of men. Accustomed to fight on their own native hills, under cover of the jungles, it was supposed that they would be most useful in defending entrenchments. They were all armed with a good rifle and a kamma, or large dagger, suspended by a belt round their waists. They were truly reported to be excellent marksmen, always taking a cool and deliberate aim before they fired. Each Chief brought a certain number of followers, who appeared willing enough to serve; but at the same time, like the Bashi-Bozouks, they distinctly stated that nothing would have induced them to do so, except the confidence they placed in the British Government, whose representative, they well knew, would take care that no injustice should be done to them, as had too often been the case before.

It may not perhaps be considered out of place here to mention a circumstance indicative of the religious fanaticism under which the Turks labour, and which, even in a moment of extreme danger, they allow to exercise unbounded control over their actions. The great festival, called the Ramazān, which lasts for forty days, commences in the month of May, and they are enjoined by their religion to abstain wholly from water or food of any kind during the day-time.

Accordingly, a day or two before the commencement of the fast, the senior British officer at Kars—and, as such, the representative of Her Majesty's Commissioner, then in Erzeroom—waited on the Mushir, and pointed out to him, in the strongest possible terms, the disastrous consequences likely to ensue, in the present instance, from a strict adherence to this religious custom, the propriety of which, under ordinary circumstances, he would not have presumed to gainsay.

If the men were to abstain from eating and

drinking during the day, it necessarily followed that they must occupy themselves the greater part of the night in cooking and eating their food. This want of sufficient natural rest, together with the injurious effects arising from being for so many hours without anything to eat or drink, would most effectually prevent them from working with any energy on the fortifications, and greatly reduce their strength, at a time when there was almost a certainty of having to encounter the enemy.

Nevertheless, the Mushir hesitated to issue any order on the subject, though it was clearly explained to him, that in a passage of the Khoran it is distinctly stated that, in a time of war or urgent need, the fast may be dispensed with. At the same time, he expressed his readiness to overlook any breach of the ordinance among the troops. But this was insufficient; for although both officers and men acknowledged the necessity which existed for having the fortifications finished as soon as possible, yet they were *Turks*, and, consequently, by no means averse to enjoying a little idleness at any price, more especially when it could be obtained under the cloak of religion: and they would undoubtedly have made the fast an excuse for not working, though probably the greater part of them would not have kept it. Under these circumstances, there was no course left to pursue but to refer the matter to Her Majesty's Commissioner at Erzeroom, which was accordingly done.

This representation elicited the following letter from General Williams to Vassif Pasha:—

"*Brigadier-General Williams to Vassif Pasha.*

"EXCELLENCY, "Erzeroom, May 19, 1855.

"Colonel Lake has sent me a copy of the letter he addressed to you relative to the danger of weakening your garrison, especially after its severe attack of scurvy, by permitting the men to fast during the Ramazān. I most fully agree with Colonel Lake in the advice he has tendered your Excellency in my name, and as travellers and soldiers before the enemy are released from this religious duty, and as the safety of your soldiers depends on a steady continuance of work on the fortifications, and the utmost vigilance at night, I hope your Excellency will look with a favourable eye upon the advice I now respectfully offer for your consideration.

"I have, &c.,
"(Signed) W. F. WILLIAMS."

In the mean time, however, the Mushir relented, and was convinced of the expediency of issuing an order, desiring the garrison to consider the Ramazān, for the present, a dead letter.

On the 7th of June, General Williams and his

personal staff arrived at Kars. On the following day he inspected the troops, and expressed his satisfaction at the very visible improvement in their appearance. It is true their clothes were shabby, as well as most of their appointments; several regiments were without knapsacks or greatcoats, having lost them at the battle of Kuruk Déré the previous year; and, notwithstanding the frequent applications to Constantinople, they had never been replaced. On the whole, however, the troops were in good condition, and in excellent spirits.

By this time the intentions of the enemy no longer remained doubtful, and every possible exertion was therefore made to add to the strength of the works; no means were neglected; but though much had been accomplished, a great deal still remained to be done.

General Williams minutely examined all the fortifications that had been constructed during his absence, and was satisfied with the arrangements, as far as they went. More might, doubtless, have been effected, had time allowed, and had the Engineer Officer been provided with proper means and assistance, in both of which he was, as before stated, very deficient.

On the 9th of June, the enemy advanced, and encamped near the village of Zaim Keui, about eight miles from Kars, situated on the Kars-Tchai.

The Turkish cavalry outposts had been thrown out on the heights overlooking the village, with orders to keep the garrison informed of any movement that might take place in the enemy's camp. It was highly necessary, in order to insure their being on the alert, that an officer should visit the outposts frequently, and this duty was intrusted to Lieutenant-Colonel Lake, who, on the morning of the 14th (accompanied by Dr. Sandwith, as his interpreter), proceeded to the spot, arriving there before daylight. He found that, during the night, the pickets had been thrown forward, much nearer to the enemy than was intended; and when day broke, a regiment of Russian cavalry was observed steadily advancing towards them. The patrols were immediately called in, and as the whole outpost consisted only of two hundred and fifty badly mounted and worse armed cavalry, together with about fifty Bashi-Bozouks, it was considered advisable to retire.

At this moment, Colonel Baron Schwartzenberg, who had the general superintendence of the cavalry branch of the army, arrived on the ground, and the Turks began to retreat, steadily and in good order, until the Bashi-Bozouks, finding the enemy coming on at a gallop, took fright and fled. The panic then seized the rest of the detachment, who, headed by many of their own officers, and disregarding all orders, put spurs to their horses, and the flight became general. They were closely pursued by the enemy, who kept up a sharp fire. At the same moment, another body of Russian cavalry appeared on the left hand, evidently approaching with the intention of cutting off the retreat of the Turks. It was not until the latter were nearly within reach of the guns of the fortress, that the officers were enabled to rally them, when they were formed on the rise of a hill, and the enemy, after a short time, retired; the loss on either side being very trifling.

A certain amount of good resulted from this affair, as it fully proved how little confidence could be placed in the cavalry which formed part of the garrison of Kars. All the blame, however, of this disorderly retreat must not be thrown on the men. Had they been well horsed and armed, and better officered, they would assuredly have felt some confidence in themselves, and have retired in a more soldier-like manner. As it was, no commands nor entreaties availed to induce them to keep their ranks, and it was a mercy they were not all cut to pieces.

The following letter from General Williams to Lord Clarendon gives an account of this affair, as well as other interesting details of the enemy's movements :—

"*Brigadier-General Williams to the Earl of Clarendon.*

"My Lord,   "Kars, June 15, 1855.

" Since I last had the honour to address your Lordship our entrenchments have been materially strengthened by connecting the redoubts on the heights behind the town by an épaulement, and by closing the gorges of those on the plain in front of the town. I refer your Lordship to the sketch of these works which I had the honour to forward from Erzeroom. Since Colonel Lake arrived in Kars he has shown great skill and industry in improving the defective and hastily-thrown-up works of last year. In the labour consequent on these efforts, the troops have evinced the greatest zeal and good humour, and I can with truth assure your Lordship that I never saw works executed with greater rapidity nor in a neater manner than by our infantry, whose discipline has been most carefully attended to by Captain Thompson.

" I have intrusted the defensive works on the heights behind Kars to Major Teesdale, and those on the Kāradāgh to Captain Thompson: on these officers devolve the safety of the outposts by night as well as their various duties by day; Colonel Lake taking upon himself the outposts and pickets of the works on the plain, and also occasional visits to the advanced posts, which have been placed under Baron de Schwartzenberg.

"Yesterday Colonel Lake, accompanied by Dr. Sandwith, who interpreted for him, was attacked at the advanced posts, those posts having been incautiously pushed forward before he arrived on the ground; the Colonel's party retired with the loss of nine men killed.

"The enemy's army has been encamped since its arrival in this vicinity at the villages of Zaïm and Akché-Kalla, at the distance of three and four hours respectively; his detachments have penetrated to Ardahan, from whence ours had been withdrawn, destroyed some entrenchments erected last year, and purchased corn; the enemy has also made an incursion into Childir, and, indeed, is master of the country lying between this and the Russian frontier as far west as he chooses to push his foraging parties.

"Yesterday a large force detached by the enemy to seize Ardahan returned to camp at Zaïm, and the spies report an immediate attack on our entrenchments. Their numbers have now assumed a more probable form, and I believe thirty thousand of all arms, including irregulars, to be about the truth.

"I have, &c.,
"(Signed)   W. F. WILLIAMS."

The 16th of June was the great day of the Beiram, on which it is customary for the Turks to array themselves in their best clothes, pay visits,

and perform various other ceremonies. On this occasion, however, it was considered necessary to issue orders that all such forms should be dispensed with, as the enemy was much too near, and it would not be prudent to run any risk of the garrison being taken by surprise.

It was most fortunate that this precaution was adopted, for information was brought, in the course of the morning, that the Russian army was advancing. About ten, A.M., it was seen drawn up in line of battle, on the summit of the first hill beyond the town. In front of their left were two columns of infantry, with guns in the intervals, and in front again were Bashi-Bozouks and Cossacks. The Turkish outposts, after the affair of the 14th, had been strengthened to a whole regiment of cavalry, besides Bashi-Bozouks, and at the time the enemy commenced his advance, the relief had just reached their post, so that both regiments commenced retiring together, skirmishing going on between the Bashi-Bozouks on either side.

As soon as the Turks got within range of their own guns, a strong line advanced steadily towards the skirmishers; and to drive these in, a large body of Cossacks crept round a hill which hid them from the sight of those on the plain, and then came on in line till within a few hundred yards of the Turkish Bashi-Bozouks, when they broke and made a charge upon them and the regular cavalry. The moment they came within range, the guns of the Kāradāgh opened fire, quickly followed by those of Hāfiz Pasha Battery, which, notwithstanding the distance, made very good practice.

This checked the Russians. The Turks then rallied, and were turning back, when the enemy began firing with rockets to cover their retreat; but they fired wildly, and did very little harm. The loss on the side of the Turks was inconsiderable, amounting, perhaps, to eight or ten killed. The enemy's loss could not be correctly ascertained, as the Cossacks carried off nearly all their dead and wounded. They left a good many horses lying dead on the ground, so that their loss, in all probability, equalled that of the Turks. The Bashi-Bozouks skirmished well on this occasion, until driven in by the Cossacks of the Line, who charged most gallantly. They came much nearer than prudence allowed, and having galloped over a mile of heavy ground, arrived with their horses quite blown. At this time, had the Turkish cavalry behaved as they ought to have done, they might, by advancing steadily on the scattered Cossacks, have inflicted considerable loss upon them; but, instead of this, the moment the enemy came within pistol-shot, they broke and fled towards the works.

The general opinion in camp was that the affair in question was an attempt on the part of the enemy to get into the lines by a *coup de main*, their intention being to drive in the cavalry outposts, and then rush through in the confusion, mixed up with them, and expecting to find the greater portion of the garrison indulging in the pleasures of the Beiram.

Trifling as this engagement was it had a beneficial effect on the troops, and tended to give them confidence. They were quickly at their respective posts the moment the alarm was given, and behaved with great steadiness; but the artillery were at first inclined to fire at too long a range, a bad habit, very common among the Turks.

In describing this affair, Her Majesty's Commissioner concluded in the following words:—

"The spirit of the Turkish troops was excellent,
"evincing, as they did, as much readiness in the
"defence as they had shown in the construction of
"their épaulements. If the enemy had attempted
"to carry his original intention into execution, he
"would, I confidently believe, have met with signal
"disaster.

"The precautions which I have recommended
"the Mushir to take are in nowise slackened, and
"we are now preparing for an attack of the heights
"in the rear of the city. The labour of the officers
"of my staff have been incessant, and I have to
"record my thanks to Colonel Lake, to Major
"Teesdale, and Captain Thompson, and to Dr.

"Sandwith, as well as to Messrs. Churchill and "Zohrab, the secretaries and interpreters, whose "duties are equally arduous and fatiguing."

After this, the Russians retired directly, and encamped again at Zaïm-Keui. With an enemy in such close proximity, it now became necessary to use extra vigilance, especially at night, and arrangements were made for having the several posts visited constantly by the European officers.

Captain Thompson had charge of Kāradāgh and adjacent works. Lieut.-Colonel Lake patrolled round the lower fortifications from midnight until three A.M., at which hour General Williams himself was invariably in the saddle, visiting all the most important posts. Major Teesdale had taken up his quarters just outside Fort Lake, and had the supervision of all the works in that direction. The duty at this time was very laborious and severe; torrents of rain fell incessantly; and in some parts of the camp, especially near head-quarters, the water stood almost a foot high.

Outlying pickets were placed round the entire works, about two hundred paces in front; and, considerably in advance of them, were mounted sentries, taken from the regular cavalry and Bashi-Bozouks, under the superintendence of Colonel Baron Schwartzenberg, formerly of the Austrian service. The Turkish soldiers, at first wholly unacquainted with sentry duty, soon became very active and alert, and throughout the long and tedious blockade which followed, scarcely an instance occurred of a man being found asleep on his post.

General Williams, in company with Lieutenant-Colonel Lake, daily visited all the works, and many additions were made to strengthen the defences. The stores and magazines were inspected, and an account taken of what they contained; after which they were carefully locked and guarded, the amount of provisions and ammunition being kept as secret as possible. This was found to be very limited, though every possible exertion had been made to increase it. It was ascertained that there was only a sufficient quantity of rice, flour, and biscuit to last the garrison, on even a decreased ration, for somewhat less than three months.

Provender for the horses was even at a still lower ebb, and the ammunition was so scanty, that had the place been regularly besieged, it would have been very soon expended. Under these circumstances General Williams thought it right to recommend that the men's rations should, at once, be gradually reduced, which was accordingly done. It was hopeless trying to obtain a supply of grain in the neighbourhood, for every attempt which had been made had failed. Foraging parties were sent out daily to cut grass, which was stacked as soon as brought in, but no great quantity could be collected.

A large number of cattle were also procured, and given over to the Colonels of regiments to be pastured during the day just outside the lines, and shut up in pens, made expressly for the purpose, during the night. Repeated applications continued to be made by Her Majesty's Commissioner, both to Constantinople for supplies of various descriptions, and to Erzeroom for grain and other articles, but not a single thing of any kind arrived, although, at this period, there would have been little risk or difficulty in throwing in a convoy.

A large supply of grain had been collected and stored at the village of Kupri Keui, about fifty miles from Erzeroom; and though General Williams had issued repeated instructions for having it conveyed to Kars, the Turkish authorities had neglected to carry out his orders, and the consequence was that the village was soon afterwards plundered by that portion of the Russian army which was stationed in the neighbourhood of Byazid, and the whole of the stores fell into their hands. This was a very heavy loss, and was more to be lamented from its having arisen solely and entirely from Turkish carelessness.

It is, however, due to the Mushir, Vassif Pasha, to state that he used his utmost endeavours to get supplies thrown into Kars, being fully alive to the necessity of replenishing the nearly exhausted stores. He addressed a letter to General Williams, prior to the date of that officer's leaving Erzeroom, informing him that he had made constant and urgent representations to the Medjlis at Erzeroom, as well as to the Governor of Olti, to send provisions to Kars without delay. The Governor of the former place replied that he had purchased two or three thousand somars of corn, but yet not a single grain of it was ever forwarded to its destination.

It appeared to be the policy of the authorities in Erzeroom to throw every obstacle in the way of procuring supplies. They pretended that, being then the season for cultivation, it was impossible to obtain sufficient transport; but this was a mere idle excuse, for two or three carts could have been taken from each village on the plains of Erzeroom and Passin, which would not have injured the cultivation in any way, and a convoy would thus have been secured large enough for the required purpose.

The Mushir suggested to General Williams the expediency of his exercising a supervision over that most important branch of the service, the purchase and transmission of grain for the army, well knowing how very little dependence could be placed on the exertions of the Medjlis, composed of officers who really appeared to take no interest whatever in supplying the troops with the necessaries of life.

The Pashalik of Kars had already furnished considerably more than its due proportion of grain for the army; but Sirri Pasha, the Civil Governor, a man whose honesty of purpose turned out eventually to be more than doubtful, volunteered to procure a further quantity of wheat and barley from the neighbouring villages. He started on his mission, but he neither fulfilled his promise, nor did he ever return to Kars, thus proving, beyond a doubt, that his own personal safety was far more precious to him than the good of the State.

CHAPTER VI.

Russian Army advances—Halts at Magharadjik—Appearance of the Force—Army of the Caucasus described—Enemy sends to Chiplakli and destroys Grain—Post taken—Private Letters sent into Garrison —Works extended and described—Staff of Kars Army—Feyzi Pasha — Commissariat — Peculation discovered — Townspeople are armed—Reconnaissance by the Enemy, 26th of June—Again on the 13th of July — General Mouravieff on the 1st of August proceeds towards the Soghanli-Dāgh—His return to Kars.

On the 18th of June the Russian army was seen advancing from Zaïm Keui towards Kars. Not knowing what their intention might be, the garrison was immediately placed under arms, the artillery stood to their guns, the lines were manned, and due preparation made for any emergency. Towards the afternoon the enemy had arrived in front of Kars, but far out of range of any of the batteries, marching in order of battle. Shortly before sunset they halted at the village of Magharadjik, about three miles and a half to the southward of the town, and pitched their camp.

The appearance of this force, and the steady manner in which it moved, could not fail to excite admiration among those who were watching it from behind their entrenchments, but who were, however, by no means daunted when thinking of the work which was evidently cut out for them. As far as any estimate of its strength could be formed at such a distance, it appeared to consist of about thirty-five or forty thousand men of all arms, with a large field train, but apparently no heavy siege guns.

The army of the Caucasus which had now sat down before Kars was acknowledged to be one of the finest and best-disciplined forces which the Russian empire could boast of, and it well deserved the character. It was commanded by General Mouravieff in person, an officer of talent and energy, who, during a long period of arduous service, had won for himself a name of which any soldier might be proud, and which is now as much respected in England as in his own country. He was present at the siege of Kars in 1828, and held a high appointment in the army under the command of the late General Prince Paskiewitch. He was, therefore, well acquainted with the localities and with the nature of the fortifications as they then existed; but he well knew that, since that time, great alterations had been made in the works, and that they had been considerably added to and strengthened. He was also perfectly well aware that he had to encounter very different troops from those he had assisted in defeating twenty-seven

RUSSIAN INFANTRY SOLDIERS.

years before. Still he was most probably unprepared for that persevering resistance on the part of the Turks which he now experienced, and which kept his overwhelming army at bay for such a length of time, notwithstanding all the disadvantages under which the garrison laboured.

Neither, indeed, did the Turkish authorities at Constantinople look for any great resistance on the part of the Kars army, in the event of the position being attacked, as shown in the following extract from a letter, dated 28th June, 1855, addressed by Lord Stratford de Redcliffe to Lord Clarendon :—

" The intelligence, however scanty, which comes
" in from the north-eastern frontier of Asiatic
" Turkey, is not calculated to diminish the Porte's
" anxiety. The latest advices from Trebizonde,
" which came round to me through Lord Raglan,
" describe the Russians from Gumri as being within
" a few hours' march of Kars. Their force is stated
" at thirty-six thousand—a number which consi-
" derably exceeds the previous estimate—but which
" may, perhaps, comprise the detachment which
" appears to have been directed upon Ardahan.

" Be that as it may, the Turkish forces, including
" all between Kars and Erzeroom, with the circum-
" jacent stations, cannot be safely carried beyond
" an amount of twenty thousand, if so much, and
" the Seraskier Pasha has prepared me for a retro-

" grade movement on their part; it being his de-
" cided opinion that the positions at Kars are not
" tenable against the enemy."

The position which the Russians now occupied enabled them to cut off all communication between Kars and Erzeroom by the direct route, and the only road which was now open was by Pennek.

One of the first acts of the enemy, after taking up his position at Magharadjik, was to send a strong detachment of cavalry to the village of Chiplakli, where there was a mosque full of grain, which they at once burnt. Whilst in possession of this place, the Tatar, who was bringing in the post, arrived, quite unconscious of the enemy's presence. The Russians heard the cry of the Suridji at some distance, and two of their irregular troopers, who spoke the Turkish language, went out to meet him, representing themselves to be Koords going to Kars. They chatted agreeably with the unsuspecting postman until they were fairly inside the village, when, much to his astonishment, he found that he was in the hands of the enemy. General Mouravieff very courteously sent in all the private letters by a *Parlementaire*, having, of course, previously opened and perused them.

The defences having been now completed to a certain extent, it was deemed advisable to carry them still further by fortifying the heights of

Tachmasb, which commanded Fort Lake on the west at a distance of about nineteen hundred yards. The first intention was merely to construct such open works as would serve to protect the approaches to the hills with light field-pieces, and at the same time prove useless to the assailants in the event of the besieged having to retire. This was accordingly done by throwing up a line of breastwork capable of containing two field-batteries "*en barbette*," protected by a few companies of chasseurs.

A similar work, called Lāz Tabia, was also constructed on rising ground between Tachmasb and Fort Lake, intended for a like purpose. While these works were being carried on, others in different parts of the position were also in progress. The batteries of Kāradāgh and Arab Tabia were connected by a breastwork, to protect the valley formed by the hills on which these two works stand, from a sudden attack. A breastwork was also constructed uniting the English batteries with each other, and the whole line with Fort Lake, taking advantage of some rising ground, on which a semicircular battery was erected called Churchill Tabia, capable of holding three light guns.

All the troops in garrison, except those on duty, were thus kept constantly employed, and nothing could exceed the cheerfulness and dexterity with which they worked, each battalion anxious to show

how quickly it could accomplish its task. This constant employment not only tended very materially to keep the troops in good health by giving them steady, and, at the same time, not too severe exercise, but as they saw the several works gradually rising up, they became inspired with fresh confidence in their means of defence against the superior force encamped before them.

The staff of the army at Kars was by no means in an efficient state. General Collman, an Hungarian officer serving under the Turkish Government with the name and title of Feyzi Pasha, was at the head of this department, but he laboured under many disadvantages, the chief of which was the total want of able assistance. About a dozen foreign officers were under his command, who, with two or three exceptions, proved entirely useless.

Feyzi Pasha was himself a man of energy and talent, and had done good service in his own country, from which, for political reasons, he had been obliged to fly. His situation, as Chief of the Staff, was by no means a sinecure, unassisted as he was by competent officers; and nothing but his indefatigable attention to the arduous duties with which he was intrusted could have kept matters straight.

The commissariat was under the management of a Medjlis, or Council, composed of Turkish officers selected for their intelligence, ably guided and directed by Mr. Churchill, General Williams' private secretary. The stores were visited periodically by Her Majesty's Commissioner and one or other of the English officers, in order that it might be ascertained whether an undue amount had been issued.

Soon after the commencement of the blockade it was ascertained, fortunately before it was too late to be irremediable, that the accounts of the provisions in store were totally false, and that fraud and peculation had been carried on to an enormous extent. The storekeeper, into whose charge the several magazines had been given, had either sold or otherwise made away with large quantities of flour and grain, thinking, no doubt, that he would only have to deal with those as corrupt as himself, and that he might thus escape detection; but a most searching examination was made, as far as possible, and the man's guilt was but too fully proved. It was quite out of the question attempting to measure all the flour when the storehouses were tolerably full, but towards the end of the time it was found that large blocks of stone had been mixed with it in order to make it appear a greater quantity, and thus a double deceit had been practised. The culprit was confined in irons, but died before the surrender of the place.

Such of the townspeople as volunteered their

services had arms given to them and stations on the works allotted to them. They were always on the alert as soon as the alarm-gun was fired, and showed, on several occasions, that the hereditary valour for which they had long been famed had in nowise decreased. Orders had been given that all men, not in the army, too old to bear arms, as well as all women and children, should be sent out of Kars at a time when their exit could have been made without difficulty; but these instructions, like many others, although the authorities were constantly reminded of them, were neglected until it was, unfortunately, too late, and the place was completely surrounded by the enemy, who used their utmost endeavours to prevent any one from quitting the garrison.

On the 26th of June the enemy made a *reconnaissance* in force, the greater part of the troops being under arms in two columns, advancing on the extremities of the position on the plain, that is to say, on Hāfiz Pasha and Kanli Tabias. They halted within long range of the guns, and no shot was fired by the Turks. After remaining for upwards of an hour on the ground they had taken up, and having fired one gun, the shot from which rolled harmlessly by, the enemy retired to their encampment, and all was again quiet.

On the 28th, as soon as day broke, the tents of the enemy were found to be very much thinner than they had been, and before nine o'clock in the morning the whole army was discovered to be on the move, having sent an immense quantity of baggage back to Gumri. It was difficult to conceive what their intentions were. One thing, however, seemed pretty certain,—that they did not like the look of the fortifications. The *reconnaissance* of the 26th of June was no doubt originally intended for an attack, as nearly the whole army came up; and it was afterwards ascertained that the Russian officers fully anticipated that the order would be given to advance. It was very possibly postponed on the score of their arriving on the ground too late, and finding the Turks so well prepared.

After having made this *reconnaissance*, General Mouravieff must have been convinced that the position was not to be carried without great loss; and his policy at this period was to preserve the army he commanded intact, in the event of having to oppose another force which it might be reasonably supposed would be sent to the relief of Kars.

Under these circumstances, and being tolerably well persuaded of the utter inability of the garrison to act on the offensive, the Russian General appears to have finally decided on a blockade in preference to an attack.

The enemy, after the movement before described, pitched his camp about a league further to the south, and took up a position on a ledge of rocks that rendered all approach nearly impossible. This manœuvre was at first rather puzzling, but the meaning of it soon became apparent, for they left about five thousand infantry, with some artillery and cavalry, to hold the position, while all the rest marched southwards to a place called Chiplakli, where, as before stated, they burnt a store of provisions which had been laid up in that village.

From thence they proceeded as far as Yenikeui, at which place they destroyed the whole of the magazines which had been established there. They also found a quantity of biscuit at Bardhos, which they took.

On the 6th of July, the Russian force, which had been absent, returned. The main body of the army encamped close to the village of Komansoor, a little to the northward of Azadkeui, and nearly the same distance from Kars, leaving four battalions of infantry, a battery of guns, and two regiments of cavalry, to guard the grand depôt which was established at the latter village.

On the 13th of July, the enemy made another *reconnaissance* in front of the Tachmasb line of works, and, after remaining there several hours, during which time the Russian Engineers no doubt made as minute a survey as they could of the fortifications which had lately been thrown up, they again retired.

On the 1st of August, news was brought into Kars that a very large force, consisting of cavalry, artillery, and infantry, had left the Russian camp, commanded by General Mouravieff in person, and had taken the road towards the Soghanli-Dāgh. This intelligence was soon confirmed by there being a very visible diminution in the number of tents at Komansoor. It was naturally supposed that an attack on Erzeroom was intended by this movement, but no such event took place; and whatever the General's plans were, he did not seem to have that object in view; for, after an absence of not quite a fortnight, the force suddenly returned to camp.

Mr. Consul Brant, who was at this time in Erzeroom, wrote to Her Majesty's Ambassador at Constantinople, giving him an account of this movement of the Russians; and as the letter not only gives in detail the events which took place at this period, but also shows what very little dependence could be placed on the authorities at Erzeroom in any case of emergency, as well as the utter incompetency of Turkish officers to command military operations, it is inserted at full length.

"*Consul Brant to Lord Stratford de Redcliffe.*

"MY LORD, "Erzeroom, August 3, 1855.

" I have the honour to report to your Excellency that yesterday, late in the evening, a report was spread that the Russians had reached Kupri-Keuy, and that the force under Vēli Pasha was in full retreat on Erzeroom. I did not give credit to this rumour, as we hear so many similar every day; but near eleven o'clock at night, Hāfiz Pasha called at my house, and when I heard of his being at the door, I went down; he was on horseback, and accompanied by a guard; he took me aside and told me that credible information had come that the Russians were actually at Kupri-Keuy, but he did not appear to know with certainty that Vēli Pasha had retreated before them.

" At past midnight the Defterdar sent me a letter informing me that Vēli Pasha's force was on its retreat towards Erzeroom, and inviting me to attend a Council to be held next morning. I went, hoping to ascertain the real state of matters; but I found none of the Military Pashas there, but only the members of the Civil Medjlis, the Musteshar, the two Defterdars, Civil and Military, the Armenian Bishop, and some of the chief of the trading community. The Austrian Consul was already there, and the French soon joined the Assembly. No individual took the lead; no one seemed to know the object of the meeting; and a great deal of desultory conversation took place, which tended to no result, except the issue of an order that no families should quit the city, to prevent alarm spreading, and likewise an order to send some Bashi-Bozouks to occupy a bye pass, leading from the Plain of Passin into that of Erzeroom, which had not been fortified or noticed. I remarked that this was not a Military Council, and that such questions belonged to the General commanding, and should be proposed to the Council of War. It did not seem to be clear who was the commanding officer, and nobody knew exactly whither all the Military Pashas had gone to, nor on what errand.

"On leaving me last night Hāfiz Pasha went up to the forts, and arranged for manning the guns, and mounting others, as well as placing Bashi-Bozouks in the redoubts. This morning several large guns were mounted in the forts. I left the Council without having learned anything to be depended on with regard to the Russians; but the French Consul, who had been at a village on the Plain of Passin, the day before, hearing of the Russian force being at Kupri-Keuy, came into town, and found the roads so choked with flying men, women, and children, mixed up with Bashi-Bozouks, as to render them almost impassable. All the villages were abandoned, the cattle left at the mercy of the Koords, who were driving them off, and then burning the houses. The evil of this will be very serious, even if it go no further, the loss immense, and the replacing so much food very difficult; and it is the more to be regretted, as very little foresight and attention to the army of Asia might have obviated the misery, the desolation, and the loss of property which must ensue.

"The division of Vēli Pasha, increased by the garrison here, and reinforcements, though small, which have been gradually joining, should render the Turkish force, well commanded and occupying a strong position, as it now does, on the Pass of the Dévé Boynou, one hour and a half from the city, quite capable of making a successful resistance to the Russian invading force, which is variously represented at from twelve thousand to seventeen thousand men of all arms, the most, I should say, irregulars. There are hordes of Bashi-Bozouks here, who behave as usual—cowardly towards the enemy, cruelly towards their friends, and who, useless as they are, eat up the country, and cost what would support a small, useful, regular force, which might do real service in the field, and that the Bashi-Bozouks never did and never will do.

"I have, &c.,
"(Signed) JAMES BRANT."

Subsequent to the despatch of this letter, it appeared that there were innumerable reports in circulation at Erzeroom regarding the movements of the enemy. He did not show any signs, however, of advancing, but pitched his camp at the village of Hassan-Kaleh, about three hours' distance from the entrenched position of the Dévé Boynou. The

Russian force was roughly estimated at between eight thousand and twelve thousand men, with from ten to fourteen guns; while the Turks reckoned their whole force, including those in the entrenched position, in the redoubts around the town and in the city itself, at about twenty-five thousand of all arms, the greater number being Bashi-Bozouks.

With an army of this strength and no want of guns, in a position like the Dévé Boynou, well fortified as it had been by General Williams, the authorities at Erzeroom ought to have felt tolerably secure, if attacked by the inferior force of the enemy, who, it must be observed, was unprovided with heavy siege-guns. But from Mr. Consul Brant's account, and from the pusillanimity which the military authorities of this garrison never failed to display throughout the whole campaign, it is much to be feared that the result of an attack on the Dévé Boynou would have proved fatal, and there is but little doubt that the fortress of Erzeroom would have offered only a very feeble resistance. It was most fortunate, therefore, that, after a halt of a very few days, the Russians struck their tents and retired towards Kars.

Nothing could possibly be worse managed than affairs were at Erzeroom. According to Mr. Brant, " there appeared to be great jealousy and want of " cordial understanding amongst the Commanders, "none of whom seemed to possess the requisite "qualities of judgment, military knowledge, and "courage. The Bashi-Bozouks went out of camp "and came in when they thought proper, and were "apparently under no sort of control." In short, the conduct of these irregular troops was so violent and insubordinate, that the inhabitants were frequently obliged to keep their shops closed. Possessing no single good quality their presence in Erzeroom might be considered worse than useless, for they consumed provisions which they did not earn.

The retreat of the enemy from Hassan-Kaleh is thus described by Her Majesty's Consul:—

"*Consul Brant to Lord Stratford de Redcliffe.*

"MY LORD, "Erzeroom, August 7, 1855.

"I have the honour to report to your Excellency that the Russians have retreated on the Kars road, having razed the earthworks at Kupri-Keuy, for which purpose they took with them two hundred Armenians from Hassan-Kaleh; and they further took one hundred araba-loads of grain from Government stores.

"Everything that I have stated in my three last despatches has been fully confirmed by trustworthy persons, but I have not spoken with sufficient severity of the imbecile and cowardly conduct of the Pashas; they would undoubtedly have run away if they had been attacked, although, with the number of guns they had, their position, if tolerably well defended, could not have been forced by an enemy treble the numbers of the Russians. It is pretty certain they had not above eight thousand men in all, with ten guns. The conduct as well of the Pashas as of the Lāz, destroys all confidence in the safety of the town; if attacked, it will probably, in such case, be plundered both by the defenders and the enemy; and I have thought it prudent to remove my family to Trebizonde.

"I have, &c.,

"(Signed)   JAMES BRANT."

CHAPTER VII.

Skirmishes take place daily—An Ambuscade is planned, and fails—Reasons given for passive resistance—Enemy attacks Kanli Tabia, August 7th, and is repulsed—Tachmasb Heights fortified still further—Other Works constructed—Stone Bridge thrown over Kars-Tchai—General Kméty—Hussein Pasha—Inner Line of Defence on the Plain—Construction of Fortifications necessarily rude.

TRIVIAL skirmishes took place every day, but with no result of any importance. In one of these, three brothers, sons of a poor old widow, an inhabitant of Kars, were killed while employed in cutting grass. The following day, the Turks tried hard to make a heavy reprisal, and laid an ambush, which, had it succeeded, ought nearly to have annihilated a regiment of Cossacks; but the cowardice and stupidity of the Bashi-Bozouks spoilt the whole affair. The ambuscade was planned in this manner. Two battallions of riflemen left the garrison silently at midnight, one under the command of Captain Thompson, the other under that of Major Teesdale. They marched altogether about a mile and a half to the front, and there posted themselves on opposite sides of a ravine, which was the usual line of retreat at that time for the Turkish skirmishers.

Before daylight, the riflemen had so completely hidden themselves, that, of some six or seven hundred men—which was about the strength of each battalion—not one could be seen even by a person standing in the midst of them. As soon as day broke a party of Bashi-Bozouks charged down upon the nearest Russian picket, who at once retired and began firing. With astonishing quickness a regiment of Cossacks then turned out from the Russian camp, and galloped to the front, where the Bashi-Bozouks, instead of remaining long enough to induce the Cossacks to charge them, and then, as prearranged, retiring through the defile, first ran away in the wrong direction without any make-belief about the matter, and finally formed a line on some ground where it was impossible for the enemy to pursue them, thus causing the failure of the whole plan.

It may be asked why, even at this early stage of the blockade, the garrison of Kars offered only such a passive resistance to the enemy, at a time when the field batteries were horsed, and a certain, though small amount of cavalry, such as it was, existed.

It may perhaps be thought strange that, during General Mouravieff's absence, when, comparatively speaking, so small a force remained in front of Kars, no attempt was made to attack or even to harass it. Doubtless this is a matter of surprise to many who are unacquainted with all the disadvantages under which the garrison was labouring at the time, and it is a well-known fact that the Russians themselves fully expected that a sortie would be made. The same feelings of astonishment must exist in the minds of many, particularly among military men, that no endeavour was made to prevent the close blockade which was, shortly after this time, established, and which continued until the surrender of the fortress.

The question is one of easy solution, and the answer may be comprised in a very few words. With a well-disciplined force of even far less numerical strength than that which formed the garrison of Kars, it would have been something worse than impolitic to have submitted patiently, for such a length of time, to a blockade, without making a single offensive demonstration, or attempting in any way to molest the enemy; but such was the condition of the army at the period alluded to, undisciplined, badly equipped, and in a partly disorganized state, that the result of any engagement in the open field would inevitably have been the loss of the fortress, and probably the greater part of the garrison.

The cavalry, even at the commencement of the blockade, was in such a defective state that it was utterly useless, except for outpost duty: there was scarcely one officer attached to it that knew his duty, and, unless entirely remodelled, for which there was no time, it would have been hopeless to make it effective. As regarded the artillery, their precision and quickness of firing no doubt made it very serviceable, and, with good horses, they would not have manœuvred badly; but the want of cavalry would alone have neutralized their efficiency in the field. A certain portion of the infantry, with proper exercise and drilling, might have been made tolerably perfect, had time allowed of it. A considerable improvement had indeed taken place in this arm; but, at an early period of the proceedings, all the men off duty were necessarily called upon to work at the fortifications, and were, more or less, employed in a similar manner during the whole of the blockade.

It will thus be seen that the wisest and safest course the garrison could pursue was to keep within the entrenchments, and await the arrival of that succour so long withheld, but still earnestly expected.

During General Mouravieff's absence, early on the morning of the 7th of August, a force of about eight thousand men, consisting of cavalry, artillery, and infantry was seen advancing towards Kanli Tabia. The garrison was instantly under arms, and the batteries and breastworks were manned. The moment the Russians came within range, the Turkish guns from all the works on the southern line opened their fire with great effect. The enemy continued to advance steadily for some time, evidently with the intention of trying to force an entrance at this point, though what ulterior results the officer commanding expected to derive it is impossible to conjecture; for, so long as the works on the heights remained in possession of the garrison, the safety of the place was in no immediate danger.

While this affair was going on a demonstration was made by two regiments of cavalry in front of Hāfiz Pasha Tabia, but they never came within range of its guns. After a lapse of about two hours, the whole force retired to its encampment. It was commanded by General Braemer, and it is possible that his principal motive was to endeavour to entice the Turks out into the open plain, but he found himself closer to the works than he imagined. He not only failed in his plans, whatever they might have been, but paid very dearly for his temerity in coming so near the batteries. A Russian General and several superior officers fell, and the total loss of killed and wounded was very considerable. The guns of the enemy scarcely reached the fortifications, and not a single Turk was therefore touched.

The official account of this attack is given by General Williams in the following extract from his letter to Lord Clarendon, dated August 10th, 1855:—

"I had the honour, on the 3rd instant, of ac-
"quainting your Lordship with the movement of
"General Mouravieff towards Erzeroom, and I have
"since learned that prior to that advance, the Rus-
"sian General had received a reinforcement of a regi-
"ment of infantry from Georgia, making up a total
"of thirty-three battalions of infantry. The force he
"left to observe us consisted of eighteen battalions
"of infantry, three regiments of cavalry, and fifty-
"four guns. As neither our numbers (which I
"abstain from stating) nor our organization could
"hold out a chance of success in any attack upon
"such an army as now observes us, I have advised
"the Mushir still further to strengthen his en-
"trenchments, and this counsel his Excellency has
"steadily carried out, through the zealous superin-
"tendence of Colonel Lake.

"During the absence of the Russian Commander-
"in-chief, the General in command of the corps of
"observation has kept our garrison on the alert;
"more especially his cavalry, which, from its supe-
"rior numbers and discipline, is master of the neigh-
"bourhood. But on the 8th instant, the enemy,
"losing sight of his usual precautions, advanced
"with large masses of infantry, cavalry, and artil-
"lery, to within gunshot of the Kanli Tabia, on
"the south-west angle of our entrenched camp, when
"a well-directed fire from the guns of that redoubt

"obliged him to retire with the loss of several "officers and many men."

In the course of a very few days afterwards another grand *reconnaissance* was made by nearly the whole of the Russian army in front of the Tachmasb heights.

The troops did not, on this occasion, approach within range of the Turkish guns, and after a few hours the force retired to its encampments.

It was now considered advisable to pay particular attention to this position, with a view to strengthening it, as it seemed more than probable, on many accounts, that it would be the first point of attack in the event of an assault. Accordingly, the line of breastwork before alluded to as having been constructed on these heights, was extended to the southward. At the point where the two lines form an angle, an enclosed redoubt was built, in such a manner as to be useless to the enemy in the event of its falling into their hands; and at the southern extremity of the line a small return was made, with two salient angles, for guns, "*en barbette*," to sweep the road running in front of the position.

To the northward of these works, and at a distance of about a thousand yards, a small enclosed redoubt was constructed, called Yuksek Tabia, which afterwards played so conspicuous a part in the defence of Tachmasb. In front of this work, to the southward, and on rather a lower level, a small open battery was placed, which bore the name of Yarim Ai Tabia, and to the northward a long line of fortifications called Shishanajee Lines, consisting of a battery and breastwork, was erected on a ridge of hills commanding the valley leading to the front of the English batteries, intended for the purpose of preventing the Tachmasb works from being taken in flank.

A very important position, opposite to the village of Tchakmak, and commanding the road leading from the valley to Fort Lake, was also fortified by an open battery, called Tetek Tabia. All these precautionary measures, as it was subsequently proved, were by no means thrown away; and there was not one of the works, thus imperfectly described, which was not, more or less, engaged on the day of the assault.

While the fortifications on the heights of Tachmasb were in progress, many other important works were being carried on in other places. In order to facilitate the communication between Arab Tabia and the English batteries on the opposite side of the river, and to obviate the necessity for troops having to take the circuitous route by the town, a rough stone bridge, consisting of two arches, and wing-walls, with a wooden platform, was thrown over the Kars-Tchai, at a spot where its width was about fifty feet, and its depth considerable. Stone was found in great abundance close to the site; and it may perhaps be worthy of remark, that, so steadily and cheerfully did the men labour, the whole work was completed in three days. The bridge stood well, and was afterwards of the utmost service on the day of the battle.

A battery named Williams Pasha Tabia was constructed on dead ground lying in rear of the English batteries, and close to the precipice overhanging the river. The spot being commanded neither by these works nor by Fort Lake, it was considered dangerous to leave it undefended, particularly as it overlooked the fortress and the whole of the town. It was, moreover, intended that this new battery should serve as a place of refuge in the event, as proved afterwards to be the case, of the garrison being driven out of the line in front.

Thus far the works on the heights were completed. A considerable force, consisting of about six thousand men, was encamped there, under the command of Major-General Ismail Pasha (General Kméty), a Hungarian officer of great ability, who, like Feyzi Pasha, chief of the staff, had, for political reasons, left his own country and joined the Turkish army.

The opinion entertained of this officer by Her Majesty's Commissioner is given in the following letter addressed to Lord Clarendon, soon after General Williams had returned to Erzeroom from his first visit to Kars.

"*Brigadier-General Williams to Lord Stratford de Redcliffe.*

"MY LORD,   "Erzeroom, February 13, 1855.

"I beg to bring to the especial notice of your Excellency the services rendered by Ismail Pasha (General Kméty) to this army, prior and subsequently to my arrival at its head-quarters. At the battle of Inje-Dereh he was one of the few who endeavoured, by personal bravery, to encourage the soldiers when abandoned by their officers.

"Since that battle General Kméty kept the outposts, and was the eye of the army until it went into winter-quarters; and he is still the officer in charge of the advanced posts of Kars.

"In despite of these services, General Kméty does not receive the pay due to his rank of Ferik, nor has he had a decoration accorded to him for his personal gallantry. I trust, however, that, through your Excellency's influence, both these claims will be attended to at the Seraskierat: he is one of those men who abstain from complaints or intrigues, and I make this appeal in his favour without a request on his part.

"I have, &c.,
"(Signed)   W. F. WILLIAMS."

Major Teesdale was directed to afford his assistance to this officer, and accordingly took up his position near the works where he afterwards so greatly distinguished himself. Hussein Pasha, a Circassian by birth, holding at this time the rank of Colonel, but shortly after promoted to that of Major-general, also held a command at Tachmasb, and proved a most able and zealous officer. In order to give as much confidence as possible to the garrison, it was thought desirable to form a second or inner line of defence on the plain below, and this was accordingly done by constructing a breastwork, to connect the walls of the fortress with the burial-ground in front (the enclosures of which were raised and strengthened), and carrying on the breastwork again until it joined Chicheck Tabia.

A line of fortification already existed, uniting this latter work with Yussuf Pasha Tabia, forming part of the original defence of the principal suburb. This was considerably added to and improved by increasing the dimensions of the parapet, turfing the exterior and superior slopes, and facing the interior with rough stone. A battery, called Lelek Tabia, was constructed a little to the right of Yussuf Pasha Tabia, and connected with it on one flank by a breastwork, a similar line being carried from the other flank of the new work to a steep precipice in rear, thus completing the whole chain of inner defence.

Three rows of *trous-de-loup*, between three and

four feet in diameter, and about the same in depth, were excavated a few yards in front of nearly all the batteries and breastworks; and, in short, everything was done that could be thought of to add to the strength of the place.

Probably many defects may be discovered in the works thus hastily thrown up, but if the great disadvantages under which they were constructed be taken into consideration, due allowance may be made for errors and imperfections.

The total want of an engineer establishment, which has before been alluded to; the great extent of ground to be fortified, comprising a circle of nearly ten miles; the difficulty, and in many places the impossibility, of excavating a ditch, owing to the rocky nature of the soil; and, lastly, the want of sufficient time—which rendered the preparation of plans quite out of the question—were all drawbacks to a matured and more perfect system of defence. No sooner was a work decided on than it was at once marked out, and the profiles, made on the spot, were immediately put up. Working parties were told off, and as the Russian officers, who were enabled by means of telescopes to watch the progress from their camps, afterwards remarked, the batteries appeared to rise by magic.

The able supervision of Major Teesdale and Captain Thompson, who were ever ready to afford their assistance when their other duties permitted them; the cheerfulness and dexterity with which the men worked, and the quantity of loose stone found in every direction, tended very considerably to counterbalance the disadvantages under which the Engineer Officer laboured, and enabled him to complete the fortifications to such an extent as to render the place defensible.

CHAPTER VIII.

Enemy pitches Camps at Boskali, Chalgour, and Ainalli — Desertion commences to take place—Punishment awarded—Deserter taken and Shot—Lāz Riflemen become mutinous—Their punishment—Horses sent away for want of food—Vēli Pasha's Force—Correspondence between General Williams and Colonel Lake—Instructions given to Vēli Pasha—Erivan Force advanced, and Vēli Pasha retired—A Turkish Spy found and executed—Batoom Army—Heavy siege-guns arrive from Gumri—Kanli Tabia strengthened—Correspondence about Transport—Seven hundred Horses killed.

ABOUT the latter end of the month of August, the enemy formed a cavalry camp, with a battery of eight field guns, at Boskali, situated on rising ground, to the north-west of Tachmasb, and distant from it about four miles. Soon afterwards other camps were pitched at the villages of Chalgour and Ainalli, to the northward of the position; the former consisting of cavalry, the latter of all arms. Running pickets were stationed day and night in every direction, and Kars was at length completely invested.

Up to this time only one post, bringing letters and despatches to the garrison, had fallen into the hands of the enemy, and not one messenger going out had been taken, so that General Williams was able (and he lost no opportunity of doing so) to keep the authorities at Erzeroom and Constantinople fully informed, from time to time, of all that was occurring in the beleaguered city, still clinging to the hope that some assistance might be sent ere it was too late. The men's ration was again reduced, and every conceivable plan was adopted to make the provisions last as long as possible. Desertion from the ranks now began to take place, and there were evident symptoms of its rapidly increasing.

This arose, not from fear of the enemy or from the limited supply of food, but from the intense dread which the soldiers had of passing another winter in Kars. Shut up in houses, or more properly speaking in hovels, as they had been the previous year, without even a window to admit the light, the long winter nights must have appeared interminable to them, and must have had a most depressing effect upon their spirits.

The deserters did not seem desirous of going over to the enemy, and in very few cases did they attempt to do so; their greater wish being to return to their villages, where they had left their families, and where they might hope to remain concealed until the war was over.

After the battle of Kuruk Déré desertion had taken place to an enormous extent, as many as eight thousand soldiers having escaped; and, strange to

PUNISHMENT DUE TO DESERTION. 131

say, such are Turkish apathy and want of system, that scarcely one was ever brought back to his duty, or in any way punished. It could not, therefore, be a matter of surprise that many of the soldiers, composing the garrison of Kars, serving against their will, as was more especially the case among the Rediff or Militia, should seize every opportunity of making their escape, expecting that, even if unfortunate enough to be captured, the punishment for the offence would, according to former custom, only be a few stripes, or the being compelled to serve for a certain number of years longer.

Under these circumstances, and seeing no chance whatever of being able to check a crime which so materially endangered the safety of the place, the Mushir, on General Williams' earnest remonstrance, published an order to the effect that thenceforth the punishment for desertion would in all cases be immediate death. A case very soon occurred. The unhappy man did not attempt to deny his guilt, but, offering no excuse whatever, at once confessed his intention to desert. He was found concealed outside the works, having stripped off his uniform, and laid aside his arms. He was taken before a military council, tried, condemned, and immediately shot. He evinced not the slightest degree of fear, and met his just doom with that coolness and disregard of death for which the Turkish soldier is remarkable.

This example, the first that had occurred in the army, had by no means a bad effect on the troops: many of the soldiers were heard to say it was a proper punishment for the offence. They insulted the body of the culprit in every possible way, spitting on it and calling it "giaour," the most opprobrious epithet that a Turk can use; in short, there was not a murmur of discontent uttered at this sudden change in their articles of war. It was not to be expected that desertion could be altogether put a stop to by the fear of any punishment, however severe, and consequently it continued to occur from time to time, principally among the Rediff, who, after having previously completed their appointed time, had been compelled to serve again at the commencement of the war.

Not long afterwards as many as forty men deserted in a night, having quitted their post when on duty. They all belonged to the same battalion, which was, therefore, by order of the Mushir, paraded the following day and broken up on the spot, the men being drafted in small numbers into other regiments, and the officers, on whom, no doubt, considerable blame rested, were for a time laid on the shelf. The Lāz, or irregular riflemen, now and then showed signs of insubordination, and their chiefs either did not, or pretended they did not, possess that influence over them which they undoubtedly ought to have exercised.

On one occasion, in particular, a party of these

wild mountaineers, armed with their rifles, had plundered a neighbouring village, and ill treated some of the inhabitants, who, happening to meet Major Teesdale and Captain Thompson, soon afterwards, complained to them of the circumstance.

These two officers at once rode after the delinquents, and, finding the plunder on them, desired that it should be immediately laid down. This the Lāz stoutly refused to do, and, on being remonstrated with, drew their daggers and even presented their rifles at the officers. Fortunately at that moment a party of chasseurs, having witnessed the scene from the batteries, came down and disarmed the mutineers, who were forthwith put in confinement. The chiefs, though too cunning openly to sanction such a breach of discipline, showed an evident disinclination to punish it in a befitting manner. The Mushir, therefore, at General Williams' instigation, ordered that the prisoners should be severely and publicly flogged; that their arms should be broken up in their presence (the greatest punishment and insult that could be inflicted on them); and that they should afterwards be imprisoned for an indefinite period. This sentence was carried into execution the same afternoon, and had a very good effect upon the rest of the Lāz, who had been assembled to witness it.

Finding the forage beginning to run short, and the pasture daily getting more scanty, it was considered advisable to send away as many horses as could be spared. Accordingly, several hundred of the regular cavalry were ordered to march during the night, and they succeeded in making their escape, without any loss, to Olti, and eventually to Erzeroom. This occurred previously to the place being thoroughly invested.

At a subsequent period it was found necessary to send away a second detachment of cavalry, which was accompanied by five pashas, who had no duty assigned to them, and who, with their numerous followers, consumed, of course, a large amount of the now rapidly-decreasing provisions. This party was not so fortunate as the preceding one. The superior officers escaped, but about four hundred of the men, pursued by the Russian dragoons, were either cut down or captured with their horses, the remainder making their escape to Olti.

Though unconnected with the operations being carried on at Kars, it may not be out of place to make some allusion to the Turkish force stationed near the Byazid line, commanded by Vēli Pasha, at Euch-Kelissa, for the purpose of keeping in check the portion of the Russian army called the Erivan brigade, consisting of about six thousand men.

The following correspondence, which passed between Her Majesty's Commissioner and Lieutenant-Colonel Lake in the month of April, 1855, was sent to the Earl of Clarendon for his information, and the insertion of it here, though it touches upon other subjects besides the one now under consideration, may not perhaps be considered out of place.

"*Extract of Memorandum from Brigadier-General Williams to Lieut.- Colonel Lake, dated Erzeroom, April* 18, 1855.

"I have to thank you all for the exertions you are making, and am but too happy to have you where you are. I can spare but little time, as Tahir Pasha will, at my request, send off a man for Kars instanter, instead of Friday next, the day he named; you will therefore oblige me by offering to the Mushir the following remarks:—

"1. I enclose a letter which Zohrab will have translated during your visit by some trustworthy person conversant with that language; it gives positive information on the intention of the Russians to attack the Byazid line, and I am most anxious that he should call in the Ardahan detachments to Kars, where you will then have a force equal to the enemy in front; if he comes with an equal force to attack you in your lines, what would be his chance of success? I apprehend very small.

"2. With regard to the Byazid line, it is almost denuded of troops, and should the enemy break into it at Euch-Kelissa and Toprak-Kaleh, whilst the Gumri army menaces your garrison, could that garrison render us any assistance at Toprak-Kaleh and Kuprikeuy, and aid us in defending our magazines here? I think his Excellency will say 'No.'

"3. I would therefore suggest for his Excellency's mature consideration the necessity of keeping the few troops now here in hand, certainly until the men recently landed at Trebizonde shall have arrived in Erzeroom; and from Olti, and other detached places in your rear, I would advise his Excellency to look to Khaghisman.

"4. I strongly recommend the immediate assembly of the Bashi-Bozouks at Kars, and along the Byazid frontier, and the hastening of Vēli Pasha from Koordistan to the front, wherever his Excellency thinks of placing him.

"5. I suggest to his Excellency's mature consideration whether a few of the siege guns, now here, may or may not be sent to Kars to add to its defences; but as we have neither an army nor materials for besieging Gumri, put it to his Excellency if the risk of these inestimable guns should be hazarded unnecessarily; their loss would paralyse the movements of any army sent from Trebizonde to our future assistance.

"6. I leave the placing of the block-houses in your own able hands, but merely point out Kāradāgh Tabia, Arab Tabia, Vēli Pasha Tabia; these, I think, you will say are weak points, and such works would infinitely strengthen their isolated positions, and encourage their defenders. If you can add two others they might be at Canli Tabia and Suwarri Tabia; but you are on the spot to study the ground, and I shall do well to leave the whole affair to you. Those on the hills behind are, I think, out of the immediate reach of guns, and might therefore be small and slight in construction.

"7. Assure his Excellency that both by the last post and the last but one I wrote to Lords Stratford and Raglan and Clarendon on the want of support we receive from the Seraskier, and that I will again write more strongly on Tuesday next; add to this assurance my prayers that he will steadily purge the regiments and brigades of bad commanders, for I feel sure that he will yet receive perfect support and sympathy from the Sultan and the British Government."

"*Lieutenant-Colonel Lake to Brigadier-General Williams.*

"SIR, "Kars, April 20, 1855.

"I have the honour to acknowledge the receipt of your letter under date the 18th instant.

"According to your instructions, I had an interview with his Excellency the Mushir this day, and Mr. Zohrab read to him the letter you sent under flying seal. I also had the other letter read to him agreeably to your orders. I then laid before his Excellency the several remarks which you desired me to offer to him.

"With respect to the Ardahan detachment, the Mushir quite agrees with you as to the expediency of calling it into Kars, but is afraid of doing so at present, owing to the great scarcity of provisions in this garrison. Fully as I also concur in considering that this measure would be most desirable, I could scarcely urge it upon the Mushir when I knew that, at this moment, there are only fifteen days' provision in store for the troops now in garrison. I however impressed upon his Excellency the necessity of sending immediate orders to Ardahan for the detachment to hold itself in readiness to march at a moment's notice to this place, a distance which can easily be performed in three days.

"In reply to your question as to whether this garrison could afford assistance to any other place, while it was itself menaced by a force from Gumri, his Excellency is of opinion that such a measure would be impracticable.

"Under these circumstances it would perhaps be better not to weaken the garrison of Erzeroom at present as regards troops.

"His Excellency informs me that he has made out a list regarding Bashi-Bozouks, which goes to Erzeroom by this post. When it is returned, steps will be immediately taken to collect this irregular force, both at Kars and along the Byazid frontier.

"Orders have been already sent, and also an express messenger, desiring Vēli Pasha to proceed at once with the force under his command to Toprak-Kaleh.

"With regard to siege guns, we are indeed very

much in want of them here, not having nearly enough for the batteries; and looking only to our having to act on the defensive, without an idea at present of laying siege to any of the enemy's forts, the Mushir is of opinion that it would be highly advantageous to this position if you could spare a few guns from Erzeroom.

"Having now had the honour of conveying to you the opinions of the Mushir on the several remarks laid before him, I venture to add a few words on what I cannot but consider the absolute necessity of strengthening the force that at present forms the garrison of Kars. That this is a most important position nobody can, I think, deny; and, looking at the extent of the works, and the probable strength of the army that might be brought against it, I am inclined to think the number of troops is inadequate. The returns that go to Constantinople no doubt lead the authorities to believe that our force is much greater than it really is. Taking into consideration the number of non-combatants, such as surgeons and apothecaries, writers, watermen, bandsmen, &c., the amount, effective or fighting, becomes very much smaller than would appear at a casual view of the returns. In addition to all this, we must look to the number of invalids, not only the sick in hospital, but the convalescents too weak for duty. Thus, if even all the troops composing the army of Kars which could be safely concentrated here were to be assembled, we should have a force of little more than fifteen thousand service men. Supposing for a moment that this force, as I have stated it, were properly armed, clothed, and officered, still I think, bearing in mind that it has been so often defeated, it is more than ever incumbent on the authorities to take every possible precaution against another defeat, which would be most disastrous.

"I think I may say that, with an efficient force and a good supply of ammunition, in which it is at present very deficient, Kars would be able to resist any attack that could be made against it.

"I am quite aware that you have over and over again urged the necessity at head-quarters of supplying this army, not only with reinforcements, but with many articles so necessary to put it in an efficient condition, and anything I may now take the liberty of bringing to your notice is only an echo probably of your own words; but I feel it due to myself, and to the important situation which I have the honour to hold under you, to express my opinion thus freely, and to say again that, unless this force is speedily strengthened, and supplied with arms and ammunition, the consequences may be fatal.

"I am sorry to say the hospitals still continue full, the average per diem for the last week having been five hundred and seventy, and that of deaths six and a-half per diem. This, however, does not show the whole number of men unfit for duty, and several men in each regiment are ill and unable to attend drills, for whom there is no room in hospital. Steps are, however, being taken to provide increased accommodation.

"By the return of stores which I have the honour to forward, you will perceive that they are running very low. In my conversation with the Mushir to-day, he assured me that all possible steps are being taken for getting up the supply.

"Several thousand men have been employed during the week on the fortifications, which are rapidly progressing, and, I think, in a most satisfactory manner. Both officers and men pay every attention to the orders they receive. Wood is coming in for the block-houses, which I shall commence as soon as it arrives."

Vēli Pasha's detachment was about five thousand strong of all arms, and, with regard to discipline and equipment, was much in the same state as the rest of the Kars army, of which it was, in fact, a component part. The instructions which the Lieutenant-general received from Her Majesty's Commissioner were to the effect that he should, in the event of the Russians advancing, gradually retire on Erzeroom, not only for his own safety, his force being small and totally unfit to cope with the enemy in the field, but that he might strengthen that garrison, which, in case of an attack on the fortress, was scarcely sufficient to defend it.

Very early in the month of August the Erivan force advanced, and Vēli Pasha, in obedience to his orders, retired on the Devi-Boynou Pass, which, as before described, had been lately fortified by General Williams. The retreat was made during the night, and reflected considerable credit on the commanding officer, inasmuch as he succeeded in effecting it with his guns, stores, and ammunition, without any loss whatever.

From various circumstances that occurred, it appeared but too evident that the system of spying was carried on in Kars to a great extent; and as everything depended on keeping secret the quantity of provisions, the state of the troops, and, in short, every particular connected with the garrison, it was deemed necessary to put down this dangerous practice with a heavy hand. An order was accordingly published, to the effect, that any individual proved to be guilty of the crime of giving to the enemy information of any kind prejudicial to the safety of the garrison should be immediately put to death.

In a very short time after this one of the inhabitants was convicted, on the most positive evidence, of conveying intelligence to the enemy's camp. A letter was found on him, addressed by a Russian officer to an individual in the garrison,

A SPY IS HUNG. 143

stating that the information he had given as to the number of troops in Kars, the amount of stores, &c., was not sufficiently explicit, and calling on him to furnish further details immediately.

The man, on his examination, stated that he had been engaged by a certain person, whom he named, to carry a letter to the enemy; and that the document found on him was the reply, which he was going to give to his employer, when it by accident fell out of his pocket, and was picked up by a soldier, who took it at once to the proper authorities. The prisoner was tried by a military council, at which one of the English officers was, as usual, present. He offered no defence, confessing he had been persuaded to act as he had done for a few pieces of silver. He was sentenced to death, and was hung the same afternoon in the centre of the town. Crowds assembled to witness the execution, but not a murmur of discontent was heard: on the contrary, the justice of the sentence was fully acknowledged by the spectators, who expressed, in no very measured terms, the disgust they felt at a Mussulman thus betraying his country. A paper was hung round the culprit's neck, stating the nature of the crime for which he suffered, as a warning to others; and his body was left hanging for four and twenty hours. Before it was taken down, eleven newly-coined Russian imperials were found on his person, which fact, if proof of his guilt had been wanting, would have been more than sufficient to show that he had not suffered unjustly.

The greater criminal of the two, the man who had sent the information, it was found impossible to convict; for though he had long been suspected of being a spy, and was well known as a bad character, no sufficient evidence could be procured against him, except that of his victim. He was, however, kept a prisoner, and sentenced to hard labour in the public streets; no small disgrace to a man of education, accustomed to associate with officers of rank.

During the blockade many other spies were executed, and among them were a Persian and two Armenians. They all confessed their guilt, and offered no defence whatever. Fortunately, as it was fully proved by reference to the Russian officers after the surrender, every one of them was more or less guilty. Owing, however, to the great secrecy that was maintained, not one of the spies was able to give positive information as to the quantity of provisions or ammunition in store; but their crime was not the less flagrant.

At a time when desertion was very much on the increase, it became necessary to ascertain in what manner many of the soldiers contrived to escape; and it was at last discovered that there were regular agents in the town, who made a trade of assisting those anxious to fly from the garrison. It turned out to be a completely-organized system. The men were taken to a house, where they concealed their arms and accoutrements: they then exchanged their regimentals for plain clothes, and were conducted by the agents beyond the works, from whence they escaped to their own homes, provided they could pass the enemy's outposts.

It was impossible to allow this practice to continue, second only to that of spying in point of danger. It was therefore determined that every man found guilty of conniving at desertion should suffer death by hanging. The first who were convicted under this new regulation were an inhabitant of Kars, his son, and nephew. In their house were found numbers of muskets, pouch-belts, swords, and regimentals belonging to soldiers who had deserted, and their guilt was fully proved. They were all three sentenced to be executed; but on account of his great age, the punishment of the father was commuted, care being taken that he should no longer practise his nefarious trade.

General Williams, in his despatch to Lord Clarendon, dated Kars, September 14, 1855, thus notices this subject:—

"From my more recent despatches your Lordship
"will have perceived that desertion is the great
"evil against which we have to contend. In spite
"of the example exhibited to the troops in the dis-

" banding of the regiment of Redif, as detailed in
" my despatch of the 10th instant, we had no less
" than six desertions yesterday; fortunately we re-
" captured two of them; they proved to be men of
" the corps in question. They were tried by a
" Council of War, and instantly shot. On their
" trial they denounced the parties (inhabitants of
" Kars) who had instigated them to this act of
" treason, and furnished them with peasants' clothes
" to enable them to effect their purpose. Three of
" these men were seized in a house, where the
" musket of one of the prisoners who suffered yes-
" terday was found, together with the clothes and
" appointments of seven more deserters. There
" can be little doubt that these wretches are in
" communication with the enemy, as proclamations
" were found on the last-captured spy, offering any
" deserters free passage through the Russian posts
" to their homes.

" A Council of War has tried and condemned
" these men, who will be hanged to-day in the
" market-place; and the appointments of the seven
" deserters who have escaped by their agency will
" be exhibited on the gallows, as a further proof of
" their guilt.

" Your Lordship will learn with pleasure that, up
" to this moment, no Christian subject of the Sultan
" has betrayed us, all those who have so justly for-
" feited their lives being Mussulmans."

CORRESPONDENCE ABOUT BATOOM ARMY.

It was generally supposed that some assistance might have been afforded to the garrison of Kars by the Batoom army, which was said to be twelve thousand strong, under the command of Mushir Mustapha Pasha.

The following extracts from a correspondence which took place between Lord Stratford de Redcliffe and M. Pisani on the 13th and 14th of June, 1855, show the opinion of Her Majesty's Ambassador on this subject:—

"Now that Circassia is cleared of the Russians, "why should not the old idea of uniting the army "at Batoom with that of Kars be acted upon in the "present emergency? Suggest this impressively. I "am assured that Batoom may be held with a very "small force, supposing it to have works sufficient "to be relied on; but of this I am no judge.

"I have, &c.,
"(Signed)   STRATFORD DE REDCLIFFE."

"Having asked the Seraskier what number of "troops they have at Batoom, he replied, that there "is an effective number of twelve thousand men. "Upon which I observed to his Excellency that, "now that Circassia is cleared of the Russians, as "your Excellency remarks in your instruction, why "should not the old idea of uniting the army of "Batoom with that of Kars be acted upon in the "present emergency? The Seraskier said, that he not only concurs in that opinion, but even proposed it in the council, and it was because some strong objections were opposed that he did not think it right to insist; at the same time, however, he believes that a larger force can be disposed of without prejudice. His intention was to see Fuad Pasha last night, and come to some conclusion. Having seen the latter after I left the Seraskier, I urged him to settle the matter with the least possible delay. His Excellency promised to do so.

"I have, &c.,

"(Signed) Et. Pisani."

From the nature of the ground about Batoom, and the facility with which the thickly-wooded mountains could be defended, a comparatively small force would have sufficed to hold that position, and accordingly application was twice made for troops. These were positively refused at first; but, after some time, the Mushir wrote to say that five thousand men should immediately be sent to Kars. It is scarcely necessary to state that this reinforcement was never despatched, though the reason of the non-fulfilment of the Pasha's promise did not transpire. One thing was very certain, that every hope of succour became gradually less, and it appeared but too evident that the place was left to its own resources, feeble and insufficient as they were.

On the 21st of August, a convoy was seen approaching the Russian camp from the direction of Alexandropol, and it was reported that two heavy siege-guns and a large mortar accompanied it; in consequence of which it was considered necessary to strengthen Kanli Tabia, the battery at the southwest angle of the lower works, and the point which had on a former occasion been attacked. It seemed very probable that these large guns were being brought to silence this work, which had done the enemy so much mischief.

General Williams desired the Engineer Officer to lose no time in preparing the battery in question for the reception of some heavier ordnance.

The following copy of a note conveying the order to Lieutenant-Colonel Lake, who was at the moment employed in trying a spy, is here inserted as being characteristic of the forethought at all times exercised by Her Majesty's Commissioner:—

" MY DEAR LAKE. "Ten minutes past Four o'clock.

"To hang spies is, no doubt, a good thing, but in the mean time the enemy is hurrying his battering guns from the convoy to his camp, and also his escort battalions. I think we may then look out for *to-morrow morning*. I would advise the Mushir's and all those tents to be removed out of the line of fire, to the green outside of our little town gate. I hope the nine-oke guns from the two tower bastions of the town may be in Kanli by daylight. I strongly recommend you and Feyzi Bey to look to these hints, for why should the enemy press on the bullocks of the siege-guns, if he did not intend to use them to-morrow?

"(Signed)   W. F. WILLIAMS.

" To Colonel Lake."

Three of the barbettes were therefore immediately raised about four feet, additional height was given to the parapet, and embrasures were constructed. At midnight two heavy siege-guns and a twenty-two oke-howitzer were brought from the fort, placed in position in the battery, and masked with gabions. Kanli Tabia thus became a most formidable redoubt; and the increased command it obtained served to keep the enemy at a considerably greater distance when attempting to interfere with the foraging parties, a matter of no little moment, as the pasturage became more scanty every day.

The lean and wretched appearance of the horses now rendered it again necessary to reduce their numbers. The whole of them were therefore paraded for inspection; and a more miserable sight can hardly be imagined. Many of the poor brutes could scarcely drag one leg after the other, and not one was fit for the most ordinary work. The small stacks of hay which had been put up and carefully

DESPATCH REGARDING TRANSPORT CORPS.

guarded, were fast disappearing. The barley was very nearly expended, and there was no hope of a further supply. All idea of keeping up the cavalry was now at an end, and there was no chance of their being able to force their way through the Russian blockade. It was therefore determined to preserve as many horses as would suffice to move the guns to and from the several batteries, and to carry water for the troops.

No allusion has yet been made to the means of conveying the baggage of the army, in the event of their taking the field. From the commencement of the blockade, it was found utterly impossible to organise a transport corps, and mules with panniers were the only substitutes for ambulances. But it must not be supposed for a moment that these requisites had been overlooked by those whose duty it was to try and get every necessary provided. Applications without end had been made, but had met with no attention.

The following letter addressed by General Williams to Lord Clarendon shows that this important subject was by no means forgotten by Her Majesty's Commissioner :—

"*Colonel Williams to the Earl of Clarendon.*

"My Lord, "Erzeroom, January 20, 1855.

"In the interview I had with the Defterdar of the army two days ago, he informed me of the details of a project for the supply of beasts of burden for this army during the next campaign, recently decided on at the Seraskierat, at Constantinople, and sent to the authorities at these head-quarters.

"*Project.*

" 1. Twenty-five thousand horses are to be supplied from the various provinces of Anatolia.

" 2. One horse or mule is to be furnished by each group of forty-five houses throughout those provinces.

" 3. Every group of one hundred and thirty-five houses is to furnish a man who will be charged with the care of three horses.

" 4. The men so levied are each to receive one oke of bread per diem, and the horses or mules three and a-half okes of barley and four okes of straw; these rations are to be furnished by the Government.

" 5. A nazir or agent will be named by each province to make the levies and organize the establishments.

" At the end of the war these horses are to be returned to their several owners, and if, in the mean time, any of them die, or are rendered useless by labour, they will be paid for or replaced by the Government.

" Before the weather admits of any steps being taken to carry out this project, I feel it incumbent on me to point out its vices, and to lay bare the wholesale system of fraud which it is intended to cover; and to do so I must invert the series of its items or paragraphs as they stand in the project. Thus, No. 5 stipulates that a nazir will be named to go into these distant provinces to make the levies and organize the establishments; any one who is conversant with the corruption and trickery of such agents, will see at a glance the vast field for the employment of these arts. Some communities will buy off these venal men, whilst others will be oppressed with a double indent on them and their animals.

"The man in charge of three horses is to have, either on his march or in camp, an oke of bread per diem, and his horses three and a half okes of barley! Who is to supply this food for man and horse? My various reports will prove that both the driver and beast will perish together by the road-side ere they reach Erzeroom from the neighbourhood of Angora, Broussa, and Smyrna.

"How many days will the driver deputed, but not paid, by one hundred and thirty-five houses, remain by his animals under the most adverse circumstances conceivable—those of neglect and starvation? If the army cannot be kept together in camp by a chain of sentinels, how can the people of the Seraskierat count on retaining these men at their work by the promise of an oke of bread a-day?

" Any one moderately instructed in the tricks of mudirs will arrive at the conclusion that the horse or mule supplied to Government by one of these worthies, assisted by the inhabitants of forty-five houses, will be of little service to the army, if it ever reaches the head-quarters.

" To add the subsistence of twenty-five thousand horses and eight thousand three hundred and thirty-three drivers to those difficulties experienced in feeding the army last campaign, would be the grossest of faults. The authorities thus throw away the vast amount of bullock-carts and camels which can be commanded by honest payments on the part of the Defterdar of the army; those useful animals feed themselves on the road-side, more especially the camel, which can be procured in any number by contractors, and can accompany an army in any description of country, and one man drives and attends to the wants of seven of these useful animals, which carry a burden double of that of the pack-horse.

" I therefore pray that this scheme of plunder may be nipped in the bud; that the service of five thousand camels and two thousand mules or horses may be contracted for, and that the rest of the army traffic may be performed by the ox-arabas of the country, which also can be found in vast numbers.

" I make this appeal to your Lordship a few

hours only after I became acquainted with the senseless project in question, not only to plead for the army but also to save the unfortunate inhabitants of Anatolia from this last and terrible evil.

"I have, &c.,

"(Signed)   W. F. WILLIAMS."

Out of the number of horses which were paraded, such were selected as, from their age or condition, seemed likely to do a little more service. These were distributed among the several battalions for regimental purposes, reserving a sufficient number to horse five or six batteries; the remainder, amounting to about seven hundred, were sentenced to die, and were accordingly taken some distance off, where their throats were cut. Cavalry outpost duty thenceforward became a dead letter as regarded the dragoons. A few horses still remained to the Bashi-Bozouks, who, during the night, still continued to patrol some distance in front of the works. All officers were directed to reduce the number of their horses, mounted orderlies were dispensed with, and every possible means were devised for keeping alive the few animals that remained. Even at an earlier period, the poor horses fell down dead in numbers all over the camp, totally emaciated; and it was with great difficulty that the bodies could be covered up before they became decomposed.

CHAPTER IX.

Garrison attacked by Cholera—Turkish medical subordinates not well educated—Post arrives September 23rd—News from the Crimea, and from Omer Pasha—His Advice to the Garrison—General Williams writes to Sheikh Shamyl, and receives an answer—Three British Officers arrive at Erzeroom—They attempt in vain to get to Kars—Their subsequent Movements.

THE garrison, hitherto so unusually healthy, was now visited by that most dreadful of all scourges the Cholera. It assumed, after a time, a virulent form, and acting, as it did, upon constitutions already enfeebled by constant watching and want of sufficient food, the havoc it made was fearful. As a single instance, it need only be remarked that, from one regiment alone, stationed on the Kāradāgh, which was considered the most healthy of all the positions, seventy-five men, attacked with cholera, were sent into hospital in one day, of whom by far the greater number died.

The hospital arrangements made by Dr. Sandwith, and his own personal attendance on the sick, are worthy of all praise; for he had much to contend against. His subordinates were, for the most part, men of limited education and little experience, not to be trusted in any but the most ordinary cases. The medicines sent up from Constantinople were of a most heterogeneous kind, and very insufficient in quantity. Among the several articles, were a large assortment of pomatum for the hair, and a considerable collection of instruments used in midwifery! other necessary and indispensable articles being utterly deficient.

There are, perhaps, few diseases in the world which exercise so dispiriting an effect on mankind in general as the cholera. In the present instance, the rapidity of its strides, the constant sight of funerals leaving the hospital, and the necessity for the men having to carry the dead bodies of their comrades, thus suddenly swept off, to their graves, could not fail to dishearten the bravest troops, to a certain extent; but, in justice to the garrison of Kars, it must be remarked that they bore up manfully against this and every other hardship they were forced to undergo. An appearance of resignation to their fate, and determination to do their duty to the last, gave promise of that invincible bravery which they afterwards displayed, and encouraged those in authority to do their utmost to hold the place until driven by famine to surrender.

There are, of course, exceptions to every rule, and

though the general conduct of the Turks was thus exemplary, there were some among them who did not possess sufficient moral courage to face disease in so frightful a form; though probably, in front of an enemy in the field, they might have proved themselves brave soldiers.

To this cause, therefore, may, in some measure, be attributed a certain portion of the desertions which took place at this period of the blockade. The number carried off by cholera amounted to about fifteen hundred men, exclusive of such of the inhabitants as fell victims to the disease.

On the morning of the 23rd of September, a post was brought into the garrison from Erzeroom, by Arslan Agha, a chief of Bashi-Bozouks. This brave man, with six of his followers, forced his way through the enemy's outposts under great difficulties, and in a manner worthy to be recorded. He was perfectly aware that any attempt to pass the patrols by stealth would inevitably fail, as the night was not very dark, and the mounted sentinels were, as usual, close to each other. He well knew the importance of the Despatches of which he was the bearer, and was convinced that nothing but stratagem would enable him to effect his purpose. He therefore resolutely approached the enemy's outposts, trusting that the knowledge of the Russian language which he fortunately possessed would enable him to deceive the patrols.

He was, of course, immediately challenged, and at once replied, in an authoritative tone, stating that the field officer on duty was approaching. Arslan Agha and his brave followers then put spurs to their horses, and galloped through the line of pickets before the Russians had time to recover from their surprise. This gallant fellow was wounded by a lance in the breast on the 29th of September, while nobly leading on his men, and died some days afterwards.

The post, which thus fortunately reached its destination, conveyed the welcome intelligence that the southern part of Sebastopol had fallen into the hands of the allied armies, and it also brought a letter for the Mushir from Omer Pasha. A salute in honour of the victory was fired at noon, and likewise another at sunset. The troops were paraded, and an order of the day read to them, communicating the joyful intelligence that had been received, which had, naturally, a most inspiriting effect; and though their outward appearance but too plainly showed how much their bodily strength was already decreased by the gradually diminished ration, the eye had lost none of its original fire, and gave evidence of a courage still undaunted.

The letter from Omer Pasha was not calculated to infuse any great amount of spirit into the troops, or to inspire the commanders with much hope of succour from that quarter. It contained the following advice to the Mushir: that he should strengthen the fortifications of Kars as much as he could; that he should take measures for laying in as large a stock of provisions as possible; and that the garrison should keep up its spirits; adding, that in twenty days he would come to their assistance.

With regard to the first part of this advice, it is scarcely necessary to say that it was altogether superfluous. Omer Pasha knew perfectly well that Her Majesty's Commissioner was at Kars, and he might therefore be very certain that every possible precaution had been taken to insure the safety of the place, as far as the defences were concerned.

It seemed strange to write in such a style to a few doomed men who had not ceased to toil for months at their fortifications.

The counsel given regarding the provisions was incomprehensible, for the generalissimo was kept, from time to time, fully informed of the state of affairs as they existed at Kars, and might have known the utter impossibility of getting the stores replenished, unless assistance were rendered from without, of which there appeared but very little prospect.

There was, however, another quarter from which if not direct succour, at least a favourable demonstration might have been expected, and that was from the celebrated Sheikh Shamyl, Prince of Daghistan, erroneously called the Circassian Chief.

At the commencement of the war he had made a successful foray towards Tiflis, and spread consternation in and around that city, but it ended in his attacking the estate of Prince Tchevtchevadze, and carrying off into captivity the two princesses of that name, Georgian ladies of the highest rank, and of great personal beauty and accomplishments.

It was on the occasion of this miserable incursion that the British Commissioner addressed to the Daghistan Chieftain the following letter:—

"(Copy.) "Turkish Camp, near Kars, Oct. 12, 1854.

"Through the friendly offices of your countryman, Haji Khalil Pasha, I have great pleasure in writing you this letter, more especially as I am able to tell you that the English and French armies, having landed in the Crimea, defeated the Russian army under Prince Menstchikoff, with the loss of fourteen thousand men. Every attack has proved successful, and the batteries were just going to play upon the city of Sebastopol. Balaclava is taken, and Anapa blown up and abandoned by the Russians. All this is very glorious, but does not eclipse the glory with which your name has been associated throughout the world during so many years. You will, I know, thank me for frankly telling you that, as your Government is now recognised by the Allied Powers, it would be regretable that the deeds of some of your warriors should bring it into disrepute, as they have done in the late attacks in the neighbourhood of Tiflis, by killing unprotected Russian ladies, and carrying other ladies into captivity into the mountains.

"Lord Stratford, as your friend and great supporter at Constantinople, invokes you, through my pen, to cause these unhappy people to be instantly sent in safety to their homes; and I add my humble voice as a soldier to that of his Excellency. I learn from your friends that these acts have been committed to induce the Russians to exchange prisoners; but I again pray you to take my advice, and trust to your arms, which have never failed you, and not to the cries of unhappy women, whom all brave men are sworn to defend.

"(Seal) THE QUEEN OF ENGLAND'S
COMMISSIONER TO THE ARMY AT KARS.
"Sheikh Shamyl,
&c. &c."

Shamyl evidently felt the force of the language adopted in this communication, and returned, by one of his trusty followers, this reply :—

"*Sheikh Shamyl to General Sir Fenwick Williams (then Colonel Williams).*

"In the name of God the merciful and clement.
"From the slave of God, Shemouil, to the illus-

trious and honourable Colonel Williams, Commissioner in the army of Anatolia. 'Imperishable may his eminence and dignity be.'

"We received your letter, and understood its purport and meaning. We rejoiced to hear of the successes of our ever-victorious arms over our virtueless enemies, and the prostration of their pride in every engagement that has taken place. May the Lord be praised!

"After that, we thank you for the notice you take of our dignity and honour, and for giving us a place amongst worthy men; and though we may not be that in truth and reality, God forbid that we should do anything which might be considered disgraceful by the Mohammedan laws or by the exalted government. We had liberated the women (Princess Tchevtchevadze and her companions) before the arrival of your letter, and had you been acquainted with the true circumstances you would not have found fault with us; for everybody knows that we are always humane; that we expend our breath in reciting the holy words of the Lord of the Creation, and scorn the enmity of the infidels our foes. Our great solicitude and prayer to the Almighty is the pleasure of making your acquaintance, and we never had that opportunity until now. It may be that God the all-gracious will grant us this favour.

"(Sealed)   SHEMOUIL.

"*Friday, the 12th of the month of Redjeb,* 1271."

However just may be the celebrity obtained by this man in combats with the Russian troops in his own mountain fastnesses, it is very evident that beyond those precincts he wielded but a slender power; otherwise he most undoubtedly would have availed himself of a moment when Tiflis was utterly stripped of Russian troops, and when a few thousand of his hardy mountaineers, skilfully led, would have made themselves masters of that city, or, at all events, would have caused a most serious disquietude to the Russian Government.

But independent of this, Shamyl had received back from St. Petersburgh his lost son, at that time a Russian officer, attached to the institutions of Russia, and accustomed to a civilized life. He had been received with infinite joy by his father, who accepted, no doubt, with a corresponding pleasure, a large sum of Russian gold, which accompanied this long wished for restitution of his first-born.

While speaking of this extraordinary man, Shamyl, it must be admitted, from his conduct during this war, as well as from more recent events, that he has been vastly overrated by the British public, who had fondly looked upon him, not only as a Chief of great genius and consummate ability, but also as a man incorruptible, as regards the acquisition of worldly wealth, when placed in the balance against his religion and his renown.

It should be mentioned, that in consequence of

an application from General Williams to the English Government, the services of three more British officers—namely, Major Stuart, and Captain Cameron, on the retired list of Her Majesty's army, and Major A. L. Peel, of the 52nd Light Infantry—were placed at his disposal, and were ordered to join forthwith. The two former of these officers arrived at Erzeroom on the 28th and 29th of August, 1855. They immediately waited on Mr. Consul Brant, who confirmed the intelligence they had received at Constantinople to the effect, that, owing to the strictness of the Russian investment, any attempt to get into Kars would be hopeless. Anxious, however, to use their utmost endeavours to join General Williams, they were determined to leave no chance untried. Fully alive to the necessity of proceeding with caution, and possessing no local knowledge or experience, they were unable to form an opinion of their own, and were therefore obliged to defer to the judgment of others, which, however, was in every instance opposed to their wishes.

Having learnt, on the 5th of September, that Tahir Pasha, President of the Military Medjlis at Erzeroom, an officer of considerable intelligence, who had been educated at Woolwich, and spoke English fluently, was about to proceed to Olti, Major Stuart requested permission to accompany him.

Mr. Consul Brant had, at General Williams' request, endeavoured to impress upon the mind of

Tahir Pasha the necessity of exerting himself, and of using his utmost endeavours to throw supplies into Kars. The Pasha, as usual, promised great things; and in order to remove all odium from himself, tried to throw the blame on others. There was, no doubt, much truth in all he said; but at the same time, had one energetic and determined General possessed spirit and independence enough to take the initiative and assume a command, the responsibility of which all the other officers appeared to be afraid of, affairs would have presented a very different appearance, and Kars would have stood some chance of being relieved.

Mr. Brant, ever alive to the interests of the State, and resolving upon leaving no stone unturned, addressed the following letter to Her Majesty's Ambassador at Constantinople:—

" Consul Brant to Lord Stratford de Redcliffe.

" MY LORD, " Erzeroom, September 3, 1855.

" I received a letter from Kars of the 25th August, in which General Williams begged me to urge Tahir Pasha to do something for their relief, observing that a regiment of cavalry having gone from Kars and passed the Russian posts, it might return, each horseman bringing in two bags of barley. I waited on Tahir Pasha, and he promised that he would leave nothing undone to relieve the garrison.

"At Olti, about half way, there are stores of everything, but the Commander there, Aali Pasha, is credulous and timid, and is prevented from making attempts to throw in supplies by exaggerated reports he hears of the danger of the undertaking and the certainty of failure. Tahir Pasha observed that Aali Pasha, by his timidity, paralyzes those under him who have more energy than himself, and he begged me to represent to General Williams that there is not a single officer amongst all the forces out of Kars who has spirit or enterprise enough to make an attempt at introducing relief, though he were promised promotion for success, as I had suggested.

"Tahir Pasha said that he would go himself to Olti and see what he could do, and Major Stuart and Captain Cameron expressed their wish to accompany him, and do their best to assist in an attempt to get into Kars with a body of cavalry carrying barley.

"There are three regiments now outside Kars, reckoning about one thousand two hundred men, beside some irregular horse, so that by a successful effort a considerable supply might be introduced, and I should expect that such a body would be too strong to be stopped by any outposts it might encounter, if the trial were made secretly and by the least-frequented paths.

"General Williams dare not express himself clearly as to his exact position in regard to the stock of provisions; but from what he does say and from what I have heard from other quarters, I much fear that they are beginning to run very short, and that if such efficient succours as would oblige the Russians to retreat do not speedily arrive, or supplies cannot be introduced, it will not be possible to hold out until the snow obliges the enemy to retire.

"Omer Pasha was reported to be about to land immediately at Redoute-Káleh with thirty thousand troops; but I yesterday heard that he would not embark from Constantinople before the 1st Muharem, I believe ten days hence; and when matters begin once to be deferred, there is no saying how often they may be again postponed, while every minute's delay may bring on the catastrophe which is sought to be prevented.

"I would therefore represent to your Excellency the necessity of stimulating the Turkish Government to hasten forward succours, for if Kars be taken, Erzeroom must of course fall, and the losses these events would occasion the Turkish Government are such as would be beyond its power to repair, and, besides, an enormous sacrifice of blood and treasure, a very large army, and a year's campaign, would be required to recover the two cities, which in the hands of Russia might become impregnable.

"I have, &c.
"(Signed)   JAMES BRANT."

Permission to accompany Tahir Pasha having been granted, Major Stuart, with Captain Cameron, who also gladly availed himself of the same opportunity of pushing forwards in the direction of actual hostilities, started about midday on the 7th, taking with them, as an interpreter, Captain Selim Effendi, a Hungarian refugee in the Turkish service, and a small cavalry escort. As might naturally be supposed, the people of Erzeroom were not long in hearing of their intended journey, and it was afterwards ascertained that the Russians were apprised of the movements of these British officers with the least possible delay. It was their intention to proceed by the post road; but the officer commanding the escort, who acted also as guide, not knowing the country well, bore off to the left before reaching Hintz, and took them by another line, which, as they advanced, became more difficult, from the frequency of steep mountain passes and rough defiles.

In some places the scenery was most picturesque and beautiful, being bold, diversified, and wild. The valleys were fertile and well irrigated by running streams, which were carefully distributed by artificial water-courses; but the officers were painfully struck by the absence of everything that could indicate the abode of man. There were neither flocks nor herds; there was no cultivation, except in the immediate neighbourhood of the few wretched villages through which their route lay, and this air of general desolation was augmented by the scarcity of trees.

The travellers met on the road many strong parties of peasants, who, with their wives, children, their sheep and oxen (reduced to a mere handful), were moving off from the sound and reach of war.

Early on the morning of the 9th of September, Major Stuart and his companions arrived at Olti, which, from its situation and natural strength, is considered one of the most important military positions in the country; but neither troops, guns, nor defensive preparations of any kind could be observed.

From Olti the party proceeded, after a rest of a few hours, towards Pennek, halting at the encampment, which was situated about a mile and a half from the town, and the site for which was admirably chosen, being at a short distance from the Pennek-su, on a piece of level ground, close to which brushwood, suitable for fuel, was growing in great abundance. The officers were much struck with the order and regularity of the tents, and, on closer inspection, all the internal arrangements were found to correspond. Their first duty was to pay their respects to the officer in command, Major-General Ali Pasha, who received them with every demonstration of respect and friendship.

He stated that the force under his command consisted of about three thousand cavalry, of which number half were regulars and half Bashi-Bozouks, all being, as he frankly avowed, in the lowest state of disorganization. The fault, however, was not his. The Anatolian Bashi-Bozouks, as is well known, have almost always proved themselves worse than useless for military purposes. As to the regulars, a large proportion of them had just escaped from Kars, and both men and horses gave evidence of the hardships and privations they had undergone. There were also at Pennek four beautiful mountain guns, which were, in every respect, thoroughly well appointed. They were placed near at hand, some fifty yards in front of the commanding officer's tent.

Ali Pasha stated that he had taken every possible precaution to guard against attack or surprise from the side of Kars. A body of two hundred Bashi-Bozouks was stationed at Panshute, a mountain village three hours distant, on the road to Ardahan, and a sharp look-out was kept on the direct route through the valley, or rather gorge, of the Pennek-su, although no immediate danger was to be apprehended from that quarter.

Compared with other villages, or rather towns, in Armenia, Pennek might be considered rather an important place. It consists of some fifty houses, with a Turkish population which may be roughly estimated at four hundred souls. It is built on a slope at the foot of a precipitous rocky height, which trends from thence to the eastward, and forms the northern boundary of the opening through which the Pennek-su makes its way from the more distant mountains.

In front, or westward of the town, is a valley, which, commencing about six miles to the north, takes a bend at the place selected for the encampment, and thence extends in a westerly direction nearly fifteen miles to Olti. Not far from this bend the Pennek-su receives a tributary stream from the north, and about ten miles further on joins its waters with the Olti-su, six miles below Olti. This valley is, in parts, very fertile, and Pennek is said to be the chief granary for its produce. The harvest had been lately cut, and the people were busy winnowing and treading out the corn, which was collected in large heaps in different parts of the place. Of the soldiers recently arrived from Kars a considerable number were quartered in the houses of the inhabitants, and were amply supplied with excellent rations of bread, meat, and vegetables. Their clothes were sadly out of order, hanging in tatters or kept together by patches of divers colours. Still the men looked clean. Throughout the day scores of them might be seen bathing in the stream, while their clothes, previously washed, were hanging to dry in the sunshine. No man perhaps pays more attention to personal cleanliness than the Turkish soldier.

While at Pennek, Major Stuart and Captain Cameron fell in with a man named Russoul, a most enterprising and trustworthy foot messenger, who was employed by General Williams in conveying intelligence between Kars and Erzeroom. The idea at once suggested itself to them that under the guidance of this man they might push on, steal through the Russian lines, and so reach their destination. There were, however, some preliminary considerations which they were obliged carefully to weigh, divesting themselves, as much as possible, of their own feelings.

The most important and difficult point was how to evade the observation of the inhabitants of Pennek, many of whom, it was well known, were in the interest and pay of the Russians. Against this danger disguise of dress would have been of little avail, besides which, it would have subjected the officers to the penalty of a bullet in case of detection. Russoul himself, like a sensible man, declined giving any opinion on the subject, but promised, in case the enterprise was determined upon, to give his best assistance as far as would be compatible with the service upon which he was engaged.

It may be as well to mention here that this most excellent man, after having risked his life in conveying the post five times between Kars and Erzeroom, was, in the sixth attempt, while endeavouring to reach the former place, taken prisoner by the Russians. He was, however, soon after the surrender, at the request of General Williams, released from his captivity, and allowed to return to his native country.

Major Stuart felt it due to Ali Pasha, as commanding officer on the station, to consult him as to the possibility of his being able to reach Kars. He found the Pasha and his staff sitting in divan with the chief of the Bashi-Bozouks and the civil authorities of the place. On explaining the object for which he came they were unanimous in condemning the attempt as hazardous in the extreme, if not impossible. They talked about the value they attached to the presence of English officers amongst them, and how great would be the loss if they were to fall into the hands of the enemy.

Returning at once to Pennek, the question of going forward was again examined by Major Stuart and Captain Cameron, who, after carefully weighing the chances of success, and balancing the *pros* and *cons* to the extent of their information, were reluctantly obliged to relinquish the idea as impracticable. They therefore dismissed Russoul, trusting him with a piece of paper on which were written their names and the date, in order to inform General Williams of their being at Pennek. This reached its destination in the course of a few days, and elicited from the General the following letter, which was received by Major Stuart on the 27th of September at Erzeroom:—

"SIR, "Kars, September 19th, 1855.

"I have learned through a foot messenger who reached this camp on the 17th, that you and Captain Cameron had reached Pennek, and that you both hoped to get past the enemy's outposts.

"In thanking you and Captain Cameron for the zeal and spirit you have evinced in pushing on towards this closely-invested place, I feel it my duty to tell you my decided opinion on the chances you have in breaking through the, I may say, chains of videttes which surround us.

"I feel that any stranger unacquainted with the minutest feature of the country between this and Olti would be captured if even accompanied by an experienced guide, who would inevitably be at the first moment of attack separated from his charge, who would, in his turn, from an utter want of knowledge of topography, fall into the enemy's hands.

"Captain Cameron's zealous wish to accompany (disguised as a native) the foot messenger who brought my despatches, might, and in all probability would, have cost him his life as a spy; as the messenger in question was concealed six days within the Russian lines, ere he could find a favourable opportunity to enter our entrenchments.

"Taking all these circumstances into consideration, and feeling still uncertain what the future movements of the enemy may be towards the Soghanli-Dāgh, I am not without anxiety for Erzeroom, the heart of the country we are striving to defend. I therefore have to instruct you and Captain Cameron to return to Erzeroom.

"(Signed) W. F. WILLIAMS,
"To Major Stuart. "*Brigadier-General.*"

On the 11th of September Major Stuart and Captain Cameron waited on Ali Pasha for the purpose of considering the possibility of throwing a convoy of provisions into Kars. He expressed, with apparent sincerity, the most intense anxiety on the subject, declared that it deprived him of sleep by night and of all relish for his food, and that he was ready at once to adopt any measure that might be deemed advisable; but that, in the disorganized state of his cavalry, it would be futile to attempt anything without strong reinforcements from Erzeroom. This appeared reasonable enough, for he certainly did not underrate the merits of his troops. When asked if assistance could be obtained from Erzeroom, he replied that they had five thousand infantry there, and that they could well send two thousand of them. With such an addition, and a few guns, the Pasha said he would advance at once, break through the Russian lines, and throw provisions into Kars. He added that he had repeatedly applied for the necessary reinforcements without any success, but that if Major Stuart were to go to the authorities in person they would perhaps listen to his representations.

He accordingly started at once for Erzeroom, and on his arrival there the following morning, he went direct to the residence of the British Consul, stated to him the business upon which he came, with a request that he would accompany him to the Serai, to which Mr. Brant readily assented. They found Tahir Pasha in divan, who, when he had heard the story, and had read Ali Pasha's despatch (of which Major Stuart was the bearer), indulged in a fit of contemptuous laughter at what he called the utter absurdity of the request submitted to him. Recovering his gravity, he stated that not a man nor a gun could be spared from Erzeroom, and that no one was better aware of this than Ali Pasha himself. Thus did every attempt which was made by the British officers at Erzeroom to render assistance to the garrison of Kars fail from want of co-operation on the part of the Turkish authorities.

CHAPTER X.

The Enemy attacks Pennek—The Turks take to an ignominious flight—Captain Cameron's description of it—Disappearance of Ali Pasha—Reasons for the Attack—Supposed connivance on the part of the Turks—Major Stuart and Captain Cameron remain at Erzeroom—Major Peel arrives September 21st—News of the fall of part of Sebastopol arrives at Erzeroom—Proceedings at Kars—The Blockade continues—The Cherkess and Assatin described—Cruelty to a child—Steps taken for protecting foraging parties.

AFTER Major Stuart's departure for Erzeroom, Captain Cameron wandered about for some time examining the different arrangements that had been made, and forming the acquaintance of a few of the superior officers whom he fancied it might afterwards be desirable for him to know. It was nearly sunset before he thought it time to ride home.

It must be observed that a long low ridge divided the main portion of the valley from a kind of dip at its further end, in the hollow of which lay the village. On reaching the foot of this ridge, much to the surprise of Captain Cameron and his interpreter, they met a number of horsemen riding past at full gallop, all of them in too great a hurry to give any explanation as to the cause of their speed.

At last, one man, whose face was the very picture of fear, shouted over his shoulder, as he rode by, "The Russians have come!" Captain Cameron at once rode back as hard as he could to the encampment. The confusion he found there was beyond all description; soldiers packing up their kits; Bashi-Bozouks squabbling and tearing open the canvass of the tents, in order that they might seize whatever they could lay their hands on; others fastening their effects on the horses already picketted; while, to complete the disorder, numbers of the latter were seen running loose about the camp, kicking and struggling amongst the tent ropes, while their owners were vainly endeavouring to capture them.

Captain Cameron rode up without delay to the Pasha's tent, whom he found already on horseback, and offered his services. The Russians had by this time passed through the village and taken possession of the ridge which has been already mentioned. They lined the whole of those heights to the number of about a thousand, and had commenced throwing rockets down upon the Turks.

As there was a field-piece close at hand, with a great crowd, all having their hands crossed and standing round it, Captain Cameron very wisely thought he might take the responsibility upon himself of firing a few shots at the enemy, which, with the assistance of his interpreter, he forthwith commenced doing. The bugle in the meanwhile had sounded to "fall in," and the regular cavalry, with the instinct of the disciplined soldier, had quickly responded to its call. There they stood in a dense mass stolidly enough, and looking exceedingly indifferent as to the result of the engagement. The Bashi-Bozouks seemed to have been determined from the first to leave the rest of the force to distinguish themselves as best they might without their assistance, and nearly the whole body of them were soon seen straggling on the road towards Olti.

Captain Cameron thus graphically describes their appearance:—" It was amusing enough to see the
" cool way in which they (the Bashi-Bozouks) filed
" off, no one ever making an effort to prevent them.
" Their leaving the field to the regulars, getting out
" of their way as it were, seemed quite a matter of
" course. One ragamuffin passed me with a huge
" bag, filled to the neck with, I suppose, the spoils
" of a hundred villages, and balanced on the pummel
" of his saddle between himself and his horse's head.
" How he contrived to keep it there, manage his
" reins, carry his lance, all at the same time, has
" been a marvel to me ever since. Another had
" taken a horseless friend up behind him, and the
" pair jogged away very lovingly in this original
" fashion. Oddly enough, I had been watching
" these same Bashi-Bozouks but an hour or two
" before, as they were exercising their horses on the

"plain. After following them as I had done, now
"charging full tilt at one another, their bodies bent
"forward, their keen eyes set, their lances at the
"rest, and now wheeling round, scouring the mea-
"dows in mimic fight, drawing up on the instant
"in their headlong career, anon returning with a
"wild shout to the charge—after seeing these fine
"bearded fellows doing all this with such admirable
"ease and zest, it was almost impossible to believe
"that when it came to fighting in earnest they were
"not in the least to be depended on."

The regular cavalry stood firm, as rocket after rocket came whizzing over the plain, looking at each other like dumb animals, both officers and men. Not a word of encouragement, nor a word of command was heard. At last down came the black Cossacks, clearing the high lands, and rushing into the plain. There was a wavering in the mass of Turks—a moving to this side and that, as of a large rock loosened at its base: gradually the horses' heads, which had hitherto been facing the enemy, turned round simultaneously as if drawn to the rear by some magnetic power, till they were all brought to face exactly the contrary way. Just as the Cossacks were within two hundred yards of them, the whole body of Turkish cavalry was in motion, first at a walk, then at a trot, and at last, as hard as they could go, pressing their way into the narrow pass beyond.

Captain Cameron had rejoined the Pasha, who, with a composed and dignified air, was giving orders to his attendants about his private affairs. At last there were scarcely ten of the Turkish force left on the field, and these were quickly filing off after the rest. On Captain Cameron turning round to ask his Excellency what he intended to do next, to his great surprise he found that he was gone. With a feeling of mingled rage and disgust, Captain Cameron had nothing to do but to put spurs to his horse, and join in the general flight with those that remained. This gallant officer had done all that man could do to prevent this disgraceful termination to the affair; but being unable, from his ignorance of the language, to exert any influence over the men, and having, indeed, virtually no command over them, he found himself perfectly helpless.

The flight continued for several hours, and it was near midnight when the fugitives arrived at Olti. They entered the town through the bazaar, where there was a great stir amongst the inhabitants, as straggler after straggler came in, each hoping, by telling some wonderful tale of what he had seen or done at Pennek, to gain a lodging for the night. Many inquiries were made after Ali Pasha, but no one at that time seemed to know anything about him. His adventures, however, are soon told. He might have escaped by the fleetness of his horse, but report says, after leaving Captain Cameron, he returned from the *mêlée* in hopes of saving some of his property, which he found in the grasp of the Russians, who were plundering his tent. In his endeavours to save his treasures, he received a sword cut in the hand, and was made prisoner. He was afterwards sent to Tiflis, where he remained until peace was proclaimed, and he was liberated with the other captives.

The Russian casualties on this occasion were stated to be four killed and three wounded by cannon-shot. Of the Turks about twenty, as nearly as could be ascertained, were made prisoners. The Bashi-Bozouks did not again make their appearance, but the regulars were collected by degrees at Erzeroom, and attached to the division then under the command of Vēli Pasha.

In the official account published by the Russians, much importance was attached to this affair, and no small credit was claimed for the successful issue of the undertaking.

The presence of a body of cavalry numbering three thousand men within a day's march of the lines of a beleaguering army, has indeed a menacing sound; but when it is considered that the cavalry in question was badly mounted and armed, indifferently drilled, and imperfectly organized, it is evident that their dispersion by twelve hundred disciplined Russian cavalry was not much to boast of.

It certainly would have been a serious error to

have left them undisturbed in such an important position, where, with abundant rations and good drill-ground, the presumption was that they would be daily progressing in efficiency, and would consequently be more likely to give trouble.

A plentiful harvest, too, had been collected on the spot, and they might, therefore, have been in readiness to seize the first opportunity of throwing provisions into Kars.

Under these circumstances, the dispersion of this force, contemptible as it was, became a strategic necessity, and the measures taken to accomplish it prove that the Russians were fully alive to its importance. Besides the cavalry already spoken of, a battalion of Russian infantry was detached from Kars by a different route; but the service having been accomplished before they could reach Pennek, they were recalled. Some credit is due to the officer who led the cavalry by a tortuous mountain-path, where they could advance only in single file, through deep ravines and difficult defiles, unless he owed his success to the treachery of his adversary, and that such was the case there are strong grounds for believing.

Circumstances were reported to Major Peel when on duty at Pennek last April, which, if true, placed the matter beyond a doubt. On the 10th of September numbers of persons, including mounted Turkish officers, were observed by Major Stuart coming along the valley-road to Pennek. One of these, according to information which was supplied to Major Peel by a Turk of high respectability residing in that village, went to Ali Pasha, and reported to him that the Russians were advancing. The Pasha affected not to believe him; and when the man persisted in his statement, he flew into a rage, and ordered him to be bastinadoed. "Don't " punish me now," said the man, " but keep me a " prisoner; and if the Russians are not here to-" morrow then punish me as much as you like."

This reasonable appeal only exasperated the Pasha's rage : the man was severely beaten, and the Russians burst upon Pennek on the morrow.

But it was not from Ali Pasha alone that the Russians are supposed to have received this negative aid; it is to be feared that a large portion of the inhabitants of Pennek and of the surrounding country were in their interest, and acting for them as spies. It was subsequently reported that they had the earliest intimation of every movement contemplated by the Turks, and especially of the proceedings of the British officers.

With such a general feeling acting in their favour throughout the country, and with devoted partizans in the camp and divan, one ceases to be astonished at the success of the enemy in coming unawares on Pennek.

Painful as it is to suspect that treachery can

exist in the breast of any man, more particularly of an officer holding a high and responsible situation, who has sworn allegiance to his Sovereign, when such a miscreant is found, it is quite right that he should be held up to public scorn. Ali Pasha was, unfortunately, not the only individual of this description on whom suspicion fell. The following extract from a letter, dated 19th September, 1855, addressed to Lord Stratford de Redcliffe, points out in plain terms the grounds on which Her Majesty's Commissioner founded his accusation against Bahlool Pasha :—

"The large force detached from the Russian "army, which I informed your Lordship was "operating in the neighbourhood of the Soghanli-"Dagh, was seen by my foot-messenger about "eight days ago marching in the direction of "Penjrood in Geuleh, where Haji Ali Pasha and "several other officers who had recently left Kars, "were stationed, for the purpose of pasturing the "cavalry and artillery horses which accompanied "them, and for seizing a favourable opportunity "to get barley into our camp.

"Haji Ali Pasha, with his attendants, having in-"cautiously ventured too far from these detach-"ments, was taken prisoner, and is now in the "Russian camp, opposite our entrenchments.

"This is the second Pasha who has been taken

" in this manner; Bahlool Pasha, the hereditary
" Chief of Byazid, having fallen into the enemy's
" hands near Euch-Kelissa about two months ago.
" I should state to your Lordship that by Prince
" Paskiewitch's official reports on the last war, this
" very Bahlool Pasha allowed himself to be taken
" prisoner in Byazid, and whilst in the enemy's
" hands exerted himself as an active partisan in
" their favour by intriguing with and rendering
" neutral several of the Sultan's Koordish subjects.

" The similarity of the game played and playing
" by this man forces me to bring him to your Ex-
" cellency's notice; the more so, as several of the
" Koordish bands of horse under Vēli Pasha during
" the recent unsuccessful operations of the Russian
" General-in-chief against Erzeroom, disbanded and
" fled to their homes without firing a shot.

" Another very serious coincidence is the conduct
" of the principal Mussulman inhabitants of Erze-
" room during the late panic. There is no doubt
" that they would have treated with the enemy if
" the forts around the city had not restrained them,
" and prevented an attack from the Russian army.
" I can only conclude that, as in 1829, Russian
" gold was ready at hand to effect its work.

" The Christian notables and their flock alone
" (under their Bishop) showed true loyalty, and I
" have thanked them, through his Reverence, in
" the name of the British Government."

In an account of the capture of Byazid by the Russians in 1828, written by Monsieur de Fonton, the following passage occurs regarding the conduct of Bahlool Pasha: " Déjà, vers le mois de Février, " Balul Pacha, qui commandait le Pachalik et les " forteresses de Baïazeth, prévoyant une rupture " entre la Russie et la Porte, et craignant d'être " accablé par les forces concentrées alors contre la " Perse, avait cherché à entrer en relations avec les " autorités frontières, pour se mettre sous la protec- " tion de la Russie. Sans accepter formellement " cette proposition, afin de ne pas provoquer une " agression prématurée de la part du Séraskier, le " Général-en-chef Russe parvint à maintenir le " Pacha dans une espèce de neutralité ; il put encore " assurer son flanc gauche, en n'employant que le " faible détachement sous le Général Major Prince " Tchevtzevadre."

It is hardly possible to believe that this act of open treachery on the part of Bahlool Pasha was unknown to the Turkish Government, and yet it is equally difficult to imagine that, with the knowledge of his guilt before them, they should allow him to remain at large with the chance of his again affording assistance to the enemy, which there is every reason to fear he did. All that can be said is, that most probably money was used to bribe those in power as corrupt as himself.

After this disgraceful affair at Pennek, there was nothing left for Major Stuart and Captain Cameron but to remain at Erzeroom, awaiting instructions, and observing, as far as possible, the course of events.

On the 21st of September, Major Peel arrived in Erzeroom from England, accompanied by Mr. Evans, late of the 6th Dragoons, whose zeal for the service had induced him to come out to the theatre of war in Armenia. They travelled from Trebizonde in company with Dervish Pasha, an active, intelligent officer, who brought with him a high reputation from the Danube, and who was soon after appointed to the command of a division.

The glorious news of the fall of part of Sebastopol reached Erzeroom on the 17th of September, and was hailed with a salute of a hundred and one guns from the citadel. On the evening of the 21st a grand entertainment was given by the medical staff in honour of the event, when the distinctions of religion, race, and country, were for the time merged in social union.

It is now necessary to revert to what had been going on at Kars during this period. Day after day and week after week had passed, and no signs appeared of any steps being taken to succour the garrison. The enemy remained perfectly quiet, contented with keeping up a rigorous blockade, and doing their best to prevent cattle grazing out of the range of the guns. It seemed more than probable that the intention of the Russian General was to take the place by famine, as he could see perfectly well from his camp the various additions and alterations which were daily being made to the fortifications, all tending to strengthen the defences, without taking any steps to prevent the work going on.

The garrison, however, was not lulled into a feeling of security by this apparent listlessness on the part of the enemy. Frequent desertions continued to occur, and spies still infested the place. There was, however, no relaxation of discipline, and the punishment of death was often necessarily inflicted.

The weather was becoming every day much colder, particularly at night, and the soldiers on duty, owing to the ragged state of their clothes, suffered most severely. The consequence was that the hospitals were getting gradually more crowded. Many of the troops were unprovided with great-coats, but fortunately some sheepskins had been kept, and these, stitched roughly together, served as cloaks for night-work, the sentries going on duty taking them from those whom they relieved. In many cases the red stripes had been taken off the men's trousers to patch their jackets with, and, in short, nothing could exceed the miserable condition of their clothing. Some few regiments, it is true, were rather better off than others, but they were all more or less in the state described. Their shoes were even more dilapidated than their coats, and the soldiers were only too glad to get strips of leather and sew them together as a covering for their feet; for this purpose a piece of the hide of nearly every horse that fell was cut off from the back, just above the tail.

The enemy at this time was, as before stated, unusually quiet, but skirmishing still continued to occur from time to time, the troops principally engaged on the side of the Russians being Cossacks of the Line, the perfection of light cavalry. When the position of Ainalli was taken up, General Baklanoff, the famous Cossack, went there to command, and he used occasionally to come out with a black flag, having a death's head and cross-bones upon it.

The regiment usually opposed to the Turks in these skirmishing expeditions was about nine hundred strong on an average, and divided into squadrons called "sotnias," literally, "hundreds." Their discipline was not perhaps as good as that of dragoons, but they still performed all the simple manœuvres required of them with the greatest precision, and always marched in the best order. They were composed of men entirely drawn from what is called "the Line," that is to say, the chain of military posts which had been established all along the northern side of the Caucasus to keep in check the still unconquered tribes of Circassians.

The followers of Shamyl are really Daghistānlis, although generally called Circassians: the tribes which give the most trouble are the Cherkess and Assatin. Being incessantly at war, and from their infancy carrying arms, the inhabitants of the Line have become, perhaps, the most warlike people of Russia. Their dress is completely Circassian. The cap is made of shaggy sheepskin, and their cloak is an almost circular piece of goat-hair cloth, impervious to wet, and so arranged as to hang round the neck, and swing at the pleasure of the wearer, according to the direction the wind or rain may be coming from. It usually hangs on the left shoulder, so as to keep the bridle-hand warm, and leave the sword-arm free. The neck is quite uncovered; a brown caftan worn over a tight, long-skirted tunic; close-fitting leggings, tucked into parti-coloured boots of soft leather; and sometimes a warm sash, complete the costume. Their arms are a rifle, worn over the shoulder, in a case made generally of the skin or tails of wild animals; a long heavy sabre, in a gaily-ornamented sheath; a large dagger, hanging in front, called a "kinjal;" and a pistol, with a good-sized ivory knob at the butt, worn behind in the belt, and attached by a leathern thong.

Such is their habit of carrying arms, that, with all these weapons, their movements are quite free, and as their ammunition is carried on both sides of the breast, in small bone cases, their facility of loading and firing from the saddle is very great. They are very brave, and as hardy as wild beasts. These were the men with whom the Turkish foraging parties, usually under the direction of Major Teesdale, were almost daily skirmishing. The use of rockets has been introduced with the greatest success as a support for these light troops, and they scarcely ever make a movement, even in small bodies, without a detachment of rocketeers.

Brought up as savages from their infancy, some of these Cossacks will not scruple to commit the most barbarous actions. As an instance of this, on one occasion, during the earlier period of the blockade, a party of them made a dash at a small village by the river side, called Karaba Kilissa, and though the inhabitants offered not the slightest opposition to them, they beat a little boy, twelve years of age, very cruelly with their whips, and finally shot him, the ball passing through his thigh and breaking the bone. It was heart-rending to see the poor old mother weeping over her dying child. He was packed up in an araba, or country cart, and sent down to the hospital, where he was attended by Dr. Sandwith. Every possible care was taken of the little sufferer, but he died under the amputation of the shattered limb.

The total want of cavalry was very embarrassing when foraging parties sallied forth to cut what little corn or grain still remained in the immediate neighbourhood. It was, of course, dangerous to take out guns without proper support, as the opposing force was solely cavalry and artillery. To remedy, in some measure, this deficiency, Major Teesdale mounted fifteen of the best chasseurs, with an equal number of troopers, to hold their horses when they dismounted, thus forming a little squadron which did excellent service on many occasions, until no spare horses remained.

CHAPTER XI.

The Enemy advances, September 29th—Preparations to resist the Attack—Action commences—Yārim-Ai Tabia taken—Yuksek Tabia in danger—General Kméty—General Kavalieffsky killed—Vassif Pasha and Têk Tabias open fire—Fight at Tachmasb—Chasseurs—Attack on English Batteries—They are taken by the Enemy—Fire opened from Fort Lake and Kāradāgh—Reinforcements sent to former Battery—Enemy is driven out of English Batteries—Russians retreat.

AT about four A. M., on the 29th of September, it was reported to General Kméty, by the officer in charge of the outposts, that while going his rounds in front of Tachmasb, he fancied he heard a rumbling noise, like that of wheels over stony ground, in the direction of the enemy's main camp. It has been already stated that for some time prior to this period, owing to the regular cavalry being almost entirely dismounted, the outpost duty was carried on by the chasseurs. It was not, therefore, a matter of astonishment that earlier or more detailed intelligence of any movement that was taking place had not been brought into the garrison.

The night was, moreover, by no means bright

enough to render objects discernible at any great distance, so that a certain doubt necessarily existed for some time as to what was going forward. For several days there had been no movement whatever in the Russian camp worthy of notice. All the villages in the neighbourhood of Kars had been taken possession of by the enemy, and the inhabitants sent to a distance, so that the garrison was deprived of even the scanty information which had formerly been brought in from time to time by the peasants. The principle of being prepared at any moment for every case of emergency had been too forcibly instilled into the minds of the several authorities by General Williams to be neglected in this instance, and all necessary preparations were immediately made.

The troops were under arms, the guns manned, and every officer at his post, in a very few minutes after the alarm had been given. Information of this suspected movement on the part of the enemy was sent instantly to General Williams, and the same necessary precautions were taken in turning out the troops, and manning the batteries below, as well as those on the Kāradāgh; and the inhabitants of the town, armed and equipped, lost no time in repairing to their appointed stations.

Lieutenant-Colonel Lake had, as usual, been patrolling all night round the lower works, and Major Teesdale, since three in the morning, round the line

THE ACTION COMMENCES.

of English batteries; but neither of them had seen any symptoms whatever of a movement in the Russian camp. Major Teesdale had just reached his tent, and was in the act of dismounting when he was startled by a gun flashing through the darkness directly in front.

This was so extraordinary an event, that he at once galloped off to the battery from whence the sound proceeded. He asked the officer at the gun what was going on, and was then told, for the first time, that the Russians were advancing. Nothing could be seen in the valley but a darker shade across it than usual. It was now half-past four. The guns continued to fire steadily from the Tachmasb works on the approaching mass, and soon all uncertainty ceased, for the Russians, finding that they were discovered, set up a yell from twenty thousand throats. The whole black valley seemed to be alive with the multitude that came rushing on in apparently irresistible numbers.

The fire ran along the whole line of the defences almost at the same moment, and showed the busy figures of the Turks hastening to every assailable point; and before the noise, caused by the incessant firing, became so great as to drown all human voices, the cries and screams of the wounded were heard with fearful distinctness amidst the general uproar.

The Russians were now close to the works: the

guns in the batteries, however, were already in full play, and being loaded entirely with case shot, and assisted by the rolling fire of musketry that at once broke forth from the parapet, swept the enemy completely from the front. The columns thus split, and swerving to each side, on the left of Yuksek Tabia, overwhelmed the small open battery called Yarim-ai Tabia, marked in the plan No. 16, and on the right forced its way round, and got amongst the tents in rear.

As soon, however, as the soldiers, who had been posted at Yārim-ai Tabia, took refuge in Yuksek Tabia, the redoubt in which Major Teesdale was commanding, and reported its occupation by the enemy, the fire of two guns and a portion of the infantry were immediately directed upon the interior of this work, which was speedily cleared of its occupants, who then took refuge on the reverse side of the parapet, from whence they kept up a most galling fire on the defenders of Yuksek Tabia.

Whilst this conflict occupied the attention of the Turks on the left front of the battery, the portion of the Russian column, which had passed by on the right, silently re-formed amidst the darkness, and, led on by an intrepid officer, rushed upon an almost undefended point in its rear. So sudden was the assault, that almost before a company could be rallied to resist it, the Russians were swarming like bees upon the parapet, and many of them were already inside the works. This moment was the most critical for Yuksek Tabia. The Turks, attacked on all sides, and bewildered by the firing which raged around them, wavered for a moment as the black figures of their enemies seemed to swoop down among them whilst jumping from off the parapets.

Every moment was now of such vital importance, that, ceasing his efforts to draw the attention of those who were fighting in front to their assailants in rear, and shouting to the few who were around him, Major Teesdale rushed up into the salient already occupied by the enemy. This sudden impulse probably saved the battery. Those who had already penetrated into the work were in a moment struck down on the platform; and their gallant leader, as he was about to cross swords with Major Teesdale, received a ball in the centre of his forehead, and fell backwards. Still the gallant young volunteers who composed the column of attack came rushing up, but the deadly and deliberate fire from within kept them in check, and their bravest already lay thickly in and on the edge of the little ditch which surrounded the work. But another mass was seen coming to their support, and it became evident that succour of some kind must be given to the few who opposed them. Seeing this, Major Teesdale left them fighting with unflinching perseverance, while he went to try and bring a gun from the front.

Fortunately, he found that one, belonging to the reserve, having lost its way in the darkness and confusion, had taken refuge in the battery, and stood limbered up and inactive. Leaving two men with orders to supply nothing but grape, he managed, with the help of four of the gunners, to run the piece up into the salient. The dead and wounded were dragged from the barbette, and the gun brought into action. It was pointed at the thickest of the approaching force, which was but a few yards from the muzzle. Six times the iron shower tore through their ranks, and left long lines of dead and wounded on its track. The column then, in utter confusion from the rapidity of the fire, broke, and fled past the redoubt, down the hill.

Day had just dawned; the force which had been disposed of was the centre of one of three which attacked simultaneously. On the left, Tachmasb Tabia, with its flanking line of breastwork turned, seemed but a huge mass of smoke and fire. On the right, a column of eight battalions had rushed upon the Rennison lines. Here the brave Hungarian General, Kméty, commanded in person. The third regiment of Arabistan and the battalion of Hassa-Sheshanidji, or chasseurs of the guard, lined the two faces of a re-entering angle into which the enemy penetrated, and made straight for the gate at the extreme end. Leaving the guns which protected their flanks to do their work until the enemy was close upon them, the Turks then opened a converging fire upon the head of the column, and, though many of the front rank fell, the rest still moved up from the rear, pressing forward those in advance; but they could not withstand the deadly fire of the *élite* of the old soldiers, who deployed, and protected by a breastwork did not fire a ball in vain.

This horrid carnage continued until the Russians, stopped by a mound of dead bodies, and dislocated by the repeated discharges of grape, were brought to a stand-still. The Turks then leaping over the breastwork, and led on by the gallant Kméty, finished with the bayonet the utter rout of their assailants. This column left eight hundred and fifty corpses upon a space not exceeding an acre in area. Their General, Kavalieffsky, fell mortally wounded. General Prince Gagārine, who next took the command, received several wounds, from which, however, he ultimately recovered. In this attack nearly every Russian superior officer fell.

It will now be necessary to turn to the events which were taking place on the plain below. Simultaneously with this attack on the heights of Tachmasb, a force consisting of cavalry, artillery, and infantry, appeared advancing against Canli Tabia, marked No. 22 in the plan, and, when far out of the range of the heavy guns in that battery, the enemy opened fire with their field-pieces.

The great fear was that the Turks, if left to themselves, would return it, and thus waste much valuable ammunition, which could ill be spared. Lieutenant-Colonel Lake was therefore directed to proceed at once to the battery, and finding that the Russian force remained perfectly stationary, firing only at intervals, it became very evident to that officer that it was merely a feigned attack, intended to prevent the possibility of any large reinforcements being sent to the heights above.

After leaving strict orders with the Turkish officer in command on no account to waste any shot by firing at the enemy before he came well within range, Lieutenant-Colonel Lake, by desire' of General Williams (who, with the Mushir and Fēyzi Pasha, the chief of the staff, had taken up a central position in Lelek Tabia, marked No. 25, from whence he could issue such orders as were from time to time necessary), proceeded at once to Vassif Pasha Tabia, marked in the plan No. 19. From this battery, and from Têk Tabia, marked No. 20 (the latter under direction of Mr. Churchill), a sharp and continuous fire was opened with heavy guns against a detachment of the enemy's artillery, which had been drawn up on the left flank of the Tachmasb line of works.

The Russians suffered considerably from this

cross-fire, which, at intervals, they attempted to return, but without much effect, owing both to the inferiority of their powder, compared with that of the Turks, and to the difference in the calibre of their guns.

While all this was going on, the enemy obstinately persevered in their attempt to take Tachmasb and Yuksek Tabias. A few moments' breathing-time had been afforded to the defenders on the right and centre of the Line, after the fearful struggles in which they had been engaged, and these were devoted to rallying the men and putting things in as much order as possible for a renewal of the fight, for the fire still raged on the left with undiminished violence.

Day had now fairly broken, and the Russians, after having turned the left of Tachmasb, had managed to get up sixteen guns, and place them in position under Colonel de Saget, the fire from which fell heavily on Yuksek Tabia, without that garrison being able, from the confusion at Tachmasb, to reply to it. In fact, the force which had carried Yarimai Tabia, and which was now keeping up a fight from the exterior of that work, and from among the rocks on which it was placed, concentrated such a fire upon the battery, that for a time the Turks were almost paralyzed by the shot, which fell around them without intermission; but the artillery by which they were thus mercilessly plied with grape were in their turn reduced to silence, and finally obliged to leave the field by the well-directed fire, before alluded to, from the guns of Vassif Pasha and Têk Tabias.

Scarcely were the defenders of Yuksek Tabia freed from this crushing fire, when General Kméty, at the head of four companies of chasseurs, came up from the Rennison Lines. Running into Yarimai Tabia, and springing like chamois amongst the rocks, these gallant soldiers made short work of the few Russians who still held their ground there, and then re-forming, went gaily on to Tachmasb.

Major Teesdale had remained in Yuksek Tabia, and had directed the fire of the guns upon the column opposed to his right, which, after having been reassembled out of range and under cover of some hills, was endeavouring to come up to a second attack, under the command of Colonel Prince Dondukoff-Korsukoff. Each time that it attempted to debouch, the shot from the battery fell with such precision against the head of the column, that, after several futile attempts, it retired and was seen no more.

While the attack was thus vigorously carried on against this position, another column, consisting of eight battalions of infantry, two batteries of artillery, and all Baklanoff's division of cavalry, were suddenly observed advancing against the line of works called the English Tabias, marked in the plan Nos. 5, 6, and 7, under the command of the Cossack General in person, who, it was afterwards affirmed by the Russians, had managed to gain during the previous nights a perfect knowledge of the batteries he was to attack. This fact is just possible, owing to the almost total want of outposts at this period of the blockade.

From the nature of the ground in front of these works, it was impossible to see an enemy approaching until he came nearly within range of grape. The fault of these batteries, as regards their site, has been already alluded to, as well as the reason why they were not taken down and reconstructed; but there was another, and still greater defect connected with them, that of being very much undermanned; this was, however, wholly unavoidable, owing to the scarcity of troops available for duty.

Fort Lake was tolerably well garrisoned, but the semicircular open work marked No. 8, in which there were only two light field-pieces, and the other English batteries, each mounting three guns, also light field-pieces, with the exception of Thompson Tabia, in which there were two of heavier calibre, contained only a handful of men, about three hundred regular troops, whilst the intermediate breastworks were partially lined by the Lāz irregular riflemen, and the town Bashi-Bozouks.

The attack on this position commenced at $6^h\ 45^m$

A.M. The moment the enemy reached the rising ground in front of the batteries, they unlimbered their guns, and began cannonading the works. After firing three rounds, the infantry charged the breastwork between Teesdale and Thompson Tabias (marked Nos. 5 and 6 respectively in the plan). They immediately effected an entrance, the Turks having been seized with a panic, and having retired in a body, after offering but very slight resistance, into Williams Pasha Tabia, marked No. 9, which had been built partly for that purpose on the edge of the cliff above the river, and accessible from beneath by a rugged path. Here the regular troops were joined by many of the townspeople from below, who by this time came flocking to the scene of action.

The Russians now lost no time in making a breach in the entrenched line, sufficiently large to admit their artillery, which they at once brought in. They immediately opened fire and began to shell the town, fortunately, however, without doing much damage, owing to the shells all bursting high in the air. Several guns were directed against Fort Lake, causing a certain amount of damage to the block-house, though to no great extent, and killing a Field-officer and a great many men. At the same time, the enemy's infantry took possession of the deserted batteries, and piled their arms, Churchill Tabia, the semicircular work before alluded to, still remaining in the possession of the garrison, being completely protected by Fort Lake and Williams Pasha Battery.

The position taken up by the Russian artillery was commanded by one particular spot in Kāradāgh, the battery on the opposite side of the river, marked in the plan No. 3. Captain Thompson, who had the direction of that work, taking advantage of the circumstance, most judiciously caused a heavy gun, which was in another part of the battery, to be removed to this spot, and to open fire on the enemy. At the same moment two large guns were run up, "*en barbette*," on the east face of Fort Lake, which, together with a very heavy gun at the north-east angle, commenced a quick and well-directed cannonade.

In the mean time, as soon as Teesdale Tabia fell into the hands of the enemy, the largest of the guns in it was turned against Arab Tabia, on the opposite bank of the river, marked No. 4, but was soon silenced by the heavy artillery of that redoubt, under the direction of Lieutenant Koch, a Prussian officer of great intelligence.

The loss of the English Tabias spread like wildfire, and was well calculated to throw a certain amount of gloom and discouragement over the garrison, for it was well known that Fort Lake and these dependent works formed the key of the whole position. If this strong redoubt had once fallen into the hands of the Russians, its commanding situation would have rendered it utterly impossible for the troops to hold out for many hours.

The enemy was no doubt well aware of this fact, for General Mouravieff was an officer not very likely to forget the nature of the ground, with which he had become so familiar during the campaign of 1828-29, and hence his anxiety to gain and keep possession of the fortifications by which these hills were defended. As soon as the attack and capture of the English batteries were known, the one following the other within the space of ten minutes, Lieutenant-Colonel Lake, who up to that period had been directing the fire from Vassif Pasha Tabia, proceeded, without a moment's delay, to Fort Lake, and assumed the superintendence of the operations which were being carried on at that position.

General Williams, at the same time (seeing the urgent necessity which existed for sending immediate assistance to strengthen the weak garrison, which had been thus unfortunately surprised and driven out of their batteries), with the promptness and decision for which he was so conspicuous during this eventful day, forthwith ordered reinforcements to be sent from the reserve below. Selecting the bravest of the Anatolian troops, consisting of four companies of chasseurs under the command of Colonel Kadri Bey, an officer of great zeal and intelligence, and one on whom every reliance could be placed, he spoke a few words of encouragement to them and desired them to proceed to the scene of action, which they accordingly did, crossing the river by one of the permanent stone bridges, and climbing up the hill, thus entering Williams Pasha Tabia by the rear, unseen by the enemy.

At the same moment—that is to say at about $8^h. 30^m.$ A.M.—a battalion of infantry was sent out from Fort Lake, and a detachment of eleven hundred men was despatched by Captain Thompson, from Arab Tabia, in anticipation of General Williams' order, which had been sent to him at the commencement of the action, across the bridge which had been lately thrown over the river. The Russians were now fiercely striving to carry Williams Pasha Tabia, and, by the fire of their artillery, to engage that of Fort Lake; but the guns of this latter work swept the front of Williams Pasha Tabia of its assailants, and the three reinforcements arriving simultaneously at each extremity of the Line gallantly charged the enemy, who had taken possession of the English batteries, and drove them out at the point of the bayonet; the Russian artillery having been about a quarter of an hour previously forced to retire from the position they had taken up by the murderous cross fire which they had so courageously withstood for nearly an hour and three quarters, notwithstanding the loss of a great number of men and horses.

The enemy in retreating took with them five of the Turkish guns, two of which were afterwards regained, having been left at a short distance from the works, and they spiked the others which remained. During the retreat of the Russians a regiment of their dragoons made a most gallant and perhaps unprecedented charge against the breastwork, which was by that time again lined by riflemen and Bashi-Bozouks. They were received with a tremendous fire, and the confusion which ensued from the horses falling into the triple line of *trous-de-loup* running the whole length of the works, baffles all description. The cavalry then covered the retreating column, and the whole retired in excellent order, the guns from the batteries Nos. 6, 7, and 8, having by this time been unspiked, continuing to play upon the Russians until they were out of range. The cavalry remained a long time in the valley within reach of the heavy guns in Teesdale Tabia, which kept up a sharp fire, but at length they disappeared and the line of English batteries, now retaken, was no more attacked. The loss on the side of the Turks was very considerable both in officers and men. Among the former were several of rank. The slaughter among the enemy was fearful, and in Thompson and Zohrab Tabias the number of dead bodies (upwards of two hundred) showed how obstinately the Russians endeavoured to retain the advantage they had gained.

CHAPTER XII.

Not a shot fired from the Citadel—Action continues at Tachmasb—Daring act of a Russian Battalion—Order given to the Enemy to retire—Retreat is commenced—Impossibility of pursuit—Gallant conduct of Officers—Messrs. Zohrab and Rennison—Names of Officers who distinguished themselves—Conduct of Turkish Troops—Gallantry of the Enemy—Burial of the slain—General Williams notices conduct of his Staff—Probable loss on the side of the Enemy—Hospital arrangements—General Williams' official Despatch regarding the Battle.

By some unaccountable accident not a shot was fired from the citadel at the enemy when in possession of these works, and while he was engaged in shelling the town, although two large guns could have been brought to bear on him without difficulty.

This neglect arose probably more from ignorance and want of presence of mind than from cowardice, for the officer in command was not exposed to any danger. He gave no excuse for his conduct, and was therefore disgraced after the battle was over. Had the guns of the citadel opened on the enemy's artillery it never could have stood its ground as long as it did, and much loss of life might thereby have been saved.

Meanwhile the battle on the heights of Tachmasb was carried on with the same persevering and indomitable courage.

Word was brought there that all the English Tabias were in the hands of the enemy, and that the fight was for the possession of Fort Lake. It appeared, moreover, doubtful if the heroic garrison of Tachmasb Tabia itself, under the command of the gallant veteran Kerim Pasha, and the brave Hussein Pasha, could much longer withstand the repeated assaults of the fresh troops which were being incessantly brought against it. Great, therefore, was the joy of the Turks to see the dark masses of the Russians retiring from the English lines, and the shot from the batteries once more plunging amongst them. They then knew that their rear was secured, and that if they could only hold out all was safe.

At this moment a battalion of the enemy debouched from the right flank of the Tachmasb breastwork, apparently with the intention of repeating the manœuvre which had so nearly succeeded at Yuksek Tabia; but from this latter redoubt the Turks opened such a fire of grape upon the Russians, that, in spite of the efforts of their officers, who were bravely urging them on, they again took refuge inside the Line. Here they were met by some reserves from below, which cut off their retreat towards the left. They therefore took the direction of the small work called Tetek Tabia, marked No.

12 on the plan, which commanded the village of Tchakmak, and which contained two guns.

It appeared, at the moment, that their intention was to take this work so as to afford an easy passage for the column of General Baklanoff, which, having retired from the English lines, was then nearly opposite to it, and which might have made a considerable diversion in the rear of Tachmasb. When, however, these troops had proceeded a few hundred yards, a most fearful cross fire opened upon them from Fort Lake and Yuksek Tabia, and they had, at the same time, to encounter a small body of chasseurs stationed on rising and stony ground near which they had to pass.

Notwithstanding all these difficulties they effected their retreat in good order, though with a loss, as it was afterwards acknowledged, of two hundred and fifty men. For this gallant act Colonel Kauffmann, the officer in command, was decorated with the cross of St. George. This battalion was finally dispersed by the garrison and guns of Tetek Tabia, upon which they unexpectedly came. General Baklanoff's artillery from the opposite ridge fired its last shot in support of these troops, and then left the ground.

In spite of success on every other point, the fight still continued to rage with unabated fury around Tachmasb Tabia, marked No. 17. General Kméty had taken up three companies to the assistance of this garrison, and Major Teesdale had sent three more, accompanied by a gun; but their losses were scarcely filled up by this reinforcement, and their own ammunition was expended. Incredible as it may appear, the last hour of the battle was sustained by the ammunition of the Russian dead. Sallies were made for no other purpose than to obtain the needful supply, and at one time part of the garrison were employed in stripping off the pouches of the fallen on one side of the redoubt, and throwing them to their comrades, who were thus enabled to repulse the enemy on the other side.

Such fighting as this deserved to be crowned with success; but the Russians fought with equal obstinacy, until, of the whole infantry of that large and splendid army, only two battalions remained that had not been engaged. Then, indeed, the last shadow of hope having vanished, the Russian General gave the order to retire; but it was too late.

General Williams, seeing that the moment had arrived for making a vigorous attempt to drive the enemy off, now despatched a reinforcement from below directly towards the Tachmasb Line; and Lieutenant-Colonel Lake, who had previously received written instructions from the General, " in the event of his having more troops in his " quarter than necessary, to send some in any " manner he pleased to Tachmasb Tabia," seeing that there was no likelihood of the attack on the

English batteries being renewed, sent a battalion of the second regiment of Anatolian regular infantry from Fort Lake in the same direction, under charge of Major Selim Agha (Lieutenant Tüköri, formerly of the Hungarian army), a most gallant and distinguished officer, and Aide-de-camp to General Kméty. These two forces met just as they were ascending the hill leading to the scene of action; and immediately, in the most determined manner, charged the enemy and drove him from the interior lines.

Tired of acting so long on the defensive, Major Teesdale now led a charge against the enemy's chasseurs and stragglers, who, favoured by the nature of the ground, still kept shooting the Turks at their leisure. On reaching the exterior of Tachmasb Tabia, they found themselves confronted with a regiment of the enemy, fresh men probably, and firing heavily along their front: it was the last remnant of the Russian infantry. The interior of the works had just been cleared, and the brave garrison of Tachmasb Tabia, under their gallant chief Hussein Pasha, rushed furiously out of the redoubt to take their share in the close combat thus commenced by their comrades, and the Russian regiment seemed to melt before them. In a moment the ground was covered with the killed and wounded, and the remainder were seen flying in utter confusion.

The Turks could not be stopped until they had passed the road at the bottom of the hill; but the affair was over, and a few more shots amongst the fugitives were fired, as a band struck up, and the Hassa-Sheshanidji (rifles of the guard) were dancing in triumph amongst all the horrors of a battle-field.

In utter confusion, and with hanging heads, the bulk of the Russian infantry straggled away from the scene of action, passed by the masses of their cavalry, and only rallied in some sort of order when far out on the plain to the left of the hills which faced the Tachmasb position. It was impossible to pursue the retreating columns. Utterly destitute of cavalry, and with scarcely horses enough to drag a dozen guns, and they in a weak and exhausted state from want of proper nourishment, the Turks were compelled to remain upon the Lines from which the enemy had just been driven.

The foregoing description conveys perhaps but a feeble idea of all that took place on this memorable day. It is as impossible to describe every circumstance that occurred, as it would be to notice every individual act of courage and devotion shown by the officers and men. General Kméty, Hussein Pasha (a Circassian officer), and Major Teesdale, who all held most important posts, particularly distinguished themselves by the coolness and bravery they displayed, which had a most beneficial effect on the

Turks under their respective command, who, from their position, undoubtedly bore the brunt of the battle.

Not less distinguished for the ability and judgment he evinced, and which contributed in a great measure to the happy termination of the attack on the English batteries, was Captain Thompson, who exercised, with untiring zeal, the superintendence of the garrisons of Kāradāgh and Arab Tabias. The brave Colonel Yanik-Mustapha Bey, who was at the commencement of the battle stationed in Fort Lake, was the first to go to the support of Tachmasb. Too much cannot be said in praise of this officer. Though severely wounded in the cheek during the early part of the action, he never quitted the field, nor did he absent himself from his duty in consequence.

The noble and gallant conduct of General Kerim Pasha, the Reis, or second in command, was most conspicuous. Beloved by the men and respected by the officers, his presence among them in the hour of danger, and the coolness with which he issued his orders, inspired the garrison with confidence, and excited the admiration of all. He received a contusion, and had two horses shot under him.

Colonel Kadri Bey (afterwards promoted to the rank of Major-general), of whom mention has been before made, proved himself, on this occasion, a brave and good officer.

The active part taken by Mr. Churchill on the day of the battle is brought to notice by General Williams in his official despatch. A few words must be said regarding the conduct of Messrs. Zohrab and Rennison, who, though non-combatants, showed an amount of courage worthy of men brought up to the profession of arms. The former of these gentlemen, attached to Lieutenant-Colonel Lake as interpreter, remained with him during the battle, and was constantly employed in conveying orders and instructions to the several positions under that officer's command.

Major Teesdale, in speaking of his interpreter, Mr. Rennison, states that "this young man per-
" formed most excellent service during the block-
" ade, and was in the whole of the action on the
" 29th September, during which his clothes were
" shot through. He was invariably present in all
" the skirmishes in which I was engaged, and his
" strong health and willing spirit enabled him to
" serve to the last moment, when he would gladly
" have joined us in captivity rather than separate
" himself from those with whom he had been so
" long associated."

There were many others among the Turkish officers, besides those already mentioned, who, though in less responsible and therefore less conspicuous situations, still proved how well they understood and could perform their duty when their

DISTINGUISHED CONDUCT OF OFFICERS. 219

energies were called into action. Among these were the gallant Colonels Zacharia Bey, Kurd Ali-Bey, Lieutenant-Colonel Temir-Bey, Majors Omer Effendi, Mehemet Effendi, and Hassan-Agha, Captains Halil-Bey, Aarif-Agha, Ibrahim Agha, Mehemet Effendi, Bekir-Agha, and Hassan Agha, with Lieutenants Koch (formerly in the Prussian army), Gratoffsky, a Polish instructor of infantry, who was wounded in the back while laying a gun in Fort Lake, and Mussa Agha.

Many of these brave officers fell mortally wounded, and all more or less distinguished themselves. General Hussein Bey received a contusion, and had his clothes riddled by balls in several places. Major Teesdale, while in Yuksek Tabia, received a bruise on the leg from a case shot, which, owing to a thick boot which he had on at the time, did him no further injury. Major Selim Agha, Aide-de-camp to General Kméty, while gallantly leading the reinforcement from Fort Lake to Tachmasb, received a ball in the arm which shattered the bone. Thanks, however, to the great skill and attention of Drs. Sandwith and Schneider, the limb was saved, though the brave young officer was, in consequence of his wound, confined to his quarters during the remainder of the blockade.

Too much cannot be said in praise of the Turkish soldiers, whose steadiness and courage under such heavy and continued fire would have reflected credit on troops far better trained and disciplined. The practice of the artillery was perfect. It is not saying too much when it is asserted that the precision and celerity of their fire were never surpassed in any affair of a similar kind. Nor were the infantry, particularly the chasseurs, at all behindhand in this respect: scarcely a single shot was uselessly expended, and the number of dead bodies lying around the batteries sufficiently showed how true their aim had been. The inhabitants of the town fully supported the character they already possessed for hereditary valour, and every individual capable of bearing arms came cheerfully to his post.

The number of Turkish troops actually engaged on this occasion did not exceed ten thousand fighting men, while that of the attacking force amounted to between thirty and thirty-five thousand of all arms. It must therefore be allowed that the defence is worthy of record in the annals of military history, particularly when it is considered that the garrison had been living for several months on less than half rations, and, besides, had to contend against disadvantages more than enough to dispirit the bravest heart.

But while this just meed of praise is bestowed on the officers and men composing the garrison, the firmness of the enemy, who, under their distinguished Commander, stood, for more than seven hours, exposed to such a heavy fire of artillery and musketry, is scarcely less remarkable. They fell by thousands in front of the batteries and breastworks, which they failed in storming, and the number of gallant Russian officers (stated at two hundred and fifty) who were killed and wounded, shows, better than words can tell, the example they set their men.

As soon as the garrison had obtained some food (for they had fought without eating a morsel from half-past four till nearly noon), and had in some measure reposed after their immense exertions, they began, of their own accord, to pick out their fallen comrades from amongst the heaps of their enemies; and in nearly all cases the Turkish soldier was buried where he lay, the same afternoon, by his own comrades, who built little mounds of stones to mark the spot on which their friend had fallen, and where he slept his last sleep. But few wounded remained, for, unhappily, but little quarter was given on either side. Those who lived received all the attention which a very limited hospital staff could bestow upon them.

Night at length closed in upon the horrid scene, but brought little repose to the officers and men of the garrison, for a fresh alarm soon drew them from their tents, and left them to find what rest they could for their exhausted minds and bodies upon the bloody and trampled ground which they had fought for all the day.

There must, on all occasions of this kind, be a certain amount of difficulty experienced in fixing anything like an exact amount of the killed and wounded on the side of the enemy. For upwards of three days the greater part of the garrison were employed in burying the dead who had remained in heaps on the field. It was sickening work in itself; and for many days afterwards it was almost impossible to walk about the field of battle on the ordinary duties without, at every moment, treading on the black and clotted mass that marked the spot where some brave fellow's life-blood had oozed away. Many bodies were, doubtless, carried off by the Russians, who have been at all times proverbial for using their utmost endeavours to recover their killed and wounded.

Among their officers, two Generals were killed, and three wounded. There were also many superior officers killed among the number of those who fell, and four wounded officers of inferior rank, two of whom soon afterwards died, became prisoners. About one hundred and fifty Russian soldiers were also taken, most of whom were wounded, and conveyed to the hospital, where they met with every kind of attention.

General Williams, in his first letter to Lord Clarendon, dated on the day of the attack, after briefly describing the affair, thus speaks of his own personal staff:—

" The Mushir will doubtlessly at a future moment bring before his Government the conduct of those officers who have distinguished themselves on this day, a day so glorious for the Turkish arms.

" On my part, I have great gratification in acquainting your Lordship with the gallant conduct of Lieutenant-Colonel Lake, Major Teesdale, and Captain Thompson, who rendered the most important service in defending the redoubts of Vēli Pasha Tabia, Tachmasb Tabia, and Arab Tabia. I beg to recommend these officers to your Lordship's protection.

" I beg also to name my secretary, Mr. Churchill, an attaché of Her Majesty's Mission in Persia: he directed the fire of a battery throughout the action, and caused the enemy great loss.

" I also beg to draw your Lordship's attention to the gallant bearing of Messrs. Zohrab and Rennisson, who, as interpreters to Lieutenant-Colonel Lake and Major Teesdale, rendered very effective service. Dr. Sandwith has been most active and efficient in the management of the ambulances and in the hospital arrangements."

It will be utterly impossible to give even a faint idea of the scene which presented itself immediately after the battle. Every single dead and wounded Russian had been stripped by the Turks, which was not to be wondered at, seeing that they were themselves nearly in rags, and a good coat was too great a prize to be thrown away, although it had two or three bullet-holes in it.

The ditches of the batteries were almost filled with bodies, many of which were in a most mutilated state, some without heads, and others without arms or legs. Every possible precaution was taken by General Williams to insure the decent burial of the brave men who had so nobly fought for their country in this sanguinary affair, the close proximity of the place where they fell to the fortifications having rendered it inexpedient to invite the Russians to come and perform the last rites over their gallant comrades.

The number of the enemy who were buried after the battle was stated, by those who superintended the interment, to be rather more than six thousand three hundred, besides which many who were killed and wounded at a distance from the works were taken away by the retiring columns. The total loss of the enemy in this engagement is stated to have been about eight thousand nine hundred.

On the side of the Turks, the loss was naturally very much less than that of the attacking force; but it was still considerable, and tended to diminish, to an inconvenient extent, the ranks already thinned by the effects of cholera, which had lasted such a length of time in the garrison, and which still continued to prevail, although in a mitigated form. Of the regular troops one thousand and ninety-three were killed and wounded, and about three hundred of the armed inhabitants and Lāz riflemen. A great number died afterwards of their wounds, most of which had been received at close quarters, and were, consequently, of a very severe nature.

The hospitals soon became crowded to excess, and great inconvenience was experienced from the want of sufficient accommodation. Houses in the town were fitted up in a rough manner for the reception of as many as could not be taken to the hospital, and every possible arrangement was made, under the able superintendence of Dr. Sandwith; but the paucity of beds, and the total deficiency of many articles necessary for the comfort of the wounded, could not be remedied.

It was not until the 3rd of October that General Williams could find time to write a detailed despatch. On that day he addressed the following letter to the Earl of Clarendon :—

"*Brigadier-General Williams to the Earl of Clarendon.*

(Extract.) "Kars, October 3, 1855.

" I had the honour to announce to your Lordship on the evening of the 29th ultimo the glorious victory gained on the morning of that day by the Sultan's troops, on the heights above Kars, over the Russian Army commanded by General Mouravieff, and I now beg to furnish your Lordship with the principal incidents of that sanguinary battle.

"Your Lordship will perhaps recollect that in my despatch of the 28th June, I stated that the Russian General, after his second demonstration against the southern face of our entrenchments, which is flanked by Hafiz Pasha Tabia and Kanli Tabia, marched south, and established his camp at Boyouk-Tikmeh, a village situated about four miles from Kars. Knowing that General Mouravieff served in the army which took Kars in 1828, I conceived his last manœuvre to be preparatory either to a reconnaissance or an attack upon the heights of Tachmasb, from whence the Russians successfully pushed their approaches in the year above cited.

"Whilst, therefore, the enemy's columns were in march towards Boyouk-Tikmeh, I visited those heights with Lieutenant-Colonel Lake, and, after studying the ground, decided upon the nature of the works to be thrown up: these were planned and executed by Lieutenant-Colonel Lake with great skill and energy. I enclose, for your Lordship's information, a plan made by that officer of the town and its neighbouring heights, which are situated on the opposite side of the river Kars-Tchai, over which three temporary bridges had been thrown to keep up our communications.

"Your Lordship will observe that whilst our camp and magazines in the town were rendered as safe as circumstances would allow, the hills above Kars commanded all, and were therefore the keys of our position.

"The entrenchments of Tachmasb, being those nearest the enemy's camp, demanded the greatest vigilance from all intrusted in their defence. General Kméty, a gallant Hungarian officer, commanded the division which occupied this eminence: he was assisted by Major-General Hussein Pasha, and my Aide-de-camp, Major Teesdale, who has acted as Chief of the staff.

"Throughout the investment, which has now lasted four months, the troops in all the redoubts and entrenchments have kept a vigilant look-out during the night, and, at their appointed stations, stood to their arms long before day-dawn.

"In my Despatch of the 28th ultimo I informed your Lordship of the arrival of the news of the fall of Sebastopol, and of the landing of Omer Pasha at Batoom. I also acquainted your Lordship with the fact that the Russian General was engaged in sending off immense trains of heavy baggage into Georgia, and showing every indication of a speedy retreat. This in nowise threw us off our guard, and Lieutenant-Colonel Lake was directed to strengthen many points in our extensive and under-manned lines; and amongst other works, the Tabia bearing my name was constructed.

"At four o'clock on the eventful morning of the

29th, the enemy's columns were reported to be advancing on the Tachmasb front. They were three in number, supported by twenty-four guns; the first or right column being directed on Tachmasb Tabia, the second on Yuksek Tabia, and the third on the breastwork called Rennisson Lines. As soon as the first gun announced the approach of the enemy, the reserves were put under arms in a central position, from which succours could be dispatched either to Tachmasb or the English lines.

"The mist and imperfect light of the dawning day induced the enemy to believe that he was about to surprise us; he advanced with his usual steadiness and intrepidity, but on getting within range, he was saluted with a crushing fire of artillery from all points of the line: this unexpected reception, however, only drew forth loud hurrahs from the Russian infantry as it rushed up the hill on the redoubts and breastworks. These works poured forth a fire of musketry and rifles which told with fearful effect on the close columns of attack, more especially on the left one, which being opposed by a battalion of four hundred and fifty chasseurs, armed with Minié rifles, was, after long and desperate fighting, completely broken, and sent headlong down the hill, leaving eight hundred and fifty dead on the field, besides those carried off by their comrades.

"The central column precipitated itself on the redoubts of Tachmasb and Yuksek Tabias, where desperate fighting occurred and lasted for several hours, the enemy being repulsed in all his attempts to enter the closed redoubts, which mutually flanked each other with their artillery and musketry, and made terrible havoc in the ranks of the assailants; and it was here that Generals Kméty and Hussein Pasha, together with Major Teesdale, so conspicuously displayed their courage and conduct. Lieutenant-General Kerim Pasha also repaired to the scene of desperate strife to encourage the troops, and was wounded in the shoulder, and had two horses killed under him.

" The right column of the Russian infantry, supported by a battery, eventually turned the left flank of the entrenched wing of the Tachmasb defences, and whilst the Russian battery opened on the rear of the closed redoubt at its salient angle, their infantry penetrated considerably behind our position.

" Observing the commencement of this movement, and anticipating its consequences, Lieutenant Colonel Lake, who had taken the direction of affairs in the English Tabias, was instructed to send a battalion from Fort Lake to the assistance of the defenders of Tachmasb, and at the same time two battalions of the reserves were moved across the flying bridge and upon the rocky height of Laz Teppè Tabia. These three reinforcing columns met each other at that point, and, being hidden from the enemy by the rocky nature of the ground, confronted him at a most opportune moment; they deployed, opened their fire, which stopped, and soon drove back the enemy's reserves, which were then vigorously charged with the bayonet at the same moment when General Kméty and Major Teesdale issued from the redoubts at Tachmasb and charged the assailants. The whole of that portion of the enemy's infantry and artillery now broke, and fled down the heights under a murderous fire of musketry. This occurred at half-past eleven, after a combat of seven hours.

"In this part of the field the enemy had, including his reserves, twenty-two battalions of infantry, a large force of dragoons and Cossacks, together with thirty-two guns.

"Whilst this struggle which I have attempted to describe was occurring at Tachmasb, a most severe combat was going on at the eastern portion of the line called the English Tabias.

"About half-past five o'clock, A. M., a Russian column, consisting of eight battalions of infantry, three regiments of cavalry, and sixteen guns, advanced from the valley of Tchakmak, and assaulted those small redoubts, which, after as stout a resistance as their unavoidably feeble garrisons could oppose, fell into their hands, together with the connecting breastworks defended by townsmen and mountaineers from Lazistan, whose clannish flags, according to their custom, were planted before them on the épaulements, and, consequently, fell into the enemy's hands; but ere the firing had begun in this portion of the field, Captain Thompson had received orders to send a battalion of infantry from each of the heights of Kāradāgh and Arab Tabia to reinforce the English lines. This reinforcement descended the deep gully through which flows the Kars river, passed a bridge recently thrown across it, and ascended the opposite precipitous bank by a zigzag path which led into the line of works named by the Turks Ingliz Tabias—the English Batteries. Their arrival was as opportune as that of the reserves directed towards Tachmasb, which I have had the honour to describe in the former part of this despatch; these battalions, joined to those directed by Lieutenant-Colonel Lake, gallantly attacked and drove the Russians out of the redoubts at the point of the bayonet, after the artillery of the enemy had been driven from those lines by the cross fire directed from Fort Lake, and from Arab Tabia and Kāradāgh by Captain Thompson. This officer deserves my best thanks for having seized a favourable moment to remove a heavy gun from the eastern to the western extremity of Kāradāgh, and with it inflicted severe loss on the enemy.

" After the Russian infantry were driven from the English redoubts, the whole of their attacking force of cavalry, artillery, and infantry retreated with precipitation, plied with round shot from all the batteries bearing on their columns. During their temporary success, however, the enemy captured two of our light guns, which the mortality amongst our horses, from famine, prevented our withdrawing from their advanced positions. He also carried off his wounded and many of his dead; yet he left three hundred and sixty-three of the latter within and in front of these entrenchments; and his retreat occurred at least an hour before the assailants of Tachmasb were put to flight.

"During this combat, which lasted nearly seven hours, the Turkish infantry, as well as artillery, fought with the most determined courage; and when it is recollected that they had worked on their entrenchments, and guarded them by night, throughout a period extending to nearly four months—when it is borne in mind that they were ill clothed, and received less than half a ration of bread—that they have remained without pay for twenty-nine months, I think your Lordship will admit that they have proved themselves worthy of the admiration of Europe, and established an undoubted claim to be placed amongst the most distinguished of its troops.

"With regard to the enemy, as long as there was a chance of success he persevered with undaunted courage, and the Russian officers displayed the greatest gallantry. Their loss was immense; they left on the field more than five thousand dead, which it took the Turkish infantry four days to bury. Their wounded and prisoners in our possession, amount to one hundred and sixty, whilst those who were carried off are said to be upwards of seven thousand.

" As the garrison was afflicted with cholera, and I was apprehensive of a great increase of the malady should this melancholy duty of the burial of the dead be not pushed forward with every possible vigour by our fatigued and jaded soldiers, I daily visited the scene of strife to encourage them in their almost endless task; and I can assure your Lordship that the whole battle-field presented a scene which is more easy to conceive than to describe, being literally covered with the enemy's dead and dying.

" The Turkish dead and wounded were removed on the night of the battle. The dead numbered three hundred and sixty-two, the wounded six hundred and thirty-one. The townspeople, who also fought with spirit, lost one hundred and one men.

" His Excellency the Mushir has reported to his Government those officers who particularly distinguished themselves—a difficult task in an army which has shown such desperate valour throughout the unusual period of seven hours of uninterrupted combat."

CHAPTER XIII.

Cholera again breaks out—Gloom spread over the Garrison—Omer Pasha's silence—Officers receive the Medjidié—Turkish rank conferred on British Officers—Provisions begin to run short—Difficulty of sending out a Post—Evil resulting from neglect of orders—People caught in their attempt to escape from Kars—Turks found lying dead on the road—Increasing sickness of Troops—Addition to the Works.

Thus gloriously for the Turks terminated this gallant, though unsuccessful, attack by the Russians on the 29th of September. It will be imagined, probably, that the brilliant success which they had gained would have elated to the highest pitch both officers and men; but the incessant toil which the events of the battle necessitated scarcely left them time to reflect upon the importance of that action, and, moreover, great anxiety was added to their already over-taxed minds by the cholera, which had for a moment ceased, again breaking out with renewed violence. As many as seventy or eighty men a day died of this fearful complaint.

Just at this period, and with all the deaths from wounds received in battle, and from the usual causes, it became difficult to find men enough to bury the dead. The supply of meat, moreover, had gradually dwindled away, until it entirely ceased; and the men now existed wholly on farinaceous food, given them in very insufficient quantities. The nights, too, were piercingly cold; and, in short, it seemed as if the great excitement of the battle had been too much for the minds of all after such protracted anxiety, and a gloom appeared to be spread over the place from the moment the last shot was fired. There was every reason to hope and expect that the victory, together with the arrival of Omer Pasha on the coast, would have the effect of causing the blockade to be removed, and that supplies would be at once thrown in from Erzeroom. Days, however, passed by, and no signs of succour appeared, nor was anything known in the garrison regarding the movements of the Generalissimo who had promised to relieve it.

The Russian army remained immoveable in the same positions that it occupied previous to the attack. No movements of an offensive character were made, but Kars was as closely blockaded as ever by the cavalry, which had suffered too little on the day of the battle to be rendered less effective than it was before. The arrival and departure of convoys at and from the enemy's camp were watched by the garrison with the utmost anxiety. He appeared to be principally occupied in sending away his wounded to Gumri. His carts and arabas were so constantly on the move backwards and forwards, that it was naturally supposed he was sending off his heavier baggage preparatory to a move.

It was very difficult to make out what General Mouravieff intended to do. He had suffered a terrible defeat, and it scarcely seemed likely that he would again try to take the place by storm. There were occasional rumours of succour coming from Erzeroom. The reports which, from time to time, arrived regarding the movements of Omer Pasha were brought in by peasants living near the frontier, or else by people sent out from Kars especially for that purpose. The Generalissimo himself, although he landed with the ostensible object of creating a diversion in favour of the beleaguered garrison, never gave them the smallest intimation of what his movements had been or what they were to be. Twice, and twice only, did he write. The first letter has been before alluded to as containing advice regarding fortifications and provisions: the second was a cold, formal, and simple acknowledgment of a despatch from General Williams, conveying intelligence of the glorious victory of the 29th of September, and offering his warm congratulations thereupon to the Commander-in-chief of all the Turkish forces.

On the 17th of October there was a large

assemblage of officers in the tent of the Mushir. They were sent for to receive the Order of the Medjidiyé, for their distinguished services on the day of the battle. By virtue of the authority vested in him by His Imperial Majesty the Sultan, the Mushir distributed the decorations through the hands of Her Majesty's Commissioner to the Turkish as well as the British officers assembled for the occasion.

The following letter from General Williams to the Secretary of State for Foreign Affairs states the Class of the Order with which each officer composing his staff had the honour of being presented, the General himself receiving the First or highest Class. In addition to these, Lieutenant-General Kerim Pasha received the First Class of the Order; Major-Generals Kméty and Hussein Pasha, the Second Class; Colonels Fēyzi-Bey (General Kollmann) and Baron Schwartzenberg, the Third Class; and several officers of inferior rank were also invested at the same time with the Order.

"*Brigadier-General Williams to the Earl of Clarendon.*"

" MY LORD, "Kars, October 31, 1855.

" In my despatch of the 3rd instant, in which I had the honour to detail the movements of the battle on the heights of Kars, I omitted to state that the enemy in his retreat left a tumbril on the field.

"I have now great pleasure in stating for your Lordship's information that immediately after the battle his Excellency the Mushir, in virtue of the authority with which he is invested by the Sultan, conferred the Second Class of the Imperial Order of the Medjidiyé on Lieutenant-Colonel Lake, for his distinguished services on that day; on Major Teesdale, Captain Thompson, Mr. Churchill, and Dr. Sandwith, the Third Class of that Order; and on Messrs. Zohrab and Rennison he bestowed the Fourth Class.

"As these decorations were received in view of the position which their courage and conduct so materially assisted in defending, I trust that your Lordship will obtain Her Majesty's gracious permission to accept and wear them.

"His Excellency the Mushir has also named Colonel Lake a General of Brigade in the Turkish Army; Major Teesdale a Lieutenant-Colonel, and Captain Thompson a Major in that army; and his Excellency assures me that he has written for the confirmation of those ranks so honourably won by the officers in question.

"I have, &c.,
"(Signed)   W. F. WILLIAMS."

Her Majesty's Commissioner addressed the officers in a complimentary speech, thanking them, in the name of the Sultan, for the valuable services they had rendered His Imperial Majesty on the 29th of September, which had so materially contributed to the success of the day.

General Williams and the officers of his staff were much gratified at the receipt of the following letter from Lord Clarendon conveying the approbation of Her Majesty and the British Government of their services on this occasion :—

" *The Earl of Clarendon to Brigadier-General Williams.*

" SIR, " Foreign Office, November 2, 1855.

" I have received your despatch of the 29th of September last, announcing that General Mouravieff, with the bulk of his army, had at day-dawn that morning attacked your entrenched position on the heights above Kars, and on the opposite side of the river, and that, after an engagement which lasted nearly seven hours, the enemy was driven off in the greatest disorder and with considerable loss.

" I beg to congratulate you upon this brilliant and important victory, which reflects the highest credit upon the garrison of Kars.

" It is my agreeable duty to convey to you, and to the British officers under your command, the cordial approbation of the Queen and of Her Majesty's Government, for the energy, the perseverance, and the valour with which, for many months, and under circumstances of extraordinary difficulty, you have laboured with Lieutenant-Colonel Lake, Major Teesdale, and Captain Thompson, together with Mr. Churchill and Dr. Sandwith, to sustain the spirit and discipline of the Turkish troops, and to place the defences of Kars in a state to resist successfully the attack of the Russian army.

" I shall not fail to recommend these officers to the Queen for the rewards due to their gallantry.

" I am, &c.

" (Signed)   CLARENDON."

It is but justice due to the patriotic feelings of the Turkish Government to insert the following letter addressed by it to the Mushir, Vassif Pasha, commanding the army at Kars, conveying the approbation of the Sultan, as well as that of his Ministers, to all those engaged on the 29th of September.

" *Address from the Porte to the Defenders of Kars.*

" (Translation.)

" The signal victory which you have gained by the grace of God, and under the auspices of His Majesty the Sultan, is an event which will fill a bright page in history. The courage and valour displayed on this occasion by your Excellency, the officers, and soldiers of the Sultan's army under your command, and by the inhabitants of Kars, are deserving of universal praise. They have been duly appreciated by His Imperial Majesty, who has graciously extended his royal favour towards yourself, the army under your command, and the people of Kars, in reward of the brilliant service rendered by them.

"The sufferings undergone by the Imperial forces beleaguered in Kars have troubled the sleep and repose of all of us, and we have never ceased to pray for their safety and success. We were conscious of the zeal and intrepidity which animated your Excellency, and of the infinite mercy of God, and found consolation in this reflection. On the other hand, we worked day and night in devising means to oblige the enemy to raise the siege, and the joyful tidings of this victory has infused new life into us. Such a service rendered to our gracious master is a glory to the state and to the nation, and His Majesty has permitted that we likewise, as companions, should offer our thanks and congratulations to our brethren, who have been made worthy of so great a victory. We therefore, from the bottom of our hearts, offer our warm thanks and congratulations to your Excellency, and all the officers and troops of the army, our brothers; and by that you will convey the same to all of them, with our prayers for their prosperity and salvation."

Provisions were now running so short, that it was no longer difficult to calculate how many days or weeks the place could hold out, in the possible event of no assistance coming from any quarter. The last bullock was killed on the day of the attack, and from that date the soldiers ceased to taste any wholesome animal food. A great change in their appearance became every day more and more visible. Their step was less firm, and their eye was less bright, but scarcely a murmur of discontent was heard. It is true that desertion continued more or less, and nothing but the strictest adherence to discipline at this time could have enabled the authorities to keep the garrison together.

It was, even at this late period of the blockade, difficult to imagine that troops who had done such good service, and already endured hardships beyond description, would be utterly forsaken, and the hope that, ere it was too late, some steps might be taken for their relief, still kept the devoted garrison from succumbing to what appeared their inevitable doom.

Ignorance of the exact state of affairs could not be set up as an excuse for the apparent apathy on the part of those whose duty it was, even for the sake of humanity, if for no other reason, to strain every nerve for the purpose of sending assistance to the now starving troops.

It had become very difficult to send a post to Erzeroom through the enemy's pickets, which, shortly after the battle, had been doubled all round the works; and the men, no longer fatigued by the forays which had previously been of almost daily occurrence, were more than ever on the alert. General Williams had, however, most fortunately arranged a cipher with Her Majesty's Consul at that place before he came to Kars, and by these means he made known the miserable plight the garrison was reduced to, urging the authorities, in the very strongest terms, to use their utmost exertions to send relief. Duplicate and triplicate copies of these short, though important and comprehensive despatches, left the garrison almost every day. Written in very small characters, and inserted in a quill, they were given to a peasant or other messenger, with orders, if he found he could not escape, to throw them away. This was frequently the case, but still either the original or one of the copies invariably reached its destination. What effect these constant communications had upon those to whom they were addressed, through the Consul, it is needless to state.

It has been previously remarked that at the very commencement of the affair, and long before the place was invested, an order was issued to the effect that such of the townspeople who were, either from age or infirmity, unable to bear arms, and were therefore useless in a garrison, together with all women and children, should quit the place, and retire to the adjoining villages.

The execution of this order was never properly insisted upon by the Turkish authorities, although they were constantly reminded of it by General Williams; and it was only when too late that the evil consequences of this inattention began to be felt. Every family had, it is true, made some provision for its support prior to the place being blockaded, and had collected sufficient grain to last some months; but this supply came to an end very soon after the attack on the 29th of September, and it therefore became necessary to feed the inhabitants from the stores which were intended solely for the garrison.

Several attempts were made by the people to leave Kars and seek for assistance elsewhere. With that utter want of foresight for the future which is the peculiarity of Eastern fatalists, they had obstinately remained in their homes; nor was it until the last mouthful of food was expended that they perceived what ruin they had worked both for themselves and for the garrison. Now that the fears of actual starvation drove them from their houses, impeded as they were in their movements by the women and children, they were nearly always captured and unrelentingly driven back into the place.

The same people were occasionally caught several times in trying to escape, and General Mouravieff used to threaten them with all sorts of punishment if they renewed the attempt. He was, however, far too humane to carry his threats into execution.

The duty of issuing a certain amount of grain to the almost famishing inhabitants was intrusted to Mr. Zohrab, first-class interpreter, who had a difficult and sometimes a very troublesome task to perform, inasmuch as it was necessary, on the one hand, to guard against imposition, and not to give to any but those who required assistance to keep them from starvation, while, on the other hand, there was the danger of refusing to give when such aid was positively necessary. This service was performed by Mr. Zohrab with great zeal and ability, and was continued by him up to the last, even though latterly completely prostrated and confined to his room by a severe attack of illness.

It was indeed a most melancholy sight to see the poor creatures daily crowding round the interpreter's room, eagerly urging their claims for a handful of grain.

The Civil Medjlis assembled daily, and was attended by Mr. Churchill, General Williams' secretary, who was untiring in his attention to this onerous and responsible duty. It is impossible to speak too highly of the manner in which he superintended the proceedings of the council, and his presence had a most beneficial effect. The members were composed of officers of great energy and intelligence, who were at all times ready to listen to and act upon his suggestions.

The cholera, which up to this period had committed great ravages, now, most fortunately, began to disappear; but famine soon supplied its place. Each day several victims to this most fearful scourge were taken to the hospital, and few, if any, ever left it alive. It was by no means a rare thing to find soldiers lying dead on the roads, while others were scarcely able to walk without assistance. Very frequently, when obliged to come down from the upper batteries, either on duty or for some private purpose, the poor fellows have been, from weakness and exhaustion, utterly unable to return. It was no uncommon sight to see dead bodies being washed and prepared for burial in the middle of the bazaar.

As soon as possible after the battle, the men were again employed in adding to the fortifications, but they no longer worked with the same expedition or energy as before; and this was not to be wondered at, for each day there was a visible decrease in their vigour, arising from the want of proper sustenance. Nevertheless, several new works were completed, and much additional strength was given to the place. A small star fort, marked A in the plan, was thrown up on the left extremity of the Tachmasb line, it having been sufficiently proved, on the 29th of September, that something stronger than an open work was required to prevent this flank from being turned.

Experience had also shown that the line of English batteries, unless garrisoned by a much larger force than was allotted to this position on the day of the attack, stood in need of being strengthened by new works, and accordingly another star fort, marked B, nearly similar in size and shape to the one just described, was constructed midway between, and in rear of, Thompson and Zohrab Tabias. The open battery for three heavy guns and a mortar, marked C in the plan, was thrown up in order to protect Arab Tabia and to sweep the ground lying between it and Kāradāgh behind the breastwork connecting these two batteries. It was so constructed as to be useless to the enemy if it happened by any accident to fall into their hands, being commanded in rear by the citadel and Tēli Tabia at the north-east angle of the fortress.

CHAPTER XIV.

Parapets raised in places—Sentries withdrawn from the front—Reported advance of Selim and Omer Pashas—Effects of starvation—Cold becomes intense—Difficulty of carrying fuel to the Heights—Conduct of Feyzi Pasha—Enemy begins to hut himself—Attempts made to keep up the strength of the Troops—Annoyance from the Enemy at night—Garrison kept on the alert—Barrack constructed.

As the garrison was now so much reduced in strength by death and sickness, and as it was, consequently, impossible to man the breastwork below in an efficient way even with the aid of the dismounted cavalry which were told off for this duty, it was considered desirable to raise the height of the parapet in certain places. This was accordingly done along the whole south line between Hāfiz Pasha and Kanli Tabias, and every possible precaution was taken to prevent a night surprise, which, now that the garrison had become so much weakened in bodily and numerical strength, was the evil chiefly to be dreaded and guarded against.

As the desertions which still continued to take place were principally among the sentries in front of the works at night, it was deemed necessary to withdraw them from that position and keep them entirely behind the breastworks, having a certain number of officers patrolling along the lines from sunset to sunrise. In addition to these, an officer and a small party of men were placed at stated intervals a few hundred yards in front of the lower works, in order to keep a look-out, not only on the movements of the enemy, but on the men that attempted to desert from the garrison.

On the heights of Tachmasb it was found so utterly impossible to keep the men on sentry within the lines from deserting that a number of officers were induced, by promise of promotion, to shoulder the musket and do the duty of common soldiers at night. This service they performed well and efficiently until the surrender of the place.

Towards the end of October a messenger came in bringing despatches from the Seraskierat in Constantinople confirming the good news which had been previously reported in garrison of Selim Pasha being on his way from Trebizonde with a powerful and well-equipped force to its assistance. The General was described as a brave and energetic man; and on the 31st of October letters were received from him addressed to the Mushir dated from Erzeroom, and announcing his arrival at that town. He stated that he was at the head of a fine army, consisting of cavalry, artillery, and infantry, all in the highest spirits. They received the news of the victory of the 29th of September at a place called Massat-déré, near Baiboort, and Selim Pasha added, that, so delighted were his troops to hear of this glorious event, they begged to be led on at once without halting to fight for their gallant comrades.

This good news, as it may well be imagined, infused fresh spirit into the garrison. Various were the rumours as to the strength of the succouring army; and it was supposed by the Turks, not without reason, that the Russian General with this force in his rear, and Omer Pasha advancing, as it was constantly asserted, on Kutais, must, ere long, raise the blockade.

The effects of starvation were becoming daily more and more apparent. Men were seen digging up small roots out of the ground, which they eagerly devoured, the earth still clinging to them, their hunger not even allowing them to wait whilst they washed it off. The quarters of the English officers were literally besieged by the inhabitants of the town, craving most piteously for a morsel of food. As much as could be spared was given to them each day, but their anxious countenances and emaciated appearance plainly showed how insufficient it was. Women were seen at night tearing out the entrails of dead horses, over which, the men being too weak either to bury them, or drag them out of the lines, a light coating of earth had been hastily thrown. Some of the women even took their children to the Medjlis, and laid them down at the feet of the officers, saying they had no longer any means of supporting them.

General Williams ordered horses to be killed near his quarters during the night, and the flesh was sent to the hospitals for the purpose of making soup for the sick. A few bottles of this luxury, which it had really become, were also served out to the surgeons in the camp, and the soup was administered with great effect upon men who dropped at their posts, or were found senseless in the morning.

It may be stated that the religion of the Turks forbids them to use the flesh of the horse for food, and to get over this difficulty, the Sheik-Islam of the town was applied to. His answer was, that what the Khoran laid down man could not alter, but that he himself should never reprimand any one for transgressing the law under existing circumstances. Many of the soldiers were, therefore, only too glad to add a small quantity of this unpalatable food to their scanty rations, and thus in some measure satisfy the cravings of hunger.

About this time the Russian irregular cavalry made a practice of burning all the rank and dry vegetation which covered the country around Kars; and although this did no kind of harm, it produced a very dismal effect at night to see the red flames extending sometimes for miles, and the dark figures of the enemy moving about in the smoke.

Towards the middle of November, snow began to fall, and General Mouravieff, as if to show his determination never to change his position, began to construct pyramids of stones to mark the road from his own tent to Alexandropol. So intense did the cold now become, that to sleep under canvas, except in numbers, became nearly impossible. Most of the superior officers, therefore, burrowed holes behind their tents, and made a sort of subterranean cabin wherein to sleep. A small fireplace was constructed in it, and it became by no means an uncomfortable quarter.

At this time, Lieutenant-Colonel Lake and Major Teesdale used to take it in turns to remain out all night at the Head Quarters, so as to be able to send in a report to General Williams the moment anything occurred in camp. The Mushir had at length taken to sleep in a house about a hundred yards in rear of his tents, and had prepared for the use of these two officers the bell tent, in which he formerly remained at night. Here, when not patrolling, they were comparatively comfortable.

The stock of wood, of which the greatest care had been taken, at last came to an end, and the task of destroying the deserted houses of the town was now added to the labours of the soldiers. The cold at

DIFFICULTY OF CARRYING FUEL TO THE HEIGHTS. 253

night became so very bitter, that it was absolutely necessary to have a small fire in some place, where those who had been engaged during the night should find a certain degree of warmth to restore life to their benumbed bodies. It must, however, be recollected that the town lay at the edge of the plain, and that the extreme positions were three miles distant on the hills. Horses and mules had long ceased to be of any service except for food, and no amount of wages could tempt the starving townspeople to relieve their defenders of the onerous duty of carrying up fuel to the tents. The apathy consequent on great exhaustion induced many of the men to neglect providing themselves with fire-wood, and the result was, that numbers were daily found in the tents quite inanimate.

General Williams had most fortunately bought up all the sugar, coffee, and tobacco which could be found in the place, and these he distributed to the several regiments at stated periods. Every possible contrivance was resorted to in order to make the stores last until the expected succour should arrive.

A certain quantity of biscuit, flour, and wheat (five drachms of each per man) was daily issued to every battalion for the purpose of making a kind of soup for the troops, as it was naturally supposed that the ingredients in this form would be more satisfying. As Dr. Sandwith justly observes in his narrative, " This soup was maigre indeed, containing rather "more than an ounce and two-thirds of nutritious "matter."

The English officers were directed by Her Majesty's Commissioner to visit the kitchens at a certain hour, just before the dinners were ready, in order that they might taste the soup, and see that no roguery took place among the cooks or other individuals through whose hands the provisions necessarily passed. The allowance of bread issued to the soldier was a hundred drachms daily per man not quite three quarters of a pound: this, and the soup above described, was all the nourishment that the unfortunate men received, except, indeed, those who, less scrupulous than others on the score of religion, preferred eating horse-flesh to gradual though almost certain starvation.

No one deserved greater praise at this period of the blockade than Fēyzi Pasha (General Kollmann). Holding only, at that time, the rank of Colonel in the Ottoman army, he had occupied the post, as before stated, of Chief of the Staff. His subordinates, from unavoidable circumstances, were not, with perhaps a few bright exceptions, of that assistance which they ought to have been. Thus the whole labour and anxiety of this responsible situation fell upon the shoulders of this zealous and indefatigable officer. Never for one single hour of the whole twenty-four was he permitted to rest in peace, until it became a perfect wonder to every one who witnessed his exertions, how he contrived to carry on his duties without breaking down under such incessant and protracted labour. His tent also was the point to which all couriers, spies, deserters, and others were brought for examination.

As these arrivals were always at night, the English officer on duty never left the camp without having, just as day broke, smoked a pipe with the Pasha, in order that he might convey to General Williams the latest news that had been received from these various sources.

Day after day elapsed, and no symptom of the approach of Selim Pasha's army appeared. The garrison again began to get disheartened, and when any word of encouragement or comfort was spoken to them, they shook their heads mournfully and in an incredulous manner. The enemy showed no signs of retreating, but, on the contrary, seemed to be making preparations for remaining some time in their position. Every day, huts were seen to rise in the several Russian camps, and nearly all the horses were put under cover. Large convoys of provisions arrived from Alexandropol almost every week or ten days, and it became but too evident that whatever Omer Pasha or Selim Pasha's movements might be, they were not of such a nature as to frighten General Mouravieff.

Rumours that he meditated another attack became very prevalent, and the Turks were frequently heard to pray that the reports might be true. They began to think that nothing else could save them. Quite prepared were they again to defend their works, and to show that their courage was not daunted by all the hardships they had gone through, forgetting, at the same time, that their weak and enfeebled state would render a second assault far more dangerous than the former one had been.

In proportion to the daily increasing misery in the town, was the vigilance of the enemy redoubled. With little to oppose or annoy it, the irregular cavalry swarmed round the works, and some of their posts were but just out of range of the Turkish guns. Once, indeed, the garrison tried to surprise one of the Russian pickets, under cover of the darkness, in order to deter them from coming so close to the place; but the attempt failed, and, after marching about for half the night, they returned from their fruitless errand.

General Williams was now unceasingly employed in nursing the remaining strength of the men. The town had been searched over and over again to drain the last remnant of concealed stores, and the officers subscribed to furnish some slight assistance to the military chest, which was as empty as the stomachs of the men.

Scarcely a night passed that firing was not reported to have been heard in the direction of the Soghanli-Dāgh. In this state of uncertainty, and with a natural foreboding of evil, it was not the easiest task which fell to the lot of the English officers to go about with a smiling face and a confident air, doing their utmost to encourage and console the desponding.

Much of the duty had now to be done on foot, as the Turkish officers were almost all dismounted, their horses having eaten the stuffing of the last sofa or divan, and they having, in their turn, been consumed by their masters. The stud, also, of General Williams and his staff, in spite of the provident store which had been laid up at the commencement of the blockade, was obliged to be greatly reduced, and many of those that remained were too weak to be of much service.

For a long time the health of Captain Thompson had been gradually failing, but he nevertheless kept steadily at his post, until the cold and exposure had entirely unfitted him for exertion. He at last consented to come into the town, and was put under the immediate care of Dr. Sandwith.

About this period the garrison was constantly alarmed by parties of the enemy coming within a certain distance of the lower works, between midnight and three in the morning, when the nights were dark, firing upon the few sentries who were outside the breastwork, and letting off rockets in all directions, occasionally bringing up a battery of Cossack artillery, which, after firing a few rounds in the direction of Kanli Tabia, retired. These night alarms had the effect, which there was no doubt they were intended to have, of harassing the troops in garrison very considerably, as it was, of course, necessary to keep them under arms till daylight.

Many a poor fellow, as he stood in the ranks of the reserve, or at his post in the batteries, might be seen shivering with cold, or heard coughing heavily, as if his last days were drawing near, which, indeed, proved to be but too often the case. No sooner was the first shot fired than General Williams and those of his staff who were not already on some night duty or other were in a moment on horseback, and galloping through the darkness to the Mushir's tent, which was the rendezvous to which all hurried independently.

The Mushir himself, Kerim Pasha, the Chief of the Staff, and all the superior officers stationed below, were always quickly at their posts. Having waited to hear the last shot fired, and see the last rocket flying through the air, they dragged out the remainder of the long and weary night, until the cold grey dawn showed that the Russians were quietly at rest in their comfortable huts. Then, and not till then, were they enabled to get to their quarters, and snatch a few moments' rest before commencing on the labours of another day.

In order to divert the men's minds, and to prevent their thoughts from dwelling too much on their present miseries, and the dark prospect before them, the Engineer Officer was directed by Her Majesty's Commissioner to employ those off duty in constructing a barrack immediately in rear of the fortifications of the principal suburb, so that there might be some cover for the troops during the approaching winter, in the possible though not very probable event of Kars being saved.

Many of the houses in the immediate vicinity of this spot had been destroyed for the purpose of providing fuel, and the stones were therefore available for the required building. It was, however, very difficult to persuade the poor half-famished soldiers to work, though a certain small amount of money was issued to them every day. The consequence was that the work progressed but slowly, and it was only just completed when the place surrendered.

It will now, perhaps, be as well to turn to Erzeroom, and describe what had been going on at that place during the period of these stirring events at Kars.

CHAPTER XV.

Orders sent to Erzeroom by General Williams—Interview between Major Stuart and Vēli Pasha—The latter declines advancing without orders—He refuses to state the number of his Troops—The Condition of his Army—The State of Selim Pasha's Force—Vēli Pasha at length advances—Major Stuart visits Selim Pasha—Reputed character of the latter—Excuses made by him for his delay—General Williams writes to him, and offers him some advice—He is urged in vain to advance—Impossibility of collecting Bashi-Bozouks.

On the 19th of September, General Williams wrote to Major Stuart directing him to release Major Olpherts—who had, at his own request, been transferred by the authorities in England to the Turkish Contingent—from his duties at the head-quarters of Vēli Pasha's army, at that time encamped at the fortified position of Dévé-Boynou, and also instructing Captain Cameron to superintend the construction of the forts and lines of defence around Erzeroom.

Accordingly, on the following day, these three officers rode out to Vēli Pasha's camp, where the necessary introductions took place: they also paid their respects to Mehemet Pasha, the Vali of the province, who, in order to avoid the heat and dust of Erzeroom, had taken up his temporary quarters at the same place.

On the 3rd of October, reports reached Erzeroom of "a terrible struggle at Kars, ending in the de-"feat and almost total annihilation of the Russian "army."

Although the value of Turkish reports was too well known to be implicitly trusted, yet from the positive manner in which the rumour in question was reiterated, it was considered deserving of some notice. Accordingly, without loss of time, Major Stuart waited on Vēli Pasha, who professed full belief in the truth of the statement, although no official confirmation of it had, up to that time, been received.

A long conversation then ensued, as to the part which ought to be taken in the event of the report being confirmed. The consultation ended by the Pasha engaging to advance from Dévé-Boynou with four thousand infantry, five hundred regular cavalry, the same number of Bashi-Bozouks, and five field batteries of six guns each. It was arranged that the troops should be put in motion the very day that despatches should arrive establishing the fact of the victory, and that subsequent operations should be regulated by the movements of the Russian detachment at Delibaba, where it had been previously ascertained that there was a force consisting of infantry, cavalry, and a few guns but in what number it had been impossible to obtain any correct information.

Major Stuart, at this interview, thought it necessary to inquire whether Vēli Pasha possessed the power of acting independently on his own judgment, without any reference to the authorities at Kars. To this question he received, without hesitation, an answer in the affirmative.

Despatches from General Williams and the Mushir were received at Erzeroom on the night of the 4th of October, and early on the following morning Major Stuart again waited on Vēli Pasha, accompanied by Major Peel and the other British officers. Their surprise and disappointment may well be conceived on finding that the Pasha's views had since the last interview undergone a total change. He now said he could not move without orders from superior authority; that his infantry only numbered two thousand five hundred men instead of four thousand, as he had previously stated; and that the Russian force at Delibaba was stronger than his own.

Although arguments and remonstrances were unavailing, Major Stuart very properly considered it his duty to state his views in writing to Vēli Pasha, and he accordingly sent them to him the following morning, despatching a copy, at the same time, to General Williams, from whom, on the 16th of the month, he received the following answer, in cipher :—

"Kars, October 12th, 1855.

"It is highly objectionable, in the present state of Vēli Pasha's army, to advance further than Kupri-kui. Erzeroom must be held until winter puts an end to all movements; for so long as the Russian detachment of Byazid exists, it would be dangerous for Vēli Pasha's army to move on Kars. On the contrary, the movement on Kupri-kui will paralyze those of the Russian detachment of Byazid, for it has been reported that that detachment was intended to reinforce General Mouravieff's army for a second attack on this place. Announce, of course, that your army is to march on Kars.

"(Signed)   W. F. WILLIAMS."

The want of confidence which Her Majesty's Commissioner placed in Vēli Pasha's army was fully justified by the condition in which it then was. Every application on the part of his representative at Erzeroom for a "present state" was evaded or refused by Vēli Pasha. In reply to any verbal questions, he would affirm that he could scarcely parade three thousand infantry and one thousand regular cavalry; whereas, the observations made by the British officers, together with information obtained from other quarters, raised the number of the former to at least six thousand, and of the latter to fifteen hundred, besides ten or twelve hundred Bashi-Bozouks. It is true that these troops were scantily clothed, badly armed, and but indifferently drilled. The cavalry were in a deplorable state: the horses were all out of condition, and many, from age, were quite unfit for service. Most of the troopers were without boots or warm trousers: their sabres were short, and they were clumsily armed with old flint carbines, which they could not use. The artillery, however, were an exception to this general state, being, in every respect, fairly appointed. It must be observed, that the men were, for the most part, stout, active fellows, wanting nothing but proper discipline, as well as good clothes and arms, to make them an efficient force.

The transport service was in the worst possible condition. In the early part of the year a large number of pack-horses had been collected, stated by some at sixteen thousand, but not half of them now survived, and they were dying by scores daily, from neglect and starvation, on the heights of Déve-Boynou. The effluvia from their carcases became insufferable throughout the camp, until the Pasha was induced, by frequent remonstrances, to give an order for them to be buried.

From this brief sketch of Vēli Pasha's army, given by Major Stuart, who had frequent opportunities of judging of it, from time to time, by personal inspection, it is very evident that it was not fit for active operations against a watchful and resolute enemy. It is doubtful, therefore, if much blame ought to be attached to this General for any disinclination he may have evinced to make a forward movement, with a view to succouring the beleaguered garrison of Kars.

The Turks at Erzeroom were now in daily expectation of the arrival of Selim Pasha, who had been appointed, as before observed, to the command of the army at that place. In a previous part of this narrative, the report of this officer's advance, at the head of what he termed a large and well-equipped force, has been alluded to. It will now, therefore, be necessary to show what was the real state of the case.

Selim Pasha arrived at Trebizonde on the 11th of October, with eleven hundred men, the first instalment of the promised succour, and after a detention in that town of ten days he set out for his command. Long and anxiously was he looked for, as, from his reputed energy and courage, great things were anticipated on his arrival. It was, indeed, partly to the effect of his counsel that the British officers attributed the change that about this time came over Vēli Pasha and the Military Medjlis at Erzeroom. New life seemed to be suddenly infused into them, and an immediate advance towards Kars was determined upon.

On the 20th of October a battalion of infantry and a field battery were sent from Dévé-Boynou to Erzeroom, and on the morning of the 22nd the force commenced its forward movement, those fortified heights having been left without a single man or gun, contrary to the urgent remonstrances of Majors Stuart and Peel, who, it should be observed, accompanied Vēli Pasha, while Captain Cameron remained behind, to look after the forts and defences of Erzeroom. The first day's march across the plain of Passin was to the village of Korusjuk, a distance that only occupied two hours. There the force encamped and halted several days, Vēli Pasha alleging that he could not proceed further without orders from Selim Pasha, whose arrival at Erzeroom was expected hourly.

At length, on the 25th, this long-expected General arrived, and on the following morning Vēli Pasha pushed on to Hassan-Kallah, where the main body of the cavalry were encamped. Here again was another tedious halt, which was said to be in accordance with orders received from Selim Pasha. The weather being fine, and the ground favourable, the troops were drilled every day. Not much could be said in praise of their movements, but in the manual and platoon exercise they showed themselves, like the rest of the Turkish army, equal to the best troops in the world.

On the 29th of October it was reported that the Russians, who were said to have fallen back some days before from Deli-baba, had again advanced to their former position. On the 30th Vēli Pasha shifted his ground and moved to Alvara, a small village one hour's distance from Hassan-Kallah, in a southerly direction. On the same day there was a skirmish between the Turkish and Russian patrols, in which the former lost three men and four horses killed, the enemy being, nevertheless, driven back.

The order for this retrograde movement came from Selim Pasha, and, being unable to comprehend the motive or object of it, Major Stuart at once rode into Erzeroom for the purpose of seeing this officer. His reception on the following morning was most cordial, and, judging by the Pasha's declarations, no one could apparently be more alive than he was to the necessity of prompt and decisive action. With respect to the movement of Vēli Pasha's camp, he was afraid, with such inefficient troops as he had, to allow him to push forward. He stated that he hoped shortly to furnish them with new clothing and arms, and on the arrival of his own reinforcements, which were then on their way from Trebizonde, he would take immediate steps to perform his part in the war. This, Major Stuart's first interview with the new Commander-in-chief, was not altogether satisfactory, but, making the best of it, he returned the same afternoon to Alvara.

On the 1st of November, in consequence of a report that a party of Russians had, on the preceding day, made their appearance in the plain towards Kupri-keui, it was determined that the Turkish force should remove still further out of harm's way. Accordingly, early in the forenoon the camp was struck, and they fell back to the foot of the Dévé-Boynou, pitching their tents upon a piece of level ground not far from the village of Taher, where they remained until the approach of winter closed the campaign, and obliged them to return to Erzeroom.

It has been stated that Selim Pasha arrived in the capital on the 25th of October. He had been preceded by flattering reports of courage and energy, which of course led to corresponding expectations on the part of those he was about to reinforce. It was thought that his delay of ten days at Trebizonde might possibly have been unavoidable, owing to the numerous arrangements which it was necessary to make there, and which he might have wished to superintend himself, with respect to the troops said to be following him from Constantinople.

As to his having been nine days on the road to Erzeroom, all that could be said in extenuation was, that Pashas are great personages; and, according to Eastern notions, it is undignified to travel with an appearance of haste. Every allowance, therefore, was made for him; but the confidence of the people in Erzeroom began to give way when they found that the Pasha allowed eleven days to elapse before he visited his troops, distant, at that time, only a few hours' ride. More than once, when the matter was hinted to him, he said that his time was occupied from morning till night in correcting the evils resulting from the vicious administration of his predecessors, in superintending the issue of new arms and clothing to the men, and in establishing a proper system of interior economy.

There was some truth in all this. Several bales of new clothing, which had been lying for months in store while the troops were in rags, were at length distributed; and a large number of useless flint fire-locks were replaced by Minié rifles and percussion muskets. Increased attention also was given to the rations of the soldiers, and several of the contractors were sharply brought to task, owing to the inferior quality of the bread and meat which they had undertaken to supply.

It soon became notorious, that, in carrying out these beneficial measures, Selim Pasha incurred the ill-will of some whose duty it was to give him every support; in fact, it was but too evident that there were two distinct parties in the Divan.

On the 5th of November the Pasha proceeded to Taher, and for the first time inspected the troops under his command. On that occasion Major Stuart asked him for a "parade state," but it was again refused. He however calculated the men present on the ground at nearly nine thousand.

On the 6th of November, despatches dated 31st of October arrived from Kars. The copy of one of these addressed by General Williams to Selim Pasha deserves, from its importance, to be transcribed at full length, as it shows pretty clearly how little Her Majesty's Commissioner imagined, up to that moment, that the statement forwarded to him by the Pasha regarding the force which he was bringing up to the succour of the beleaguered garrison of Kars was wholly without foundation.

" EXCELLENCY, "Kars, 31st of October, 1855.

" I have heard your letter to his Excellency Vassif Pasha read with the greatest pleasure, and beg to congratulate you on your arrival at Erzeroom.

" The whole tenor of your letter is calculated to give this army increased courage, and to inspire it with a hope of a happy termination of the campaign.

"I trust that not a moment will be lost in directing the succouring army under your Excellency's command upon Kars, and from the sagacity which you have already shown in the conduct of war, I feel sure that at every halt, every precaution will be taken in selection of positions, and the temporary strengthening of them, always putting the enemy to extra loss in attacking, and taking into consideration the advantage which the Russians would have through their numerous cavalry, were your Excellency to offer them battle in an open plain.

"A battalion carrying trenching tools would be most useful, and as many Bashi-Bozouks on horseback as the sudden call of the moment will enable your Excellency to collect.

"If a few soldiers, joined to the Erzeroom-lee Topjees, and inhabitants, be left in the forts around Erzeroom, I apprehend that the greatest part of Vēli Pasha's army will be available for the reinforcing of your columns.

"I beg to assure your Excellency of my greatest respect and consideration, and pray for your protection for the English officers now in Erzeroom, who will accompany you in your advance.

"(Signed)   W. F. WILLIAMS.

"To his Excellency Selim Pasha."

It may be as well to state that the letter addressed to Vassif Pasha, and which is alluded to by General Williams in the above despatch, was the one written from near Baiboort on the 23rd of October, and which gave a most exaggerated account of the means at Selim Pasha's disposal for the relief of Kars, together with strong assurances calculated to inspire hopes of speedy succour.

Acting on the instructions received from General Williams by the same post which brought the above despatch, Major Stuart at once proceeded to the Serai, accompanied by Mr. Brant, H.B.M.'s Consul, and the English officers then in Erzeroom.

Selim Pasha had evidently been much disturbed by the letter he had just read, and seemed to feel the weight of the responsibility he had drawn upon himself by his boastful misrepresentations. To all the questions which were put to him as to his intended movements, he replied in vague and unmeaning generalities, chiefly dwelling on the difficulties he apprehended from the Russian detachment at Delibaba, which he stated to consist of five thousand infantry, six guns and cavalry in proportion. This, it must be observed, was a misstatement on the part of his Excellency, whether wilful or not was best known to himself; for at the time alluded to it was known that there were at Delibaba not more than fifteen hundred infantry at the very utmost, three hundred and fifty Cossacks, six guns, and about forty dragoons.

The Pasha was urged, but in vain, to advance to the entrenched position at Kupri-keui, which would at once develop the real intentions of this Russian force, and demonstrate whether or not it would be in the power of the Turks to operate still further. The strongest arguments in support of this movement were submitted to him, but all that he would promise was, that he would attack the Russians at Delibaba as soon as two thousand Bashi-Bozouks were collected in their rear to cut off their retreat.

This was nothing more nor less than a grave mockery, for the greater part of that number of irregular horsemen would have to be collected throughout the surrounding country, a work of some weeks at least, but more probably of months, if it could be accomplished at all. Indeed, it was subsequently learned that an order to this effect was given, which resulted in two hundred and fifty being assembled at Erzeroom in the following January!

CHAPTER XVI.

English Officers continue to visit Selim Pasha daily—False account of expected reinforcement—Major Stuart writes to Selim Pasha—His reply, and statement of his Force—The Pasha's arguments not well founded—General Williams writes to Major Stuart—Mr. Consul Brant's opinion of Selim Pasha—He urges the expediency of sending up another General—Some account of Omer Pasha's movements—The feasibility of a retreat from Kars is discussed—It is at first decided upon—All hope of succour is at an end, and a retreat is at length found to be impossible—The vigilance of the Enemy is increased.

From the tenor of the accounts which were constantly arriving from Kars through various channels, it became highly necessary that the British officers should not relax a moment in their efforts with the Turkish authorities. Day after day, therefore, they waited on Selim Pasha, and at length, on the 9th of November, they extracted from him a promise to advance.

The 14th was named as the day on which to put the troops in motion, and all the necessary arrangements were accordingly made; but the 14th passed and nothing was done. On the 15th the Pasha stated that he was in daily expectation of the arrival of additional reinforcements, and that a fortnight previously he had been advised by the Seraskierat of their departure from Constantinople.

A second instalment of a thousand men had arrived at Erzeroom, and a third detachment of the same strength was then on the road, coming slowly along at the rate of three hours a-day. These, however, were not the troops referred to by Selim Pasha, but a whole division ready equipped for the field, which, it need scarcely be observed, was imaginary, no force of the kind having left Constantinople, or being even expected. There was now at Taher and Erzeroom an available force of eleven thousand men, which, there was every reason to expect, would in a few days be increased by a thousand more; and, in addition to these, there were six field batteries well horsed and appointed. With such a force, a General of ordinary skill and courage ought to have at least attempted something for the relief of Kars; but it seemed to be more and more apparent every day that Selim Pasha did not come to Erzeroom with the intention of fighting. He constantly evaded all applications made to him by Major Stuart for a state of the army. On the 21st of November, therefore, he addressed the Pasha as follows:—

" EXCELLENCY,

"I did not write by yesterday's post to Lord Stratford de Redcliffe about reinforcements, because you did not send me a return of the force at present under your command, as you promised two days ago you would.

"From the position I have the honour to hold as British officer attached to your army, by order of Her Majesty's Commissioner, Brigadier-General Williams, I consider that I have a right to demand this return. Six times I have applied for it, but it has not yet been granted. I now ask for it the seventh time.

"On the 9th instant you told Mr. Brant and myself that the troops should advance from Dévé-Boynou on the 13th, or at the latest on the 14th. Will your Excellency be pleased to inform me what are your intentions now, as it is necessary I should let General Williams know what he has to expect from this quarter?

"Having already more than once explained to your Excellency the plan of operations which I am of opinion ought to be adopted, I shall say no more on the subject until I receive your reply.

"(Signed)   R. STUART, Major."

On the next day a return was received by Major Stuart, of which the following is a recapitulation:—

Officers	479
Medical staff	26
Musicians	122
Artisans	176
Non-commissioned officers and privates (cavalry and infantry)	4,484
	5,287
Bashi-Bozouks	1,613
Total	6,900

HORSES.

Cavalry and artillery	2,582
Transport	2,621
Bashi-Bozouk	1,613
Total	6,816

This return was accompanied by a letter, of which the following is a translation:—

"HONOURABLE SIR, "Erzeroom, November 22nd, 1855.

"On the 21st instant I received your letter, in which you ask me to state my intentions respecting the advance of my troops for the relief of Kars.

"Although we as a nation, and I, in particular, have a strong desire to act to the utmost stretch of our abilities, yet, be it known to you, that we have been disappointed at the state in which we found the arms and clothing of the Erzeroom troops. They were not as we wished them to be, but, on the contrary, were deficient in many things. We have, in consequence, been engaged since the day of our arrival until now, a period of twenty-seven days, in supplying troops with everything they wanted, and also in ascertaining the strength of our enemy. And now we may say that our troops are just furnished with what they require.

"To attack an enemy without previously ascertaining his strength, and before our own preparations were made, would obviously be very wrong according to the rules of war—would be opposed to reasonable conduct, and to the orders of our Government.

"In order to advance against our enemy we must have a force proportioned to his; but you will see, by the enclosed return, what is the number of our troops. We have only between six and seven thousand men who are able to use their arms, and we are very deficient in cavalry horses. But even supposing that everything was in good order, our troops are only sufficient to stand before the force at Delibaba; and if we leave behind a portion of them to cover Erzeroom and other places, and to protect the roads, the remainder would not be able to face the enemy.

"Should the whole of our army advance beyond Hassan-Kállah, there being two or three roads from Kars and Byazid, in case the enemy should come to Erzeroom by any of them and find the place undefended, which may God forbid, he would at once take possession of it. We think of this, and see that it would not appear right in the sight of intelligent men.

"Our plan must be either to attack the enemy or to keep them off. We do not think that we should be able to defeat them in attack; therefore it would not be reasonable to go against them. But if you say that we could fall back should we find the enemy too strong for us, this act of flying from the face of an enemy having happened here once before, when it caused great tumult amongst the inhabitants of this city and disheartened our troops, it does not appear reasonable in the eyes of wise men that it should be repeated.

"And now there are at Hassan-Kállah and beyond that place, one regiment of cavalry, four guns, some Bashi-Bozouks, and four battalions of infantry. The rest are at Neki-chair (Taher, near Dévé-Boynou).

"Until more troops arrive from Constantinople, if the enemy attack us we will fight.

"Our Government has been informed of our condition, and the state of everything, by our numerous despatches. We have also sent orders throughout the surrounding country for the collection of troops.

"We hope in God that as soon as we receive reinforcements we shall be able to advance to the relief of our besieged troops; and as we believe that you are the sincere friends of the Turkish Government, we have written thus to our dear friends.

"(Signed)   MEHMED SELIM."

There would no doubt appear in this letter, at first sight, a good deal of sound sense, and the arguments of the Pasha might have been considered irrefutable had they been based on the actual numerical strength of his army; but at the very time when he stated that his available force only amounted to between five and six thousand men, it was well known to the British officers at Erzeroom, from private information which they obtained, that the returns furnished to the Porte showed the number to be upwards of fourteen thousand, and there was good reason for believing that a still wider discrepancy existed with regard to the horses. Pay and rations were no doubt charged to the Turkish Government according to the higher number, while the lower was put forward as an excuse for inactivity and want of energy.

On the 23rd of November Major Stuart received the following letter, which General Williams had addressed to him:—

"My dear Major, "Kars, November 19th, 1855.

"Doubtless you have written to let me know how Selim Pasha is acting, and what his intentions are, but all the posts from Erzeroom have fallen into the enemy's hands, and since the capture of Sebastopol we have remained in utter ignorance of all things, politic and impolitic.

"Pray send off a messenger every day, and give him the promise of a thousand piastres on reaching me.

"If I knew that all hopes of succour from Selim Pasha had vanished, I could give you a hint of collateral relief, in the shape of artillery horses, *via* Olti; but I do not wish to distract Selim Pasha from a direct movement in our favour, and we are all ready to play our parts with our ragged veterans. My regards to your companions.

"(Signed)   W. F. WILLIAMS."

Mr. Consul Brant, seeing the very questionable manner in which Selim Pasha was acting, felt it his duty to address the following letter on the subject to Her Majesty's Ambassador at Constantinople:—

"*Consul Brant to Lord Stratford de Redcliffe.*

(Extract.)   "Erzeroom, November 19, 1855.

"I have the honour to inform your Excellency that a peasant from Kars brought me to-day a few lines from General Williams of the 12th.

" The General evidently seems to be in the belief that Selim Pasha has received the troops promised, of whose arrival at Trebizonde, however, we have heard nothing, and his Excellency has requested both Major Stuart and myself to entreat your Excellency to hasten their expedition. A Colonel arrived with a long letter from his Excellency Vassif Pasha to Selim Pasha. The precise contents of this letter I do not know, but the object was to urge on his Excellency to the relief of the garrison. Selim Pasha inspected his troops yesterday, and they mustered between five thousand and six thousand infantry: most of the cavalry were on duty at the outposts; they will amount to nearly two thousand, chiefly regulars, and besides these, they could collect one thousand five hundred to two thousand Bashi-Bozouks, if not more. The troops are in good health, well armed, and clothed, and have lately received four months' pay; and I have no hesitation in saying that such a force under an active and brave General could relieve Kars; but I have seen enough of Selim Pasha to have discovered that he is neither active, nor energetic, nor brave; and I have long feared that he would not advance. He has a new excuse for delay every day; to-day it was, that he must wait a change of weather. It is much finer than we had any reason to expect at this season, beautifully clear, though a little cold at night, and I can only say, that as finer weather cannot be expected before next summer, it is evident his Excellency will not leave Erzeroom. Selim is superior in rank to Vassif Pasha, and will not, therefore, obey his orders. The former's character was well known from his conduct in the command of the Choorooksoo army, which by neglect he allowed to perish, and yet in circumstances which demand immediate action, a slow and indolent Mushir like him is sent up. It really makes me fear that the Seraskier has no wish or intention of saving from destruction General Williams and his little band of heroes. I would therefore once more earnestly entreat your Excellency to see that a General of character be sent up, with at least a few good troops, with positive orders that they must arrive here in twenty or twenty-five days, and that every assistance the country can furnish be afforded to effect this. If a proper man be not at hand, the Porte had better avail of the services of General Cannon and his staff, who are at Trebizonde; but should the General be sent, your Excellency must insist that he have the absolute and uncontrolled command of this division, and that not one hour be lost in coming to a decision. The Russians cannot have many troops before Kars, I should think not more than twelve thousand, and they are discouraged and have no heart to fight; but in the camp it is said that General Mouravieff is of so obstinate a character that he will never abandon the siege, even though he should risk his own life, and the destruction of his whole army, by a desperate assault, or by frost or famine. He has put his troops into huts which are well constructed, and having plenty of firewood, they can stand the frost for some time yet, and too long, alas! for the safety of the garrison of Kars, which in the last extremity can do nothing but surrender; for without cavalry, and without horses for their guns, they could never, I imagine, cut their way through the enemy, who is still superior in numbers, taking into account his numerous cavalry and artillery.

"Omer Pasha is too slow in his movements to hope anything from him. About twelve days ago his Excellency was still on the coast, and although he had gained a victory, I suppose he will require time before he can resume his advance.

"I ask your Excellency, is the Kars army to be allowed to perish? Is nothing to be done to relieve it? for all that the Porte has lately done is quite insufficient for the purpose. I before pointed out that Omer Pasha's army should have been directed on Kars by way of Erzeroom, and not on Georgia, and had that been done, Kars might long since have been saved. I now fear it must surrender; and to confer honours on its gallant defenders, while they be left to perish, is a cruel mockery, and an indelible disgrace to the Turkish Government, as well as to those of the allied powers."

THE FEASIBILITY OF A RETREAT DISCUSSED. 285

In the mean time affairs at Kars were as bad as they could well be. So few days' provision remained, that it became but too evident that the place was untenable for any length of time. Omer Pasha continued perfectly silent, and the truth of Selim Pasha's statement was now more than doubtful. Unless, therefore, some very unexpected piece of good news reached them, it was very evident that the garrison would have to abandon the position they had so long and so gallantly defended under every imaginable difficulty. When this painful conclusion was arrived at, no time was lost in making the necessary preparations. The feasibility of a retreat was now discussed. Secrecy being the element of a successful sortie, the plan was only confided to the Mushir, the Chief of the staff, and General Kméty, and the necessity for taking such a step was fully concurred in by all these officers.

General Williams still continued to send messengers from Kars nearly every night, and the following despatch in cipher, dated the 19th of November, to the address of the British Consul, reached Erzeroom on the 23rd:—

" Tell Lords Clarendon and Redcliffe that the
" Russian army is hutted, and takes no notice of
" either Omer or Selim Pashas. They cannot have
" acted as they ought to have done.
" We divide our bread with the starving towns-

" people. No animal food for seven weeks. I kill
" horses in my stable secretly and send the meat to
" the hospital, which is now very crowded.

"(Signed)   W. F. WILLIAMS."

This short letter, conveying such a melancholy account of affairs at Kars, Mr. Consul Brant immediately forwarded to the Earl of Clarendon. He well knew that the case was desperate, although General Williams was too prudent to trust to an uncertain mode of conveyance any detailed intelligence, for fear of its falling into the hands of the enemy. The following extract from a despatch, dated 24th of November, 1855, must have prepared Her Majesty's Government for the news of the surrender which so quickly followed :—

"*Consul Brant to the Earl of Clarendon.*

(Extract.)   " Erzeroom, November 24, 1855.

" I have the honour to inform your Lordship that messenger after messenger has reached me for several days past from General Williams, pressing for succours. I have received short notes from him of the 12th, 13th, and 16th, all to this purport.

" To-day, a despatch came in, of which, by General Williams' desire, I have the honour to send to your Lordship a copy: I experienced the most painful feelings on perusing its contents.

That after so gallant a defence, Kars should fall into the hands of a thrice-beaten enemy, on account of the apathy of the Porte and the cowardice and imbecility of Selim Pasha, is intolerably distressing; but the consolatory feeling remains that, however disgrace may attach to those parties whose duty it was to have prevented this melancholy termination of so glorious a struggle, the brave garrison, and the inimitable director of its energies and operations, will, to the last, maintain their character for valour, skill, foresight, and every soldierly virtue; and that while noble deeds are appreciated, the defence of Kars will stand prominent among the achievements of a war unsurpassed by any other in acts of daring gallantry.

"Major Stuart has repeatedly waited on Selim Pasha, and has, in urgent terms, entreated him to advance to the relief of Kars; the Major has done so again to-day, but met with the same coolness and refusal. His Excellency will neither attempt the relief of the place, nor will he advance to cover the retreat of the garrison, and refuses even to send a strong detachment of cavalry towards Kars, which the Major and his officers offered to accompany in the hope of rendering assistance to the retiring army.

"Selim Pasha now pretends that he fears danger to Erzeroom from the Byazid division, and talks of advancing to attack it; but this is a mere pretext to cover his cowardice. I fear there is nothing to be done to help this neglected army: a retreat without cavalry or artillery, in face of an enemy who commands a large number of both, seems inevitable, and I tremble for the result.

"Omer Pasha is too distant and seems too slow in his movements to hope anything from him; from hence all relief is denied: the garrison therefore has nothing to depend upon but its own bravery, and the unflinching resolution, the consummate prudence and skill of its gallant Commander and his heroic band of European officers. Had Selim Pasha not been sent up hither something might have been effected. Vēli Pasha would have probably not attempted more than Selim Pasha himself; but if the command had been given to Tahir Pasha, which, without the presence of Selim Pasha, it was in the power of Vassif Pasha to have ordered, I think relief could have been got into Kars. But as soon as Selim Pasha arrived, all control over the troops here was taken out of Vassif Pasha's hands.

"The reputation of Selim Pasha might have led to the anticipation of what has happened; he was so well known as wanting in military knowledge and courage, as well as in administrative talent, that the Seraskier Pasha who named him should be made responsible for the incapacity of his protégé, and Selim Pasha should not be allowed to escape the punishment due to his cowardice and heartless conduct."

Retreat having been decided upon, Major Teesdale was ordered to prepare, with General Kméty, a proposition for the best line of march. Having arrived at Tachmasb, these two officers once more carefully examined the ground, with which, from their long residence on that position, they were already so well acquainted; and having determined on the most advantageous route, Major Teesdale proceeded to make, under cover of the rocks, as careful a sketch of the country as the circumstances of the case would allow.

It was intended that the garrison should have marched to Tchakmak by the road leading past Fort Lake, and have continued on the road to Chalgour, until on a level with that village. They were then to have made straight for the small camp of the Russian irregulars that occupied the southern corner of the plateau. These were imagined to be too few in number to have opposed any serious resistance to the retreating army, who, having then gained the edge of the mountain, would have struggled on to the road which passes over the summit to Guile and Pennek. How soon the enemy would have been upon them is uncertain, as it would have depended very much upon how far the intended movement had been kept secret.

It was highly necessary that the Turks themselves should be kept in ignorance, until the last moment, of the plan which was in agitation. Linen bags or havresacs were made up privately under the superintendence of Lieutenant-Colonel Lake, and when a sufficient number were ready they were issued to the men, with three days' biscuit in each, under the pretence that the troops might be called on at any hour to take the field for the purpose of meeting Omer or Selim Pashas, who were supposed to be coming to their relief.

A post now unexpectedly arrived bearing a short note in cipher from Her Majesty's Consul at Erzeroom, in which he begged General Williams not to expect any assistance from Selim Pasha, who had quietly established himself in the capital, and had notified his intention of not proceeding further.

A council of war was then held in Kars, attended by the Mushir, Her Majesty's Commissioner and his Aide-de-camp, Lieutenant-Colonel Lake, and all the general officers present in the garrison, with the Colonels commanding regiments. At this meeting General Williams, addressing the officers, gave a plain statement of facts. He told them that he had that day received a despatch from Her Majesty's Consul at Erzeroom, stating the part that Selim Pasha had acted. He informed them that no assistance could be reasonably looked for from Omer Pasha, of whose movements nothing had been heard for some time, and who, it was evident, had confined his operations to the neighbourhood of Sukum-Kaleh, without having any intention of coming to Kars. He then pointed out to them the very low ebb at which the provisions in garrison had arrived, and ended by saying that it was necessary to lose no time in taking some decided step.

After a long discussion, it was finally determined that a retreat, which was lately talked of, was now quite out of the question. The troops had become so enfeebled by sickness and want of proper nourishment, that any attempt which might, a short time before, have been practicable, to cut their way through the enemy's lines to the mountains, with the hope of reaching Olti, must have been attended with fatal consequences; nor would any commanding officer have been authorised in undertaking a movement which would inevitably have caused such a wholesale loss of life.

It must be remembered that at this time scarcely a horse remained alive. Not a single cavalry trooper was mounted, nor were there the means of horsing one field battery.

It would, therefore, have been a most unequal fight, the result of which could not be doubted for a moment, between the remains of a worn-out and partly undisciplined army (wholly so, indeed, as regarded manœuvring in the field), consisting solely of infantry, and such a force as would be brought against it, well fed, fully equipped, and efficient in every branch, with its splendid and numerous cavalry stationed in all directions, and ready at any hour to intercept or pursue the retreating columns.

General Mouravieff, too, being fully aware of the state to which the garrison was reduced, and expecting, doubtless, that some movement of the kind might be in contemplation, had redoubled his usual precautions, and had put everything in readiness to oppose its execution.

No other course, therefore, appeared to be open to the garrison but a conditional surrender. The Turkish officers, reluctantly acknowledging the sad truth which was thus forced upon them, agreed at once with General Williams that no time should be lost in arranging a meeting with the Russian Commander.

CHAPTER XVII.

An Aide-de-camp is despatched with a flag of truce to the Russian Camp—General Williams visits General Mouravieff—He announces the surrender of Kars to Lord Clarendon—Terms of the capitulation—Approval of Her Majesty's Government—General Mouravieff appreciates a brave defence—Terms are approved of by the Mushir, but objected to at first by the Turkish Officers—All is at length arranged satisfactorily—Generals Kméty and Kollmann escape—Reception of the Turks by their Enemy—Destination of British Officers—Peace is concluded.

MAJOR TEESDALE was accordingly despatched from the Council with a flag of truce to the enemy's lines, bearing a letter to General Mouravieff from Her Majesty's Commissioner, requesting an interview on the following day. On arriving at the outposts, Major Teesdale was blindfolded by the Cossacks, and was thus led for some distance towards the enemy's camp. The bandage, however, was soon removed from his eyes by an order from the Russian Commander-in-chief, and he was at once conducted to the hut forming the head-quarters of that officer. On making his wish known to an Aide-de-camp, he was immediately admitted into the presence of the General, and was by him courteously received. General Mouravieff having expressed his readiness to receive General Williams the following day at noon, Major Teesdale returned to Kars by nightfall.

Her Majesty's Commissioner, accompanied by his Aide-de-camp and Secretary, repaired the next day to the Russian camp, and at once entered upon the sad business which had caused him to demand an interview with General Mouravieff. A rough draft of the terms on which the Turkish Commander was willing to give up the fortress was then and there made out and agreed to by the contracting parties. With the nature of the capitulation, which was honourable alike both to the Russians and Turks, the public has already been made acquainted; but as it cannot be too widely known it is again given at full length, as well as General Williams' letter to the Earl of Clarendon announcing the surrender.

"*Brigadier-General Williams to the Earl of Clarendon.*

"Russian Camp near Kars, November 29, 1855.

"MY LORD,

" From the various despatches in cipher which I have addressed to your Lordship through Mr. Brant, the intelligence which I have now the misfortune to announce must have been expected by your Lordship.

" I had received direct promises of succour from Selim Pasha; and Omer Pasha's operations, until

I knew that his movements were directed towards Soukoum-Kaleh, had buoyed me up in my determination to hold out to the last moment: this intelligence from the Generalissimo reached me on the 24th instant, by the same post which brought me positive news, from Mr. Brant, of the indisposition or inability of Selim Pasha to advance further than Keupri-keuy.

"We had, up to that date, suffered from cold, want of sufficient clothing, and starvation, without a murmur escaping from the troops. They fell dead at their posts, in their tents, and throughout the camp, as brave men should who cling to their duty through the slightest glimmering of hope of saving a place intrusted to their custody. From the day of their glorious victory, on the 29th September, they had not tasted animal food, and their nourishment consisted of two-fifths of a ration of bread and the roots of grass, which they had scarcely strength to dig for; yet night and day they stood to their arms, their wasted frames showing the fearful effects of starvation, but their sparkling eye telling me what they would do were the enemy again to attack them.

"We had now lost nearly two thousand men by starvation, and the townspeople also suffered, and would have died by hundreds if I had not divided the bread of the soldiers amongst those who had bravely fought by their side. I therefore begged

VIEW OF THE RUSSIAN CAMP AT CHIFTLI-KAYA.

the Mushir to call a Council of War, which, on being told that we had only six days' rations, came unanimously to the conclusion that nothing was left to us but a capitulation; and that the debility of the men, and total want of cavalry, field artillery, and ammunition mules, rendered any attempt to retreat impossible.

"The Mushir then deputed me to treat with General Mouravieff, and I consequently waited on his Excellency on the 25th instant. He at first seemed determined to make prisoners of all who defended the place, but as the Rediff, or militia, and the townspeople formed a large portion of the infantry, I made a successful appeal to his humanity, which, coupled with the obvious measure of destroying our artillery and stores, to which we should have had recourse previous to an unconditional surrender, brought about the Convention which I have now the honour to enclose for your Lordship's information, without the expression of unavailing regret.

"I have only to add that the stipulations were carried into effect yesterday; that myself, my officers, and the regular troops composing the late garrison, amounting to eight thousand of all arms, are prisoners of war, and that the irregulars, numbering six thousand, have marched towards their respective homes.

"I and my officers are to march for Tiflis to-morrow, there to await the decision of the Emperor as to the place of our abode in Russia.

"I have, &c.,

"(Signed) W. F. WILLIAMS."

"*Précis of the Convention between General Mouravieff and Major-General Sir William Williams, relative to the Surrender of Kars.*

"ART. 1. The fortress of Kars shall be delivered up intact.

"2. The garrison of Kars, with the Turkish Commander-in-chief, shall march out with the honours of war, and become prisoners. The officers, in consideration of their gallant defence of the place, shall retain their swords.

"3. The private property of the whole garrison shall be respected.

"4. The Redifs (militia), Bashi-Bozouks and Lāz, shall be allowed to return to their homes.

"5. The non-combatants, such as medical officers, scribes, and hospital attendants, shall be allowed to return to their homes.

"6. General Williams shall be allowed the privilege of making a list of certain Hungarian and other European officers, to enable them to return to their homes.

"7. The persons mentioned in Articles 4, 5, and 6, are in honour bound not to serve against Russia during the present war.

"8. The inhabitants of Kars will be protected, in their persons and property.

"9. The public buildings and the monuments of the town will be respected.

"November 27, 1855."

If anything could lessen the pain and regret which were experienced by General Williams and the officers of his staff, it would have been the knowledge that their endeavours to do their duty to the last moment were recognised by Her Majesty and the Government in England. It was therefore with feelings of no ordinary pride and pleasure that the following letter was received by the British officers while they were in captivity:—

"*The Earl of Clarendon to Major-General Williams.*

"SIR, "Foreign Office, December 22, 1855.

"Her Majesty's Government have learned with the deepest regret that the garrison of Kars was reduced by famine to capitulate, and that, in consequence, yourself and the other British officers serving under you at that place have fallen as prisoners of war into the hands of the Russians.

"Her Majesty's Government have observed with the utmost admiration the zealous and indefatigable exertions which you made for the defence of that important position under circumstances of no ordinary difficulty, as well as the judgment and energy which you displayed in overcoming the obstacles of every sort with which you had to contend, and in inspiring the Turkish soldiery with that confidence which enabled them, under your influence, signally to defeat on all occasions the attempts made by an enemy superior in numbers and military resources to make themselves masters by force of arms of the besieged town.

"I trust that the applications which have been made to the Russian Government for your exchange may be successful, and that Her Majesty will soon again have at her disposal the services of an officer who has earned for himself so distinguished a reputation. Some time may elapse before you receive this despatch; but I think it right at once to place on record the sentiments of Her Majesty and of her Government in regard to your whole conduct during the time that you have been employed with the Turkish army in Asia; and, while sympathising with you in the unfortunate result of your honourable exertions, I have to express Her Majesty's entire approval of the manner in which you acquitted yourself throughout the whole period of your recent services.

"I have at the same time to instruct you to signify to the officers and civilians serving under your orders at Kars, namely, to Colonel Lake, to Major

Teesdale, to Captain Thompson, to Mr. Churchill, and to Dr. Sandwith, Her Majesty's entire approval of their conduct.

"I am, &c.,
"(Signed) CLARENDON."

It may perhaps be a matter of surprise to some, that, in the helpless condition to which the garrison had been reduced by famine and every other kind of hardship, any terms whatever were granted; but the Russians had already received terrible proof of the desperate valour they would have to contend with in the event of another collision taking place, and, by refusing all terms, they would only have incurred a considerable amount of loss, both in men and in the destruction of all the trophies so dear to the heart of a conqueror.

Moreover, the gallant Commander of the Russian forces well knew how to appreciate a brave defence; and so far from desiring to trample on the devoted garrison who, only two months before, had driven him from their entrenchments with such tremendous slaughter, General Mouravieff took every possible means in his power of showing how much he esteemed his enemy for the courage and perseverance they had shown in holding the place until forced by famine to surrender, after having endured privations which even he, who had passed nearly all his life in camp, could scarcely believe it to be in the power of man to sustain.

The document in question was drawn up by General Mouravieff, General Williams, Colonel Kauffman, and Colonel (now Major-General). Prince Dondoukoff Karsakoff, and it was arranged that Her Majesty's Commissioner should, on the following day, bring back the answer of the Turkish authorities to the proposed terms, with such modifications and alterations as should, on further consideration, be found desirable.

On his return to Kars late in the evening General Williams proceeded straight to the tent of the Mushir, to whom he communicated the result of his interview with the Commander of the Russian forces.

The Turkish General appeared to be perfectly satisfied with all the arrangements that had been made, and threw no obstacles in the way of the treaty being forthwith ratified.

On the following morning, however, it was ascertained that many of the Pashas, on being informed that they were to become prisoners of war, strongly objected to the terms of the capitulation. Some delay therefore took place, and General Williams was obliged to send his Aide-de-camp once more over to the Russian camp in order to explain to General Mouravieff the reason of his not being able to fulfil his intention of attending himself for the purpose of completing the negociation.

A Council of War was again assembled, composed, as on the former occasion, of all the superior officers in garrison, at which Her Majesty's Commissioner recapitulated the nature of the treaty proposed by the Russian Commander, and explained to them that the terms of it were such as they could accept with honour, and that they had no right to expect or require any of a more advantageous kind.

The Turkish officers contended that, on former similar occasions which they quoted, the garrisons had been permitted by their enemy to lay down their arms and go whither they liked. They did not, therefore, see why the same indulgence should not be granted to them in the present instance.

The reasoning of General Williams had, however, at length the desired effect, and the Turks were persuaded that there was nothing left for them but to submit patiently to their inevitable fate. The council was then dissolved, and on the following day, November the 27th, Her Majesty's Commissioner, accompanied by the officers composing his staff, together with Major-Generals Hāfiz and Hussein Pashas, and Colonel Achmet Bey, rode over to the Russian camp. The treaty was duly signed and sealed, and it was arranged that the fortress should be given up the next morning, and that the garrison should surrender themselves as prisoners of war.

It should be mentioned here that Generals Kméty and Kollmann, the two Hungarian officers who had done such good service, had, at their own request, been permitted to leave the garrison as soon as the surrender of the place had been finally determined upon, with the hope of being able to cut their way through the enemy's chain of pickets, and make their escape to Erzeroom. This they were fortunate enough to effect without accident of any kind. Had these officers trusted to the generosity of General Mouravieff, as they were urged to do by General Williams, this hazardous measure might have been avoided; but it must be remembered that they had left their own country while under sentence of death, and they well knew how fatal the consequences would have been if the Russian General had handed them over to the Austrians.

On the 28th of November, 1855, the Turkish troops, after having laid down their arms, marched out of the beleaguered city which they had so nobly defended for nearly six months, and, accompanied by Her Majesty's Commissioner and the three English officers attached to his staff, gave themselves up as prisoners of war to the Russians.

It was a melancholy sight, and one that will not be easily forgotten by those who witnessed it, and who had so lately fought by their side, to see these brave soldiers, with what little property they possessed, consisting chiefly of a change or two of linen and perhaps a few household articles belonging to their families strapped to their backs in lieu of a knapsack, dragging along their weary limbs from the scene of all their miseries, as well as of their glory, towards the camp of an enemy from whom they did not at that time know what sort of treatment they might receive.

There was not one among the poor half-starved garrison who had not, by patient endurance and resignation, shown unexampled fidelity to his sovereign; while many of his comrades, wanting in that moral courage which alone enables men to face dangers and difficulties, had deserted their posts during the blockade, and were at that moment, if not taken by the enemy while attempting to escape, enjoying comparative happiness and security in their native villages.

Nothing could exceed the feeling of depression which but too evidently pervaded all ranks as they marched slowly and heavily away, their only consolation being that they had done all that men could do, and had performed their duty nobly to the last.

The reception they met with from General Mouravieff and his army was such as might reasonably have been anticipated. The officers were received with courtesy and attention, and everything was done to make their captivity as little irksome as possible.

Preparations had been made providing for the wants of the half-famished soldiers who were reduced to such a state of weakness by want of proper nourishment that several of them fell down dead from exhaustion during the short march from Kars to the Russian camp. Many of these poor fellows, not having tasted animal food for so many weeks, could not restrain their appetites when provisions were placed before them, and fell victims to the effects of repletion.

The same kindness and good feeling, which both officers and men received on first becoming prisoners, were continued to them during the period of their captivity, in the several places to which they were conducted. The English officers were, in the first instance, sent to Tiflis, there to await further instructions from His Majesty the Emperor. Previously, however, to their ultimate destination being decide dupon, General Williams was attacked by low fever, brought on principally by the mental anxiety, as well as by the great bodily exertion he had undergone during the harassing and protracted blockade.

When the final orders arrived from St. Petersburgh, directing General Williams, his Aide-de-camp, and private Secretary (the latter gentleman having, it should be mentioned, voluntarily accompanied his Chief into exile) to proceed to Varonesh, and Lieutenant-Colonel Lake, in company with Captain Thompson, to Penza, Her Majesty's Commissioner was unable to move on account of his severe illness, and he was, therefore, permitted to remain at Tiflis with Major Teesdale and Mr. Churchill, the other two officers proceeding at once to their destination. At the conclusion of the war the British officers were released from captivity and returned to England. The Turkish officers and soldiers, who had reason to be satisfied with the treatment they had received from their captors, were also set free and sent to their own country.

CHAPTER XVIII.

Reasons for endeavouring to hold Kars—Former Invasion of Asia Minor briefly described—Fall of Kars in 1828—Conquests by the Russians in 1828-29—The position of Kars stronger than that of Erzeroom—Inexpediency of an early retreat—The results which would have followed—The probable loss which might have been expected.

THERE are one or two points connected with this lengthened and disastrous blockade which it may, perhaps, be advisable to consider, with a view to establishing the expediency, if not the absolute necessity, of holding Kars to the last moment, as well as the power which existed of sending timely succour to the beleaguered garrison.

It may be stated, without fear of contradiction, that Kars is the key of Asia Minor. It is situated near the Turco-Russian frontier, within five-and-thirty miles of the fortress of Gumri (or Alexandropol as it is more commonly called), in which place, as well as in the neighbourhood, General Mouravieff had assembled a very considerable force of all arms, and had also been engaged for some time previously in collecting, on a large scale, all the munitions of war, establishing store-houses in various places for grain and provisions of every kind.

Alexandropol, from its central position, was peculiarly adapted for the head-quarters of an army preparing to take the field, not only being in itself strongly fortified, but possessing great facilities for being provisioned by means of the interior and frontier depôts.

In the year 1828–29, when the Russians invaded Asia Minor under the late General Prince Paskiewitch, Kars was, as might have been reasonably expected, the first place of any consequence that was attacked.

After taking Akhalkalikh, a place of no real importance, the Russian General found his offensive movements impeded by the positions of Kars and Akhiska. He considered that an invasion by way of Alexandropol on the former of these places was the most politic course he could pursue. How far he was right in his judgment, subsequent events fully proved. Kars fell after little more than three days' resistance.

It is not necessary to allude further to this defeat; but it may not, perhaps, be out of place to remark a somewhat strange coincidence between the capture of Kars in 1828 and its surrender in 1855. Eminn Pasha, the Turkish Commander-in-chief on the former occasion, after having held the fortress until the Russian General was in a position to dictate terms to the besieged garrison, hesitated to accept the conditions proposed, wishing thereby to gain time, as he was in hourly expectation of promised succour. Prince Paskiewitch, however, refused even the two days demanded for reflection, and granted only one hour, at the expiration of which time the place surrendered. The fall of Kars in 1855, it need scarcely be observed, arose from precisely the same want of promised and expected assistance.

The possession of this place, unimportant in itself as a fortress, gave to the Russians in 1828 the whole of the Pashalik bearing the same name, an extremely fertile tract of land, capable of affording food of every description for the advancing troops.

After this capture the conquering army marched against Akhalkalikh, the Commander-in-chief himself making a feigned demonstration with a certain portion of his troops in the direction of Erzeroom, which had the intended effect of forcing the Turks to fall back upon the Soghangli Dāgh.

It is not intended to follow the movements of the Russian army at this period step by step, for they are doubtless too well known to need repetition; it is sufficient to observe that Akhalkalikh fell, and Akhiska was soon afterwards taken.

The Turks now found themselves deprived of their base of operations, and were, consequently, obliged to remain beyond the mountains. The Russians, on the contrary, being firmly established in possession of all the country as far as the Soghangli Dāgh, proceeded to take Ardahan, Byazid, and Toprak-Káleh. Not long afterwards, Erzeroom capitulated. The enemy then marched on towards Trebizonde, from whence they returned to Baiboort, and while besieging that place, peace was proclaimed and put an end to future hostilities.

Thus, in a very brief space of time, the Russian troops had dispersed the Turkish army, taken the capital of Armenia, and several fortresses, besides many entrenched camps, and had possessed themselves of the Pashaliks of Kars, Erzeroom, and Moosh, together with a certain portion of that of Trebizonde. It is true that their loss in killed and wounded, as well as from disease, during the period alluded to had been very great; but, considering the important successes they had gained, there is no doubt that the campaign was a glorious one for the Russian arms.

A result similar to that now described would assuredly have followed the fall of Kars in 1855, had it surrendered or been taken by storm before the state of the weather rendered it impossible for the Russian General to advance any further. The consequences might, and most probably would have been even still more disastrous to the Turkish troops, for not only was the army of the Caucasus stronger than it was in 1828, both in number and general efficiency, but the Ottoman forces were proportionably weaker, both as regarded their numerical strength and their discipline. Their spirits also had naturally been much depressed by the defeats of the previous year.

As it is desirable to look at this point in all its bearings—that is to say, the expediency or otherwise of having held Kars for so long a time under such great difficulties and disadvantages—it may be as well to consider how far it would have been politic to have abandoned that place, and to have retired on Erzeroom, either before the arrival of the Russian army in June, or at any subsequent period during the earlier stage of the blockade, while the Turkish cavalry, such as it was, still existed, and while sufficient number of horses remained to take away the field batteries.

Many arguments might be brought forward to show the dangerous consequences which would inevitably have resulted from such a movement.

It may be observed that Kars was a far stronger position than Erzeroom, and from the many natural advantages it possessed, there was every reason to believe that, with an adequate garrison and a sufficient supply of food and ammunition, it could have resisted the attack of any force which the Russians would apparently be able to bring against it. Were proof wanting of this assertion, the result of the battle of the 29th of September is surely more than sufficient to satisfy the doubts of the most sceptical.

Had it been determined to retire before the enemy at any period during the blockade, the whole of the heavy garrison artillery must at once have been abandoned. It may appear almost incredible, but so utterly destitute was the army of anything like transport, that about twenty arabas formed the whole of that department. Hence all the stores and magazines must have been destroyed, or left for the enemy to take possession of.

It would, moreover, have been a most fatal step to withdraw an army in (it might almost be said) the last stage of disorganization from a position they had been taught to look upon as their safeguard and stronghold. Dispirited as they were by defeat in every combat for three years, and their confidence in themselves utterly lost as it would doubtless have been by such a measure, what hopes could possibly be entertained of bringing them to face an enemy twice as numerous as themselves, and in the highest state of discipline and efficiency?

Having left Kars, the first position which the Turkish army could have taken up, would have been on the Soghanli Dāgh, but experience has shown that mountain ridges are for the most part untenable; and they would therefore soon have been obliged to commence a second retreat, leaving already a splendid forest, the most available part of the country, and three pashaliks, in the enemy's hands.

The so-called position of Kupri-keui is utterly indefensible. Nothing, therefore, would have remained if the retreat had once commenced, but to fall back on the Dévé-Boynou Pass, where, owing to the usual procrastination of the Turks, only one imperfect battery, and part of an unfinished redoubt, existed; but even if they had been able to make a stand at this place, it cannot be doubted but that General Mouravieff, with the numbers he held at his command, would have divided his army, and, keeping them in check with one portion of it, would have entered the plain by the other route with the remainder, and thus placing them between two forces, each equal to their own, would have forced them to retire into Erzeroom.

The people of this place. unlike the brave Karslis, are possessed of no warlike feelings, nor could any dependence be placed upon them. A great part of the population consists of Armenians, who are openly in favour of Russia; nor is this to be wondered at when the cruel and unjust treatment they invariably receive at the hands of the Turks is taken into consideration. Not only would they have been of no assistance to the army, but they would have impeded its movements. Thus, in all human probability, would the capital of Asia Minor have fallen, and it would not have been difficult to foretell the events which must have followed. Beyond Erzeroom, there was no force of any kind to oppose the further progress of the Russian army, and the whole of Asia Minor would have at once been in their hands.

It might, perhaps, be urged by those who, for the purpose of screening the authorities to whose carelessness and neglect the ultimate surrender of Kars was wholly attributable, that it was a strategical error to hold the place at all; that, with famine staring the garrison in the face, and with disease of no ordinary kind to contend against, it almost amounted to an act of unnecessary cruelty to prolong the sufferings of the devoted men, who, rather than yield to the enemy, were prepared to undergo hardships and privations almost unparalleled in the annals of warfare.

Let those who feel disposed to use such an argument bear in mind, that not only was immediate succour promised from more than one quarter, but that there was every reason to believe, up to the last moment, that such assistance was actually on its way to the relief of the beleaguered town. With these facts before them, who can any longer doubt the policy of the course which was pursued?

With regard to the importance of Kars as the key of Asia Minor, a very able despatch from Fuad Pasha, the Minister of Foreign Affairs at Constantinople, is here introduced, as showing the identity of opinion existing between the Turkish Cabinet and the British Commissioner. Fuad Pasha appeared fully alive to the fact, that had Kars fallen early in the campaign, a similar fate for Erzeroom and Anatolia would soon have followed, and obliged the armies operating before Sebastopol to detach troops for the protection of the Turkish capital. How little able those armies were to have responded to this demand upon them history has already told us.

"*Fuad Pasha to Lord Stratford de Redcliffe.*

(TRANSLATION.) "July 31, 1855.

"I have the honour to transmit herewith to your Excellency a copy of a despatch received yesterday from the imperial army of Kars.

"The substance of this despatch is, that the Russian troops which marched upon Kars have pushed a reconnaissance up to the fortifications; that they retired after a few unimportant affairs; and it is thought that the reason why no serious engagement took place is, that they are expecting reinforcements from the direction of Erivan, after the arrival of which they intend closely to invest the fortress of Kars. In this same despatch it is urgently requested that the succours which have been hitherto demanded, and which are now again demanded, may be sent without any delay.

"The position of Kars is, so to speak, the key of the frontiers of Asia; so that if (which God forbid!) it were to fall into the power of the Russians, in the first place Erzeroom would be in danger, and then the whole of Anatolia would be threatened—of that there is no doubt.

"If Anatolia were to become the theatre of war, and the enemy were to make an advance in that quarter, great evils would result, not only to the Sublime Porte, but also to the whole alliance. Moreover, the success of the Russians at Kars would be a defeat which would create through the whole world a bad impression with regard to the alliance. For these reasons the Sublime Porte has seen the necessity of taking prompt measures to prevent the anticipated danger.

"If inconsiderable reinforcements were to be sent directly to Kars, they could neither, in the present state of affairs there, unite with the forces in the town to beat off the attack of the enemy, nor operate outside so as to drive them from that part of the country; and it is equally clear that they would not be able to resist the enemy, who wishes to destroy the forces in Kars, to take that place, and to advance.

"An energetic operation, and on a large scale, seems the only means of preventing the Russians from investing Kars and advancing into Anatolia, and of compelling them to retire.

"One of the two main armies of the Porte is in the Crimea, and the other is on the shores of the Danube. The Porte does not think it at all right, as the question of the Crimea is a vital one for the alliance, to weaken the forces destined to insure the expected victory. The army on the Danube is not in a state to assume the attitude of an invading army; but it must at least remain there as a reserve, and, consequently, it is likewise not expedient to weaken it.

"All these reasons, which have been thoroughly considered, have led us to think of a prompt and energetic plan, and one likely to compel the Russians to retreat. The plan is, that an army of forty thousand men should march from Redoute-Káleh direct to Tiflis, by way of Kutais. As a means of carrying out this scheme, without disarranging the plan of general operations, we represented the importance of assembling a corps d'armée, composed of the twenty thousand Turkish troops, who, according to treaty, are to be supplied to serve in the English army, of the forces at Batoom, and of five thousand men to be taken from the army of Roumelia.

"Your Excellency has admitted the importance of the measure, and approved the plan in question, and you have asked for instructions from your Government on this point.

"According to the answer received, they approve

the substance of the proposal; but they add the following observation, that the troops of the Contingent, not being as yet in a suitable condition, it would not be right to select them for this expedition: so it has been reported to the Porte.

"On this account, and in deference to the opinion of the illustrious Government of Great Britain, as well as to carry out the plan in question, which is of the highest importance, we proposed to send the Turkish Contingent to the Crimea, to withdraw twenty thousand men from the Crimean army, and to send them to Redoute-Káleh; or, to postpone handing over the ten thousand men who, according to agreement, are to be supplied to complete the Contingent, and to send to Asia [?] ten thousand men of the Imperial Turkish army now in the Crimea, with the other ten thousand, to take part in the proposed expedition.

"The Government of His Highness has begun to provide for the measures which will be necessary for this expedition; but the official and categorical answer which is expected on this point has not yet been received, and on that account these measures have not yet been carried out; and even what has been begun of the measures depending on this question has been suspended.

"The importance of what relates to Asia has long since been explained to your Excellency, and the advantages attending operations which would have

Redoute-Káleh as a basis have been fully unfolded; and that being the case, it is useless to enter into these two points in further detail. Your illustrious Government does not agree to the employment of the Contingent on a special service. The presence of these troops in the Crimea during general operations cannot fail to make the services expected from them more sure.

"The Sublime Porte cannot find, as far as Asia is concerned, any plan more effectual than the one in question, or more capable of inspiring it with confidence. The Porte does not see the necessity of sending more forces direct to Kars, or even of quieting the troops there by sending reinforcements. These delays therefore naturally cause very great uneasiness and perplexity. The last despatch received from Kars gives a faithful picture of the importance of the question. We have made known the importance of it to your Excellency, and your Excellency has communicated to the Porte the despatch which you have received from your Court in answer to the communications made by the Porte on the subject of this expedition.

"The substance of these despatches is as follows: —The English Government is also convinced of the necessity and importance of sending assistance to the Kars army, but the succours must be sent by way of Trebizonde through Erzeroom. The troops that are sent will be compelled to halt for a short time between Redoute-Káleh and Kutais, and will be in an unhealthy spot. Instead of attacking the Russians in the rear, it would be better to strengthen the rear of the army of Kars.

"It would be superfluous to say how strongly the Sublime Porte sees the necessity of saving Kars, and, in saving Kars, of freeing Anatolia. Now the only way of effecting this is, to carry out the proposed movement from Redoute-Káleh. In fact, to save Kars, a force is required at least equal to the besieging army. Now if we must send such a force in the direction of Trebizonde, seeing that the roads are extremely bad, this force, with its artillery and munitions complete, would hardly reach Erzeroom in three or four months, and in that interval the Russians would have done all that they had to do. Therefore this plan can produce no good effect.

"If a small force were sent, it could neither relieve Kars nor defend Erzeroom. It is certain, then, that it is not possible to relieve Kars by way of Trebizonde.

"The road which leads straight from Redoute-Káleh to Kutais is perfectly level and easy. The goodness of the road is favourable to the transport of artillery and munitions, and the march of a large army by this road will be rapid and free from difficulty.

"Independently of this, as this army will be

in the rear of the Russian army, and will march straight on Tiflis, which is the very soul of the Russians in the Caucasus, as soon as it has advanced a little, the Russians will evidently be obliged to abandon Kars, and fly to the defence of Tiflis and Suram, and withdraw from Kars.

"His Highness the Sirdar Ekrem and all the officers of the Porte, are unanimously of opinion that there is no other plan of saving Asia but this, and there is no doubt that the military officers of the high allied Powers will be of the same opinion on this subject.

"As to the insalubrity of the neighbourhood of Redoute-Káleh. That place will not be the permanent abode of the army. As the march of the troops will be hurried, they will make a very short stay there; and, moreover, an army which is animated by a desire of saving its country will show itself determined to overcome all obstacles, and to brave all dangers. Therefore the observation on the insalubrity of the place cannot offer any obstacle to the prosecution of the plan.

"The survey which has been made of the coasts with a view to bases of operation, is favourable in every respect to the plan in question; that is to say, there have been found, at some hours' distance from the coast, very convenient positions with respect to climate for pitching a camp.

"In conclusion, the danger to which Asia is

exposed is very great in the eyes of the Sublime Porte, which thinks that the sole and only means, and the most effectual, to avert the storm, is to carry out the plan decided on as stated above. The Porte has, in consequence, resolved to entreat the allies very urgently to afford the assistance and facilities required in order to execute this plan without prejudice to operations in the Crimea; and for this purpose one of these two courses must be adopted: either the Contingent must be sent to the Crimea, and twenty thousand men be withdrawn from thence to be employed on this expedition, or else the transfer of ten thousand men necessary to complete the Contingent must be postponed, and the arrangement alluded to above be carried out.

"Confident in that sagacity and perfect judgment which so eminently characterise your Excellency, the Sublime Porte thinks that a representation in writing of the importance of the affair in question is all that is necessary in order that it may receive a prompt and favourable decision.

"I avail, &c.,

"(Signed)   MEHMED FUAD."

CHAPTER XIX.

The means which were undertaken for succouring Kars—Nothing required but food and ammunition to enable the Turks to hold Kars—Omer Pasha's first arrival on the coast—His movements—The rainy season puts a stop to his campaign—General Mouravieff continues to blockade Kars—The two courses which were open to Omer Pasha—Objections of the Consuls to the proposed plan—General Mouravieff's ideas on the subject—The opinion of Her Majesty's Government conveyed in Lord Clarendon's letter.

THE fact of the expediency of having held Kars until forced by famine to surrender, having, it is hoped, been satisfactorily established, the next points to be considered are, in the first place, the means which were undertaken for the purpose of succouring the beleaguered garrison—and, secondly, the course which might have been pursued with greater probability of effecting this desirable object.

Before entering on this particular portion of the subject, it may perhaps be as well to show that the ultimate fall of Kars can in no way be attributed to any fault on the part of its defenders.

The glorious defence of the place on the 29th of September clearly proves that it was not to be taken by storm so long as a sufficient number of troops could be kept alive to man the works.

Had General Mouravieff believed success to be possible, doubtless he would have attempted a second attack, rather than run the risk of seeing his forces gradually diminished by the effects of a severe and rigorous winter which was then fast approaching, or, what would perhaps have been still more disheartening, of being forced, after a blockade of nearly six months, during which period his loss in killed and wounded, as well as from disease, had been enormous, to raise the siege and retire, with the dispirited remains of his army, into winter quarters, with the almost certain prospect of having to encounter the following year, in the possible event of the war continuing, an enemy of a much more formidable character than that by which he had been defeated.

Nothing, therefore, was wanting to enable the Turks to hold the position they had so gallantly retained for such a length of time, and under disadvantages of no ordinary nature, but a sufficient supply of food and ammunition. Why they were not in possession of these necessaries need not again be alluded to in detail. Suffice it to remark, that whatever amount of blame may be attached to those, whose duty it most undoubtedly was to see that the numerous and oft-repeated requisitions of Her Majesty's Commissioner were properly attended to, none can by any possibility be attributed to him and the officers serving under his orders, who had undertaken the difficult and responsible task of defending to the last that fortress, the importance of which, as being undoubtedly the key to Asia Minor, has been fully stated.

The remarks just made refer more particularly to what might, with such ease and safety, have been effected prior to the investment of Kars by the Russian army; but the non-recognition, in a befitting manner, of Her Majesty's Commissioner on his first arrival, the jealousies and intrigues of the local authorities, and the very insufficient supply of money granted by the Turkish Government for the use of the Kars army, all tended to neutralise every effort that was made to provision the place, and to complete the necessary supply of ammunition.

Had the granaries and magazines been well filled, which might have been done with very little exertion on the part of the Government, the Turks could have defied the enemy to turn them out of their stronghold.

The point now to be discussed, as the first of those under consideration, is the nature of the steps which were taken for the relief of the garrison, after the Russians had sat down before the place.

It is sufficiently well known that Omer Pasha was sent, in the month of September, with a force of all arms, amounting to thirty-five thousand fighting men, for the ostensible purpose of succouring Kars.

What the instructions were which the Generalissimo received from his Government, or whether he was at liberty to use his own judgment and discretion in any operations he might undertake, are facts which it is not the province of this work to enter upon.

The question, however, may be asked, " Did Omer " Pasha intend to effect the purpose for which he " was sent by proceeding at once to Kars, or by " making a diversion elsewhere with the hope of " distracting General Mouravieff's attention, and " thus obliging him to retire from before the " fortress which he had invested?" If the former was his idea, it is scarcely possible to conceive a more injudicious plan than that which the Turkish Commander-in-chief thought fit to adopt.

He entered Asia at Suchum Kaleh in the month of October with the main body of his army; and it is believed that no Turkish force had ever before, on taking the field, been provided so well with money, tents, arms, and ammunition; besides which, he had at his disposal a fleet of ships-of-war and steamers, and, in short, nothing seemed wanting to render his army perfectly efficient for any service.

Leaving Suchum Kaleh, Omer Pasha proceeded along the shore to Tshimsherai or Yenitcheri, as it is sometimes called, from whence he turned inland, and after a march of nearly a month, his army arrived at Zipir Chinsk, a village about an hour's march from the right bank of the Inghour, on approaching which, the advanced guard found the enemy drawn up in considerable force on the left bank to oppose them. Omer Pasha himself joined the advanced guard on the 3rd of November, at the head of twenty thousand men of all arms, and after throwing up batteries on the 4th to distract the attention of the enemy, the Turkish troops under his orders gallantly forced the passage of the river on the day following, being divided for that purpose into two corps, acting at a distance from each other, one of which he commanded in person, whilst he confided the other to Major Simmons, R.E., the British Commissioner attached to him, which they did in a manner highly creditable to Omer Pasha and Major Simmons, as well as to the Turkish officers and soldiers under their command.

The details of this action are described in Major Simmons' official letter of the 7th of November, addressed to the Earl of Clarendon, in which he reports that Omer Pasha expressed himself in terms of the highest satisfaction at the conduct of the British officers who accompanied his force, of whom the Major particularly lamented the loss of the gallant officer who had been his Aide-de-camp from the commencement of the war in Turkey.

328 THE RAINY SEASON PUTS A STOP TO THE ADVANCE.

For his conduct on this occasion Major Simmons was promoted to the rank of Lieutenant-colonel.

After forcing the passage of the Inghour the victorious army proceeded without further interruption. An occasional halt was found necessary to allow provisions coming from Redoute-Káleh to reach the camp, but notwithstanding this unavoidable delay, and the numerous difficulties it had to encounter in its onward progress, it advanced to within twenty-four miles of Kutais.

On the 23rd of November the Turkish force arrived on the river Noga, where it halted for some days. The rainy season of Mingrelia had now set in with its accustomed violence, and the Kutais road became impassable. Omer Pasha still talked of advancing, but having soon afterwards received intelligence of the surrender of Kars, and well knowing that the army of the Caucasus would now be at liberty to reinforce the troops then opposed to him, he ordered a retreat, and thus ended his brief campaign in Asia.

Without having followed the movements of the Turkish Generalissimo step by step, enough has been said to prove that, as regards the succour which it was expected he would have afforded to the garrison of Kars, his proceedings were utterly futile. Those of Selim Pasha on the Erzeroom side were of so useless a character that they need not again be alluded to.

General Mouravieff feeling himself tolerably secure from interruption from that quarter whence he would have had good reason to expect it had the tactics on the part of Omer Pasha been different, steadily maintained his position before Kars, and pursued the policy which he had from the first adopted in order to obtain possession of the place, well knowing that it would be merely a matter of time, and that, sooner or later, famine—that invincible enemy against which not even the most determined devotion or gallantry can offer any resistance—would force the garrison to surrender.

It is true that the intelligence of Omer Pasha's arrival on the coast, and the news that the southern side of Sebastopol had fallen (arriving in the Russian camp almost simultaneously), induced General Mouravieff to make the attempt of taking Kars by assault on the 29th September. He was fully justified in supposing that reinforcements would be immediately sent, and it would therefore have been of incalculable importance to him to obtain possession of the fortress, in order that he might have nearly the whole of his force available to meet the succouring armies whenever they might arrive.

The issue of the attack, so disastrous to the Russian troops, and so unexpected by their Commander, reduced the enemy once more to the necessity of continuing the blockade, General Mouravieff having by that time ascertained that Omer

Pasha's movements were not of such a nature as to cause him any alarm, and trusting that the force under Muchranski, though very far inferior to the army of the Turkish Generalissimo in numerical strength, would still be enabled to keep it in check.

Having given a general outline, without entering much into detail, of the steps which were taken with the view to relieving Kars, and having shown the utter inutility of them, it now becomes desirable to consider what measures might have been adopted with greater chance of success.

There were two courses open to Omer Pasha when he commenced his winter campaign. The first one was to land his army at Trebizonde, and to proceed thence to Kars by way of Baiboort and Erzeroom. The second was to make a diversion by threatening or attacking Kutais.

With regard to the first-named plan of operation, both the English and French Consuls at Trebizonde, and the French Consul at Suchum Kaleh are said to have pointed out that there was plenty of time to enable the relieving army to reach Kars before the snow fell; that the road, though very indifferent, was by no means impassable; and that there was in Erzeroom an abundance of provisions, ammunition, and stores of all kinds which had been collected and laid up after the commencement of the blockade. The Consuls also pointed out that the garrison of

OBJECTIONS POINTED OUT TO THE PROPOSED PLAN. 331

Erzeroom could spare troops to hold in check the Byazid force, the same, indeed, which was at that time watched by Vēli Pasha's army.

With respect to the other course which was actually adopted by Omer Pasha, the Consuls stated that the succouring army would be overtaken by the rains under the Caucasus; that all the rivers in Mingrelia and Abasia would flood the neighbouring land from November until the following May, in the winter from rain, and in the spring from the melting snow on the mountains; and that no supplies would be obtainable from the country. It was also represented that the natives would be hostile, and that, even if the army succeeded in reaching Kutais, still Kars would not be relieved, for at a short distance beyond the former place was the mountain fastness of Gori, which would have effectually stopped any further advance.

The motives which induced Omer Pasha to decide upon threatening Kutais can only be conjectured. The result of his operations fully proved how wofully he miscalculated his chances of relieving Kars by the measures he pursued.

It will seem almost incredible, to any one who looks dispassionately at the subject in all its bearings, that any doubt should have existed in the mind of the Generalissimo as to which of the two plans alluded to offered the greater prospect of success.

General Mouravieff himself, in his despatch of the 30th of September, the day after his repulse, points out in plain terms the steps which he fully expected would have been taken for the relief of Kars.

He wrote as follows when explaining his reasons for having determined to attack the place :—

" Ayant été informé que les troupes Turques " reçurent des renforts dans la vicinité de Batoum, " et que l'ennemi se proposait de faire un mouve- " ment sur Gouriel et Akhaltchik, et en même " temps avancer d'Erzeroom sur Kars, j'ai resolu " d'attaquer ce dernier le 29."

It might almost be asked, judging from Omer Pasha's operations, whether the object of his expedition was the relief of the beleaguered city or a career more nearly connected with his own personal ambition, namely, the future invasion and conquest of the provinces of Georgia and Circassia. Surely it is but natural to suppose that so wild a scheme as the latter could never have entered the head of a General who had proved by his antecedents that he was a commander of no ordinary talent. It must, therefore, be taken for granted that in all he undertook he had in view but one sole object, that of obliging the Russian troops to retire before Kars, and thus remove the blockade.

The most feasible manner of effecting this end would undoubtedly have been by a decided and direct advance on the place itself, and not by attempting a diversion at such a distance from the spot.

The Earl of Clarendon, in the following letter to Her Majesty's Ambassador at Constantinople on this subject, states the objections entertained by the British Government to the measures at that time proposed, and eventually adopted in part for the relief of Kars.

"*The Earl of Clarendon to Lord Stratford de Redcliffe.*

" MY LORD,   " Foreign Office, July 13, 1855.

" The plan proposed by the Porte for the relief of the Turkish army at Kars, as sketched out in your Excellency's despatches of the 30th of June and 1st instant, has been attentively considered by Her Majesty's Government; and I have to state to your Excellency that it appears to be objectionable for the following reasons :—

" It would be in the greatest degree imprudent to throw on an unwholesome coast, without means of land transport, without any certainty of provisions, without an assured communication with the rear, without an accurate knowledge of the country to be traversed, or the strength of the enemy to be encountered, and with the probability of a hostile population, 40,000 men, hurriedly collected from various quarters, imperfectly disciplined, doubtfully armed and equipped, and as yet unorganized, and to expose them at once to all the hazards and difficulties of a campaign against a Russian army. They would fall ill between Redoute-Káleh and Kutais, and be defeated between Kutais and Tiflis. Moreover, the fragments to be united for the purpose of composing this army are so scattered about, that the crisis, if it is to take place, would be over long before it could reach the scene of action.

"Her Majesty's Government are of opinion that the wiser course would be to send reinforcements to the rear of the Turkish army, instead of sending an expedition to the rear of the Russian army. The reinforcements might go to Trebizonde, and be directed from thence upon Erzeroom. The distance from Trebizonde to Erzeroom is less than from Redoute-Káleh to Tiflis, and the march is through a friendly instead of through a hostile country; and at Erzeroom the army would meet supporting friends instead of opposing enemies, and supplies instead of famine.

"If the army at Kars cannot maintain that position against the Russians, it should fall back upon Erzeroom, and the whole Turkish force should be concentrated there. If the Russians are to be defeated, it will be easier to defeat them by the whole force collected than by divided portions of that force; and a defeat would be the more decisive, the further it took place within the Turkish frontier.

"Trebizonde is a port where supplies of all kinds might be landed; and Her Majesty's Government believe that it is a healthy place, and that Erzeroom is so likewise.

"Such an arrangement as that which I have described would give time for collecting and organizing the various detached corps of which the proposed army of 40,000 men is to be composed; and Her Majesty's Government entirely concur in Lieutenant-General Vivian's opinion that an army thrown on a coast without means of transport and supplies, is doomed to destruction.

"I am, &c.,

"(Signed) CLARENDON."

CHAPTER XX.

The practicability of the route between Trebizonde and Erzeroom—Particulars of the route—Letter on the subject from Mr. Consul Stevens—No necessity for heavy guns—An advance by way of Batoom considered—Objections to such a proceeding—General Mouravieff's ignorance of the amount of ammunition—Concluding remarks.

THE arguments set forth by Her Majesty's Minister, backed as they are by the opinion of Lieut.-General Vivian, an officer of talent and experience, scarcely need any further strengthening; but as there might possibly be a discussion as to the practicability of marching an army from Trebizonde to Erzeroom, the following report on the state of the road between these two places, drawn out by Her Majesty's Consul at Trebizonde, is given to show that no insurmountable obstacles existed:—

" *Report on Erzeroom Road. Addressed by Mr. Stevens to Colonel Williams, C.B.*

" Sept. 5, 1854.

"I hasten to reply to the questions which you have addressed to me concerning the marching of

PARTICULARS OF THE ROUTE. 337

a force from Trebizonde to Erzeroom in the spring. In the event of a force marching at that season, it would have to proceed by the winter road, which is calculated at one hundred and eighty miles, or sixty caravan hours. There are two other roads, but these are seldom available before the middle of June, especially if the winter has been at all a severe one. The stages of the winter road are as follows:—

Trebizonde	to	Geverlick,	6 hours,	18 miles.
Geverlick	,,	Ereupea,	4 ,,	12 ,,
Ereupea	,,	Ardassa,	5 ,,	15 ,,
Ardassa	,,	Goomosha,	8 ,,	24 ,,
Goomosha	,,	Kaleli,	5 ,,	15 ,,
Kaleli	,,	Ballahore,	6 ,,	18 ,,
Ballahore	,,	Baiburt,	4 ,,	12 ,,
Baiburt	,,	Marsat,	5 ,,	15 ,,
Marsat	,,	Hoshepoonar,	8 ,,	24 ,,
Hoshepoonar	,,	Ilejeh,	6 ,,	18 ,,
Ilejeh	,,	Erzeroom,	3 ,,	9 ,,

"The proper time for moving the troops from Constantinople would depend on the nature of the conveyance; if by sailing-vessels, in the beginning of May; if by steam, a fortnight later. Heavy artillery could not accompany the columns, but I see no difficulty for a force taking with it field and mountain guns.

"There may be one or two difficult and narrow

passes, where the former would have to be taken off their carriages for a short distance and carried, but they might be slung, or put on litters between mules, or on sleds; but even this might not be necessary: all would depend on the severity of the winter. Knowing, as I do, the nature of the road, I should say our troops could scarcely march more than eighteen miles, or six hours, daily, on an average.

"This could be accomplished with ease, by dividing the day's labour as follows—two hours before breakfast, two hours after breakfast, and the last two hours before sunset. In spring, the weather is foggy and chilly and wet at night, with a comfortable warmth during the middle of the day. No fevers prevail at that season. Water is met with everywhere, and of an excellent quality. The stations where it would be advisable to establish depôts of provisions would be Trebizonde, Gumish-Kaneh, and Baiboort. Flour, barley, oxen, and straw could be procured at all three places. Sheep must be procured at Trebizonde, as also fuel, oil, candles, rice, and vegetables; the last consisting of potatoes, onions, pumpkins, and cabbage. The order for forming these depôts should be given at least three months previous to the landing of a force at Trebizonde; and in order to secure a sufficient quantity of each article, it were well to make purchases in the course of the winter, and store them. The season for laying in firewood is October and November, when all classes supply themselves for the winter. After November it is to be had with difficulty, and only in small quantities at a time. Between Trebizonde and Gumish-Kaneh wood abounds, and a party preceding an army might prepare any quantity required. Assisted by the local authorities, no difficulty would occur in finding room for storing supplies. I would recommend the force bringing with it beasts of burden, to avoid delay. Two or three hundred auxiliary beasts could be procured here, more perhaps—but this is not to be relied upon. I state three hundred as a maximum, because, in case of emergency, the Pasha could collect that number from the peasants. I recommend any force coming this way to bring with it biscuit, rum, tea, and coffee. These are articles that cannot always be got at a moment's notice. Once a force sets out from Trebizonde, it would not meet with sufficient conveniences for baking bread on the road for any large number of men.

"(Signed) F. STEVENS."

It need only be added, that marching, as it would, through a friendly country, the succouring army would not have required to take heavy guns with it, more particularly as there was a sufficient number of them at Erzeroom.

It may be argued by some, that a still better

plan for relieving Kars would have been by landing a light corps of five or six thousand men, under the command of an energetic and determined officer, at Batoom, to proceed in the direction of the blockaded city, whilst a similar or even larger force might have been despatched to the same place from Trebizonde. These two corps, acting in concert, might have fallen upon the rear and flank of the besieging army; or at least they might have harassed it, and distracted its attention from the fortress; and there is no doubt the enemy would have been forced to retire.

Had no obstacles stood in the way of this plan, it is more than probable that the presence of a Turkish army, either in position on the mountains, or in Ardahan, through which it must have passed, would have been sufficient to have raised the entire Mussulman population in its favour. They are all armed; and it is by no means unlikely that they would have been joined by a large force of irregulars and Bashi-Bozouks. The inhabitants of Ardahan are a brave and fearless race, and would doubtless have done good service if called upon to join the advancing army.

Had the Turkish General been forced to stand the brunt of a battle with the whole of the Russian army, he would have had very considerable advantage, for General Mouravieff would have had to leave the Kars army in his rear ready to cut off his communication with Alexandropol: and even in the event of the Russians prevailing against the Turks, the former would have found it impossible to follow up the pursuit into the mountains of Adshara. In the meantime, there would have been no difficulty in throwing into Kars a supply of provisions from Erzeroom; in which latter place a sufficient quantity of stores had been collected, and carriage for its conveyance was ready on the spot.

Against this plan of operations, however, the objection might be made that the road between Batoom and Ardahan was nearly if not quite impassable. The reports on this route are somewhat conflicting; and as that on which the most reliance can be placed gives far from a satisfactory account of it, the subject is left, if necessary, for future discussion.

There can be little doubt that had an army landed at Trebizonde, and marched direct on Erzeroom, and thence to Kars, the latter place would have been saved; and it is by no means impossible that the combined Turkish forces might have then made a forward movement, and have eventually succeeded in establishing a footing in Georgia, as a preliminary step to further operations.

Having thus endeavoured to give a faithful account of this remarkable struggle, it is but justice to those concerned in it to remark, that many valuable documents, which would have borne on the subject, were destroyed, with the Archives, previous to the surrender; and thus the record of many minor but still interesting details is lost to the public.

The most remarkable feature of the contest arose from the ignorance of the enemy as to the extent of the magazines of provision and ammunition in the place.

Had General Mouravieff been aware, when he first invested it, that there were only powder and shot sufficient for three days' fighting in the open field, he would most undoubtedly have commenced his operations by a regular siege; and in that case, as the ammunition would have been all expended in about three weeks, the garrison would, of necessity, have been compelled to surrender; though no doubt they would have displayed, in the mean time, the same undaunted courage as their countrymen did at Silistria, on the Danube. There, however, the gallant defenders of the last-named fortress were supported by a powerful army in rear, their communication with which was never cut off, nor even interrupted.

The system of blockade in which General Mouravieff so pertinaciously persevered, until he felt that there was a prospect of the place being relieved by Omer Pasha, led to the battle of the 29th of September, when he was signally defeated and obliged once more to confine himself to a strict blockade, protracted on the whole to nearly six months, in which the Russians lost more men than in their operations on the Danube.

During this period, the Turkish garrison subsisted on a slender ration, drawn from a supply of less than three months' ordinary provision, while not a day passed without adding strength to the outworks of the beleaguered city. At these works, the half-famished Turks laboured with surprising constancy, and watched with a vigilance truly exemplary.

As long as history shall be read, and the art of war cultivated by mankind, the name of Kars will be a rallying-point to all true soldiers.

With regard to the Chief who prepared for, and carried through, the various phases of this remarkable defence, it has been stated, in the foregoing pages, that he was sent into Asia Minor unprotected and unaided by those whose duty it was to aid and protect him. All the difficulties he had to contend with have been recited, and the manner in which he grappled with them from the first moment, until famine compelled him to surrender, has been described.

It now only remains, therefore, to conclude with an expression of the most perfect confidence that History will do him justice, no matter whether the terms " command " or " direction " shall be considered the more appropriate to the authority with which he issued those orders so cheerfully and implicitly obeyed by every officer and soldier of the devoted Garrison of Kars.

VIEW OF THE TOWN

1. Kaya Tepe. 2. Takimsah Tabia. 3. Suwarri Tabia. 4. Tchim Tabia. 5. Eyri Lake. 6.

FORTRESS OF KARS.

www.ingramcontent.com/pod-product-compliance
Lightning Source LLC
Chambersburg PA
CBHW051034160426
43193CB00010B/932